Addressing Ableism

Addressing Ableism

Philosophical Questions via Disability Studies

Jennifer Scuro

Foreword by
Joel Michael Reynolds

And a Dialogue with
Devonya N. Havis and Lydia X. Z. Brown

LEXINGTON BOOKS
Lanham • Boulder • New York • London

Published by Lexington Books
An imprint of The Rowman & Littlefield Publishing Group, Inc.
4501 Forbes Boulevard, Suite 200, Lanham, Maryland 20706
www.rowman.com

Unit A, Whitacre Mews, 26-34 Stannary Street, London SE11 4AB

British Library Cataloguing in Publication Information Available

The hardback edition of this book was previously catalogued by the Library of Congress as follows:

Library of Congress Cataloging-in-Publication Data Available

Library of Congress Control Number: 2017957114

ISBN 978-1-4985-4074-2 (cloth: alk. paper)
ISBN 978-1-4985-4076-6 (pbk : alk. paper)
ISBN 978-1-4985-4075-9 (electronic)

∞™ The paper used in this publication meets the minimum requirements of American National Standard for Information Sciences—Permanence of Paper for Printed Library Materials, ANSI/NISO Z39.48-1992.

Printed in the United States of America

For Emma Coen

Me to my five-year-old daughter:
You know that if you ever feel frustrated because someone doesn't
understand you and what you are trying to say, you could say to them,
'Have patience with me, I have autism.'

My daughter to me:
Yes, [repeating back] 'Have patience with me, I'm awesome.'

Contents

List of Figures

Foreword

There are moments when thought brings one closer to oneself. Closer to the arrays of experience that make up one's being, but in their sheer intimacy, escape the tarrying of reflection. *Addressing Ableism*, for me, marks such a moment. It is a work that works one over, that works on who one is and wants to be.

Philosophy, it is said, begins in wonder. Wonder, we forget, arises in relief from habit. That which we regularly experience often fails to excite and provoke. That which is novel in turn provokes wonder, even when it shouldn't. Because it is a central and fundamental condition of all experience, our relationship to our body is one of habit and routine. We fail to be awe-struck by its continual shaping and founding of our world. Education and consciousness-raising was and still is required to see the many ways in which racism, sexism, cisgenderism, and colonialism, among other things, predetermine and prejudge the value and possibilities of bodies and lives across the globe. It is certainly still required with respect to *ableism*—the hegemonic, ideological fortress of ability, supporting a panoply of institutions and acolytes. "We," the *temporarily* ablebodied, must be provoked into wonder about the very forms of embodiment to which "ablebodiedness" is indexed and against which normality and acceptability and employability and nearly all *abilities* are measured. It is in light of such stakes—the very possibilities and contours of a thinking that resists ableism with as much force, consistency, and complexity as it does other forms of oppression—that one should read *Addressing Ableism*.

I had the honor of meeting Jennifer Scuro at the 2014 meeting of the Society for Disability Studies (SDS) during a session for family members of people with disabilities. Being a family member of someone or multiple ones living with disability brings about unique experiences. One is not simply an ally—one is also a sibling or child or parent-of, a dependency-laborer or lover-of. Insofar as one works in critical Disability Studies, this position is made even more ambiguous. It is strange to think of oneself as "ablebodied," as if that indicates an encrusted ontological or biological fact. "Temporarily ablebodied" is surely better, though still off. Even my "temporary ablebodiedness" is dependent on a panoply of supports without which the term would have little or no meaning. And insofar as the lines of one's concerns, loves, beings, and doings symbiotically intersect and change with those of others, the distance and stasis these labels convey are oft unapt and concealing.

For example, in speaking *for* my brother, who could not speak verbally, it was often unclear to me "who" was speaking. This is not to say my voice was his. Not at all. It is to say that the vivacity of love and care that defined our relationship and all of our joint experiences goes beyond the grammar of "speaking for" or "speaking on behalf of." It is the deep ambiguity and philosophical complexity of such experiences, judgments, testimonies, and actions that Scuro questions and illuminates so powerfully. The attentiveness to the simultaneous distance and intimacy of her role as mother, caretaker, advocate, ally, and philosopher is exemplary. In Scuro's voice, I hear a profound testimony to the constitutively ambiguous relations between one and another—a distance *constitutive* of love and care and citizenship, of a filiality beyond the biological and the myth of the autonomous individual. I hear it in the tensions and offerings, spacings and affections, that the text brings to bear upon the vast multiplicity of lived experiences of being human, of being-with others. I hear it in the testimony to experiences arising not from a disinterested spectator, but an interested thinker. I hear it in the love, anger, joy, and calm of its prose. I hear it in the insights and queries strewn across its pages. In Scuro's own prescient voice, "we have yet to understand what it is that we think we know and have only assumed."[1]

One such assumption is about *who* gets to speak about disability. Scuro is acutely aware of the fraught legacies of ablebodied thought *about* disability, especially from parents and family-members of those with disabilities. She is acutely aware of the crucial import of the disability activism maxim, "nothing about us without us." This sensitivity is reflected in everything from her practices of citation (quoting first-person experiences at length, whether from scholarly sources, blogs, or Facebook posts) to the architecture of the work (hinging in the middle with a dialogue between herself, Devonya Havis, and Lydia X. Z. Brown). It is also evident in the honesty with which she admits and assesses her own ableism throughout. *Addressing Ableism* as is an exemplary performance of Eva Kittay's assertion that "the personal is political is philosophical."

Taken as a whole, the work is a testament to the complexity and necessity of interrogating and combating ableism in all its forms. Margrit Shildrick writes, "the responsibility for enquiry and analysis [about ableism] falls... on all those who participate in the relevant structures" (2009, 15). If, as

Shildrick further claims, dis/ability is the "common underpinning of all human becoming," then that responsibility is on all humans. It falls most heavily, however, on those who are actively *benefitting* from ableism: the (temporarily) ablebodied. Yet, to even begin to understand the stakes of this responsibility is an uphill battle. As Elizabeth Barnes wryly notes, "the last time I checked, most non-disabled people are pretty personally invested in being non-disabled...when it comes to disability, I'm not objective. And neither are you. And that's true whether you're disabled or (temporarily) non-disabled" (2016, ix). Scuro contextualizes the high stakes of such an insight when she argues, "ableism is a thinking that can construct death camps and sustain (eu)genocides, without *thinking* and without *hesitation*."[2] She brings the work of multiple thinkers (including Hannah Arendt, Emmanuel Levinas, and Judith Butler) to bear on what is, in many senses, one of the touchstones of all dehumanizing thought. Her work goes to the heart of what it means to be human and how we might fashion a better, more habitable world.

Insofar as one follows Scuro's lead to simultaneously take up ableism personally, philosophically, and politically, *Addressing Ableism* has the potential to transform one's thinking and praxis. It certainly changed my own.

Joel Michael Reynolds
The Hastings Center
New York, 2017

Acknowledgments

This book could not have been written without the support of my husband, Stephen, and the unconditional love and joyful energy of my two daughters. My parents—of course my mom, Rosemarie Scuro, who dutifully transcribed my recorded notes—and my sisters, Alisa and Richele, who just know me, encourage my wildness, tolerate my nonsense and creativity, and love me all the same.

The NEH Faculty Development Committee fund at the College of New Rochelle's School of Arts and Sciences has supported aspects of this book through Summer Grants in 2013 and 2015. I am so grateful to those faculty members who originally created the fund as well as to those serving Committee members who supported my applications wholeheartedly. My colleagues and academic community have been wonderfully supportive when my work took on the direction of Disability Studies research and advocacy; thank you to Ruth Zealand, Erica (and Dan) Olson-Bang, Elizabeth Spadaccini, Kathy Mannino, Candace Barriteau Phaire, Johnnie O'Neal, Kelly Brennan, Ishita Khemka, Louis DeSalle, and Dennis Ryan for the good conversations and thoughtful collaborations. I want to especially thank Lucy Fazzino, Assistant Professor and Scholarly Communications Librarian at The College of New Rochelle Gill Library and Alan Baglia at Artists Rights Society (ARS) for their assistance in acquiring permissions. My students in the Disability Studies courses worked hard and always met me halfway with thinking in new and challenging ways, particularly Missiel Muñoz, Theresa Huth, and Revekka Halilova, but especially to my RN/BSN cohort that took on the Critical Disability Theory coursework at our DC-37 campus in downtown NYC—oh, those summer nights!

The members of the Society for Disability Studies (SDS) community have been so welcoming and generous of spirit in accepting me and my contributions. Harold Braswell was the most welcoming face at my first SDS meeting in 2013 and has been ever since. He organized the "family members of people with disabilities" caucus which has been an immense resource and support to me intellectually (and of course emotionally), particularly Douglas Kidd, Amy Smith, and Priya Lalvani. Joel Michael Reynolds and Lauren Guilmette were my philosophy partners for the 2015 SDS panel and later partnering and presenting again at the APA, as I tested out many of these ideas. I am so grateful for their friendship, personal and philosophical. I owe a tremendous debt of gratitude for Joel's constant support of this book, in his promotion of my work, and for writing the foreword to these meditations.

Thank you to Rosemarie Garland-Thompson for her very kind support of this project and to my editor as well, Jana Hodges-Kluck at Lexington Books, for her patient and kind support. I very much appreciated the support from the Emory University Center for Faculty Development and Excellence and the Emory Disability Studies Initiative for their generous invitation to speak on various chapters as they were still in development. I want to also thank George Yancy for his kind note to me just as I was completing this book, that although it was unrelated to this project, it gave me much needed encouragement. To Richard Gilman-Opalsky, Denise James, Cas Faulds, Alice Wong, Sara Brill, Das Janssen, Kevin Timpe, Melinda Hall, Bertha Alvarez Manninen, Jane Dryden, Lilyana Levy, Siri Nelson, Shelley Tremain, and Zara Bain, thank you for your openness, kindness of thought, and collegiality; I'm very grateful.

So many of the colleagues, particularly in virtual and social media communities, that I have interacted with since I've taken on the question of ableism cannot be mentioned here, but I am truly grateful to them for all of our exchanges, no matter how short and partial they may have been. I would have never engaged the Disability Studies community had it not been recommended by Lydia Brown after their presentation at our Autism Education panel in 2013, so to Lydia, of course, so much thanks. To my dearest philosophy sisters, Maeve O'Donovan and Devonya Havis, much love: I take you with me on all of my intellectual adventures. To Devonya's family, especially E.J., thank you for sharing all that you have with me and for your direct and indirect contributions to this project. Monica Vilhauer, my kind-hearted friend, thank you for always offering to share your philosophical insights.

And finally, my personal friends and allies who were always open to a conversation with a feminist philosopher: thanks for the wine, the laughs, the lightness with which we discussed our challenges, especially Lauren Duffy, Adria Peña, Nancy McCullough, Marjorie St. Hilaire, Yvonne Cullen, and the Rockett family—our extended family—especially Bernie and Katie, and, by extension of the extension—Alex and the Mirasol family.

Prologue

The Scale and Scope of Ableism

Few outside the disability community ever consider the consequences of their perceptions and limited understanding of disability, and many whose views are shaped by unsound and dangerous ideas continue to perpetuate ableism without ever having their privilege challenged and examined. Disability exists because we are largely complacent in allowing ourselves and society to perpetuate a world where disabled people are marginalized and oppressed by attitudinal and systemic barriers to access.

—Lydia X. Z. Brown, "Disability in an Ableist World" (2014, 44).

WHAT IS ABLEISM?[1]

In short, ableism is an under-determined bias that is everywhere. It is a harmful bias, often trivialized, yet, in fact, is *deadly*—especially to some bodies and minds more than others; it is a bias that widens the gap of meaning between who counts as "ablebodied" and valuable[2] as opposed to who does not.[3] Ableism is analogous (in a limited way) to other forms of systematic ideological bias and oppression: sexism, racism, classism, heteronormativity, and, arguably, speciesism.[4] Ableism is an under-recognized, more often *unrecognized* ideological bias that has yet to demonstrate itself as an oppression by ordinary standards. The invisible operations of ableism render any urgency into challenging ableism as if *negligible*; the lack of address for ableism is evident to me because even as I type this into my computer, per spellcheck, "ableism" is not recognized as a term unless I set it to be so.

As long as the social, psychological, and cultural impacts go without notice—that ableism and ableist thinking, attitudes, and institutions are not *put on notice*—there remains only delay in the ways one might address, confront, or even resist this bias. This will be the work at hand: addressing ableism means to first map out the scale and scope of this bias, provide ideas and strategies to resist the bias, and thereby open up possibilities for confronting the bias. In this regard, I would like to suggest that—although I am an "able-bodied" philosopher—these chapters that follow might come in "handy"—as an offering of a theoretical "prosthetics" that might open up non-ableist possibilities and perhaps also some novel, anti-ableist challenges.

This is to also say that these chapters focus on questioning concepts that I have found to be useful markers for mapping out the scale and scope of ableism—experience, diagnosis, intersectionality, precariousness, and prosthesis—and each chapter might be suggestive starting points for addressing ableism, hopefully instructive for future resistance and confrontation. Following Fiona Kumari Campbell (2009, 196):[5]

> Ableism is a map of a simulated territory that denotes the homelands of humanness, the dispensable beasts and changelings existing on the perimeter. Ableist landscapes communicate the values of culture, its characterological objects, and secure the transmission of the "memory" of a body of people. In these landscapes rest a form of anamnesis that orients between the past, the present and the future.

I want to suggest that this work is a starting point for a kind of *enmembering* as an anamnesis, (not just a remembering or recollecting exercise) against the fundamentally *dismembering* operations of ableist terrains.

A key element in my method for determining a bias that has gone without sufficient notice is in how I have tried to curate speculatively those ideas and narratives that might bring ableism to the fore—in a face-to-face address. To contextualize the unorthodox and strangeness of my curatorial method, if permitted, I will borrow liberally from a Levinasian phenomenology. As Levinas describes it in "Philosophy, Justice, and Love," the ethico-existential encounter with the Other in the face-to-face relation (to cite at length) is a work of love for justice against all injustice:

> From the start, the encounter with the Other is my responsibility for him [*sic*]. . . . I don't very much like the word love, which is worn-out and debased. Let us speak instead of the taking upon oneself of the fate of the other. . . . Must not human beings, who are incomparable, be compared? Thus justice, here, takes precedence over the taking upon oneself of the fate of the other.
>   I must judge, where before I was to assume responsibilities. Here is the birth of the theoretical; here the concern for justice is born, which is the basis of the theoretical. But it is always starting out from the Face, from the responsibility for the other that justice appears, which calls for judgment and

comparison of what is in principle incomparable, for every being is unique; every other is unique. . . . At a certain moment, there is a necessity for "weighing," a comparison, a pondering, and in this sense philosophy would be the appearance of wisdom from the depths of that initial charity; it would be—and I am not playing on words—the wisdom of charity, the wisdom of love. (1998, 103–104)

While these speculations are partial and not comprehensive, it is my hope that there is a fundamentally ethical function in the way these particular themes are threaded together, framed by questions, as an inquiry, with what might be best described as a "scavenger" or queer methodology. According to Ken Plummer (2003, 522):

Queer is seen as partially deconstructing our own discourses and creating a greater openness in the way we think through our categories. Queer theory is, to quote Michael Warner, a stark attack on "normal business in the academy." . . . It adopts a "scavenger methodology that uses different methods to collect and produce information on subjects who have been deliberately or accidently excluded from traditional Studies of human behavior." In its most general form this is a refusal of orthodox method.

An outcome of this method is to prosthetically provide some guidance for explicating the impacts and narrating the kinds of harms ableism exacts on bodies and minds insofar as it remains currently under-determined and unaddressed. The questions I raise in each of the chapters are to provide working banisters[6]—tools of navigation to point out how effectively ableism, instead of being prioritized and treated with urgent consideration, has been deflected and trivialized both in and out of the academy.

Add to these difficulties that those bodies and minds most subject to the viciousness of ableism are diversified by both their experience and in their relation to visible and invisible disabilities, complicating any consolidated, fair, and systematic response to this as a harmful, deadly bias. Western and particularly American ideologies of wealth, success, ownership, and individualism limits the way in which systematic ableist thinking and attitudes can be addressed—radically and whole-cloth.[7] As I finalize this book, according to *The Washington Post*, the website for The White House, under the instruction of the new Trump administration, has removed its sites related to issues, outreach and opportunities for people with disabilities.[8]

That we need to ask about the quiddity—the "what it is"—of ableism, for me, begs another question that needs further analysis, to be attended to, and more importantly with great care: *how does ableism operate?*

While popular media represents disability as a matter of novelty and fascination, often to affirm the comforts of normality, desires for normalcy, and reify the assumed privileges of ablebodiedness, the experiential and existential distance between worlds and individuals within those worlds is further culturally codified and ideologically cemented. One example most recently of this complexity is in how Meryl Streep at the Golden Globe Awards calls out (without naming) then President-elect Trump's imitation of reporter Serge Kovaleski. While seemingly on the "right side" of and in defense of people with disabilities by calling out and speaking truth to power, she, like many, missed the complicity by which ableism does its best work. As described by Kim Sauder, "If you're throwing disabled people under the bus to make a bigger message, then you're probably going to end up with a world in which that group is still disadvantaged at the end of the day."[9]

Alternatively, narratives and critiques have emerged in social media providing insight to the scale and scope of ableism with direct prompting by disability advocates: a working public dialogue under hashtags like #ableismexists, #theableistscript,[10] and most recently, #AccessibleOrganizing Matters.[11] What may be the most useful and is one of the original tests for the bias against those with disabilities for identifying ableism in its most basic operation—one that continues to be foundational to real disability advocacy—is: *nothing about us without us*.[12] From James Charlton's *Nothing About Us Without Us* (2000):

> The barriers to progress are considerable and complicated. The weight of history is burdensome. The outcome is not certain. . . . The growing number of disability activists throughout the world testifies to that . . . in the mobilization of grassroots disability activism through a common language, common experiences of oppression, a developing culture and identity, and [in] the contact with and organic formation of liberatory ideas and politics (120–21).

For me, identifying as ablebodied, this method of "address," in that I am *addressing* ableism with this project, is to work toward a paradigm shift away from thinking that disability is the disabled person's problem. We, especially those who benefit most from a world that works "for us," in which we "fit,"[13] need to change how the shape of the world works sometimes most viciously upon and against persons in both their literal and metaphorical self-determination. Similar to how racism cannot (and ought not have to) be addressed only by those people of color as they may be at the same time most subject to its viciousness and dehumanization, ableism needs to be most urgently addressed by those most advantaged by and disposed to employing it.

It, therefore, is important to note that this address does not preserve or particularly defend the language of identity politics, but rather, by outlining the scale and scope of ableism, expands the intellectual and affective demand to participate in the problem at hand: particularly how modern, Western, neoliberal ideology is at the same time an uncritical reflection of ableist thinking. "Disability"—whether or not you identify as ablebodied, or differently-abled or as disabled—functions as a world-shaping set of signs, signals, and identifications that creates alienation of bodies, minds, persons, and worlds. Think for a moment on all the ways in which the word "crazy" effectively functions as currency in the shame and blame economy of an ableist society as if benign, and yet, as Rachel Cohen-Rottenberg states it, "a critique of language that makes reference to disability is not welcome, [and so] it is nearly inevitable that, as a disabled person, I am not welcome either."[14]

This is also to say that my way of addressing ableism in this project is more philosophical than political, and although it is quite open to political application, it is first intended to free up the way we think about disability and ablebodiedness. Accordingly, I hope to present new possibilities for being in and acting upon the world. At the same time, I am queering and questioning ableism dialectically in order to decouple the discussion of disability from the operations of ableism, treating ableist thinking as linked to a more general crisis in Western ideology with due urgency: ableism requires a multifaceted and intersectional *resistance* as well as an urgent but sustainable *confrontation*.

WHAT DOES ABLEIST THINKING DO?

Hannah Arendt, twentieth century political philosopher, described the modern world as being in a dangerously social and political condition of "thoughtlessness" in the prologue to her book, *The Human Condition* (1958). Her work, insightful and uniquely attuned to the issues of the twenty-first century, contained an important plea: that there be a place opened up in the world to bring the activity of thinking back into political and social life in an everyday sense and for the "love of the world."[15] Following Arendt's injunction, and in order to understand the operations of ableism, this project is to meditatively map out the scale and scope of ableist thinking—as it is sometimes an explicit ideology, as it is also sometimes implicit in attitudes, expressed in anxieties, and usually veiled by seemingly "benign" or "benevolent" social, political, and cultural inheritances of "normal" or "natural" (read: *disablist*)[16] values and/or standards.

Addressing the role of thinking elsewhere, Arendt has stated, "We are so accustomed to the old opposition of reason versus passion, spirit versus life, that the idea of a *passionate* thinking, in which thinking and aliveness become one, takes us somewhat aback."[17] The loss of space, time, and significance for passionate thinking also continues to make our world vulnerable to totalitarianism—a situation where one may not only *not know* "what to do" and "what to think" but also believe *there is nothing to say* and that *nothing can be done*. This remains a phenomenon within Western-driven globalization and consumer-driven culture. In a world that seems so technologically powerful and "user-friendly," when situations of genuine critical need and violent conflict arise, there is nothing any "one" can really "do," and that thinking about "what to do" is rendered useless.[18] But, let's allow the honest question[19] to get asked: what does thinking really "do" anyway?

Arendt had argued in *The Human Condition* that there had been a kind of "divorce" between thinking and acting—what she called the *vita contempla-tiva*—one's thinking life—as it had emerged as wholly separable from the *vita activa*—one's active life. In her characterization of these vitae was an effort to reorganize how one's thinking life could be restored to the world as *also* an active life; having little interest in restoring the status of the removed, elite, and apolitical philosopher as the one who "does all the thinking." For Arendt, progressive ideologies "that explain everything" in which one "does not have to think, merely act," breeds conditions for psychocultural terror while grooming society for the conditions of totalitarianism.[20] Always of philosophical and political concern for Arendt were the conditions for *judgment*, such that the ways in which thinking must be, but more often is not, in real time and in real ways, also a worlded activity.

One way I want to suggest that thinking can "do" what is not done (but still needs to be done) is to selectively source how disability activists and authors have already been navigating ways to think through ableism, in order to catalog the phenomenon of how this "thoughtlessness" could actively marginalize those deemed "disabled" without an identified intention—as it can come from everyone and yet no one.[21] Ableism operates effectively, as I will argue in the final chapters, in how it *dismembers*, fundamentally contributing to the phenomenon of dismemberment. Tobin Siebers, in his book, *Disability Theory* (2008), provides a good example of how easily ableism dismembers in that disabled persons can be perceived as "narcissistic." As he states it:

> Narcissism is a form of violent hyperindividualization imposed upon victims by political bodies and other groups. That people with disabilities are automatically assumed to be narcissistic reveals not only that they are being victimized but that the perception of their individuality is itself a form of violence. . . . The narcissism of people with disabilities, then, is a political formation that inhibits their ability to act politically (45).

Siebers identifies what I think is a real error in ableist thinking—that disability is a problem ("really") only for the disabled individual. This is an assumption which Siebers also deems (quite fairly) a form of violence and victimization.

In concert with his position, I argue, the presumed "problem" of disability is not in or for the persons who have disabilities, who voluntarily represent themselves as disabled or who have involuntarily come to symbolize disability in their assumed "narcissism"; instead, it is *intimately* linked to the need for a philosophical revision of theory as well as for a full and fundamental reversal in the sustained operations of ableist thinking itself. To this I add, the violence permissible with ableist ideologies emerges as a form of thoughtlessness because no one has thought to ask: *who is really the narcissist here*? Is it the person who has come to identify with a disability or is it the ablebodied person who designates then denigrates the (abject)[22] other (but "not me"; *"never me"*) as disabled?[23]

With social media as a newly emerging tool of activism and consumption, while at the same time also a major location for inspiration porn,[24] there is a veil of anonymity that often preserves ableist rhetoric and bias, devoid of thoughtfulness and passion, filled with cliché and trite ideas, coming from "everywhere and nowhere"; "anyone and yet no one."[25] There is an uncritical ableist desire in the way these images and narratives of disabled people "overcoming" disabilities are proffered and shared. The problematic implications of this kind of fascination—what I call an "ableist affection" for the disabled "story"—can be best argued by Lilit Marcus in "Why You Shouldn't Share Those Emotional 'Deaf Person Hears for the First Time' Videos":[26]

> These "inspiring" videos continue to push one of the most problematic narratives in the history of the Deaf community: that deaf people are broken and therefore need to be "fixed." In reality, there's no such thing as a happily-ever-after.
>
> What bothers me are the maudlin videos produced out of someone's intense, private moment that are then taken out of context and broadcast around the world. What bothers me is how the viewer never learns how the individual came to the decision about their implant, which factors they took into account, whether their medical insurance covered it. Sometimes we don't even learn their names.

Instead of challenging ableist thinking, there is continued cultural production for the erasure and eradication of what is assumed the natural and objectified fact of disability: a state undesirable and broken, not needing care, but only a "fix" on the way to a "happily-ever-after." This has become a systemic way of thinking about disability that is, at the same time, inherently dangerous and unthinking—in a monochromatic, monolithic, and reductionist mode of a mob-like phobia tied to unrealistic phantasmagorias of the good life and the American (neoliberal) dream. This manifests in the wide-scale and accepted assumption that it is "better to be dead than disabled." This assumption is the punchline and plot device of many an ableist story, both fiction and nonfiction.[27]

My method for defining ableism for myself, as a philosopher by training, was to catalog a few powerful examples of provocative and useful definitions by Disability Studies scholars. I do this not to trivialize or to contradict any one of these definitions; rather, to springboard—in a Socratic style[28]—to the more abstract work of "definition." Each of these seem to me to contribute something quite valuable to the question of what ableism "is" and in order to better "scale out" its operations:

- Kim Q. Hall, in the introduction to *Feminist Disability Studies* (2011, 3) cites Susan Wendell, "ableism is a product of long-standing Western somatophobia."
- David Pfeiffer in "The Philosophical Foundations of Disability Studies," describes the problem of disability in reference to "deficit," to which he says, "Disability does not refer to a deficit in a person. Disability refers to a value judgment that something is not being done in a certain, acceptable way . . . [based] on value judgments concerning functioning, normality, and health. In other words, the term disability is based on ideology and social class" (2002, ¶7).
- Linda Ware, in "Writing, Identity and the Other: Dare We Do Disability Studies?" states that: "Cultural perceptions of disability do not emerge in a vacuum; they accrue slowly and over time, informed by normalizing discourses in medicine and psychology and reinforced by institutions and unchallenged beliefs of deficiency and need" (2001, 107).

These facets provide something of a working definition: ableism emerges from a Western *somatophobia*, in which vital needs are interpreted as *deficits* and *deficiencies*, in an *accrual* of *cultural perceptions*, such that in their overlap, together they set up a terrain in which we can think about where ableism "resides" without being directly resisted or confronted—in other words, where ableist affections may be easily exercised *unaddressed*.

Hall's calling-out of the somatophobia in Western thinking is an important component of the social construction of disability and its ideological preservation. This naming as a phobia, for me, provoked new lines of inquiry: why is it that a service professional, who might work long-term with a particularly disabled population, still privately and personally fears that same disability? Why is there a confusion between disability and illness in the care and treatment of patients?[29] More importantly, why won't ablebodied people spend time really thinking through and critically examining those deeply-seated fears about being/becoming disabled (or merely *aging*) in a way that qualitatively changes the content of these phobias, especially in the way one might need to relate to the world? Is the emotional and intellectual labor of confronting one's own "ghosts"[30] even recognized as the "good work" that needs to be done, often has yet to be done?

I follow Arendt's powerful prologue with a similar injunction against the intellectual tendencies toward "not needing to think, only to act." Whenever there is a response to need and crisis, it tends to take the form of being highly personal, apolitical, and centering in on mostly the interests of the self-preserving individual, as is the case when one must think about disability:[31] simply stated, it is most *often about me, without them.* Because the labor of revising thinking, rethinking, and thinking-through are not considered valuable forms of global or political intervention, it is then also assumed that there is limited impact on how this kind of philosophical work could predispose us for fundamental changes made in and to the mechanisms of an ableist world. In effect, even a collective kind of "doing" might still preserve the idea that there is no need for an ideological intervention that can operate alongside disability advocacy and rights history. This is especially true in awareness campaigns that only satisfy the desire to know that disabled people exist, but any work to accept, ally or advocate for and alongside people with disabilities is then pushed further to the margin, as in: "not my problem." As Kassiane S. for the Autistic Self Advocacy Network (ASAN) critically states it: "Awareness is easy. Acceptance requires actual work."[32]

Arendt described a twofold alienation in the way the modern world preserves its thoughtlessness: as a flight into the self and away from the earth into the universe.[33] Overcoming these particular *internalizing* and *externalizing* alienations, by her account, was to restore the significance of political activity, qualitatively distinct from the world-building and world-maintaining activities of labor and work respectively, into the modern world. "Activity" proper is the activity that shapes worlds anew (1958, 9). She describes an expansion of the *vita activa,* an engagement with the world that preserves human *plurality* and *natality,* qualitatively different than just our contributions to the world in terms of labor and work activities. In many of her texts, she sought ways in which we most need to dispose of thinking in stereotype, those sweeping general categories that were to serve as intellectual placeholders in lieu of thinking in pluralities, and in nuanced, novel ways: that we are all part of the category, "mankind," for instance (1973, 466).

What will follow here is the interrogation into perceived, promoted, and recognized "ablebodiedness" and what it does to feed the social and cultural imaginary as *fundamentally ableist* in its operations. These dismembering operations are twofold: as *intergenerational,* between parents/guardians and children and *institutional,* between professionals and their patients, students, or clients. This is the rationale for why it is also important to be clear that any outlining of the scale and scope of ableism is tentative though urgent, and undoubtedly should never go untested. This address of ableism—my particular style of "address"—remains time and site-specific, culturally, and politically localized.

Thinking here of the line of inquiry Primo Levi adopts when describing the phenomenon of Auschwitz in his preface to *The Drowned and The Saved* (1989), I want to note his point, which he raises as:

> a more urgent question, the question which torments all those who have happened to read our accounts: How much of the concentration camp world is dead and will not return, like slavery and the dueling code? How much is back or is coming back? What can each of us do so that in this world pregnant with threats at least this threat will be nullified?

For Levi, the threat of deathcamps and genocides survives in the way the world was now capable of "so lucid a combination of technological ingenuity, fanaticism and cruelty" (20–21).

Ableism is the ideological institutionalization for the ways disability is tolerated and not quite tolerated, in the systemic marginalization of disabled experience and self-directed narratives, and in the enforced silence against any interrogation into those value judgments that classify and distinguish the disabled from the ablebodied. I use Levi here to remind us that ableism is a thinking that can construct death camps and sustain (eu)genocides, without *thinking* and without *hesitation*.[34]

The "value judgments about functionality, normality, and health," as Pfeiffer states it, is the content of much of this emotional and symbolic fodder that establishes intergenerational and institutional boundaries for ablebodiedness. Value judgments are *communicable* and can become both implicit and explicit, further establishing unrecognized dichotomies to which all are subjected: the drowned and the saved.[35] In this kind of class division, there are those who submit to the ideological authority of what makes, for instance, normality and health, and those for whom the value judgments "drown" them into oblivion. This boundary between ablebodied and the disabled, creates a direct benefit in the form of privilege: the privileges of participating in the fabrication of a "convenient reality" and privileges what Levi calls "the construction of convenient truth [as it] grows and is perfected" (1989, 27).

Expectations and fears about the body and its connections to individuality and identity—what one should be able to do and what one should but cannot—limits discourse about political, social, and cultural possibilities for the sake of a less ableist or non-ableist future.[36] With a philosophical injunction about a non-ableist future, I hope to clarify the conditions in which non-ableist thinking may be possible and most necessary, furthering a way that can lead to world-changing political possibilities to shape the world "anew," not limited to challenging the oppressive ideological thinking about what disability signifies and what makes a person "disabled."[37] In other words, a future that is "less ableist" is not enough to cover and fully address the scale and scope of its current operation.

These unchecked biases allow clear lines of division between those "able" from those disabled, equivalent to a class division. Add to this ideological and material division, the license to arbitrarily add to the disabled classification, an aesthetics of disgust, aggression, and objectification by those who can pass or who can qualify as *able* (or ablebodied). Simply stated and as prime example, even the seemingly benign mark of being "special needs" can be reread here as just ableist-speak operating as another form of unjustified segregation and vicious discrimination between those who will and may drown from those valued as worth saving in the context of educational institutions, but only if "we" are inspired or have pity on them enough to do so.

As a philosopher, these too are my personal "ghosts": the catalogued superstitions, inherited and unpacked biases, the unspoken, and unaddressed errors that seep into the operating rationales of social structures and political mechanisms which I have learned and in which I have been raised. The ideological, biased divisions between the ablebodied and the disabled are not benign distinctions; they emerge from the material and educational conditions of exclusion and segregation and are a form of literacy—an aggregation of experiences that inscribe a reward system for "normal (read: natural) ability," functioning as semiotic currency for the ablebodied among their own class, organizing, and solidifying it into a *kind* of individual, as if that other class of "special needs" is a kindred group, yet, in this ideological "un-thinking that is a doing," as such, ableist ideology marks off a category that contains nothing one can conscientiously call "kind."

HOW IS ABLEISM TO BE RESISTED?

The form of resistance from a philosopher might be as you expect; an intellectual exercise, not immediately politically or socially tangible in the sense of disability activism, but this is an exercise not completely without social and political purpose.[38] If ableism, in its scope, is ideological—unthinking, phobic, and, without hesitation, shaping the world as I am claiming here— then what could be some of the linchpin concepts that could sustain a meditation intended to *excise* the bias? What tools might we need for a fair and thorough "thinking-through" without slipping into the polemics of "us" and "them?" How might a discussion of ideology resist further ideology?

In *Origins of Totalitarianism* (1973), "Ideology and Terror," Arendt describes the political and philosophical mechanisms of ideology—the rigor of thought based on limited conceptualizations of humanity, legitimacy, and progress—so that the lives of persons become obstacles to the movement of the ideology: "it is as though their plurality has disappeared into one Man of gigantic proportions." She prefaces this warning: "Terror . . . [comes from] the law of movement whose ultimate goal is not the welfare of men or the interest of one man but for the fabrication of mankind, [eliminating] individuals for the sake of the species, sacrifices 'parts' for the sake of the 'whole' . . . " (1973, 465–466).[39] She herself resisted being called a philosopher for such that reason. The escape to universalizations and abstract generalities in *vita contemplativa* is to ignore the labors and material conditions that are necessary to sustain a meaningful life.[40]

Natality, a powerful concept from Arendt,[41] is the idea that each individual can uniquely contribute to the world anew—as an *existential* and pre-political fact. She does not model this concept from a capabilities approach[42]—as if one needs to *do* something or have potential to do something in order to contribute to the world in a meaningful way; rather, one born into the world already belongs to it as "earth-bound."[43] Her concept of natality is not a theological concept either—as if we are earth-bound "creatures" that owe existence to a creator. As earth-bound, each individual signals a humanistic affirmation of an existential positionality and *de facto*, as existing, always already brings a challenge to our worlded, preconceived commitments: to be, as worlded, a beginning by *just being born*, *is* already *to belong*.[44]

Arendt's arguments are challenging a fundamentally flawed aspect permissible in much of Western thinking: that ideologies—good intentions aside—particularly progressive, naturalizing ideologies armed with political policy, can effectively execute and exterminate whole populations of persons. Ideologies with political teeth can become and have been violent and dehumanizing. This was Arendt's concern as well even when it came to Marxist ideology: as much as his theoretical work was a resistance to inequalities of material and economic production through capital, his work ironically translated into the totalitarian conditions and violent events of the Bolshevik revolution.[45] This is the difficulty as Arendt argues it in *The Origins of Totalitarianism*: ideologies are not benign, and, even when well-designed and intended, in certain social and economic conditions, can manifest into the political machinations and terrors of the totalitarian state.[46]

Yet, following Arendt's lead, instead of escaping from the world in an other-worldly way, we return to the question of labor: *why do we work so hard to maintain a world not worth living in?* Our earth-boundedness requires that the world we make for ourselves out from and out of the earth is *habitable* and *sustainable*: we owe this equally to everyone. These ideologies operate harms on those classified, alienated, and de-worlded *kinds* of persons (now nonpersons), not for what they *do* or how they *act*, but only for that their mere existence is deemed an offense; it is that they *are*.[47]

This also means that the honest philosopher—one who recognizes the limits of speculations and even with the best of intentions—remains at the periphery often unable to offer further practical insights; I have *no advice to give* regarding the resistance to ableist ideology. I do not have bullet points that outline: "how to spot an (dis)ableist." I am also careful to resist ableism by resisting philosophical advice-giving: philosophical discourse as "self-help," (which I realize that many non-academics and nonphilosophers might think is the function of philosophy) because most philosophically-sounding self-help advice is also often *unreflectively ableist.*

That is also not to say there is no therapeutic value to philosophical inquiry; rather, this project is about intellectual perception—a thought project and a work in progress—an opening to possibilities that are needed for the sake of those who have been rendered valueless and actively dismembered by the general somatophobia of Western culture and the accumulated "wisdom" and "best practices" of disabling medical, psychological, and service institutions which remain on a larger scale unresisted. Social systems meant to serve a public good instead drown those who resist them. Survivors of the system—the "saved," if you will—become passive to the ideological assumption and categories that remain pervasive and unchecked, subsumed into the very fabric of these same social, service, medical, and political institutions. These systems dismember in their membership; this is the wide-scale of their ableist operations—in which ableism is instituted and operational, deeply-rooted, without censure, and even "licensed and practicing."

That stated, I take resistance to be more of a personal term. While I theoretically affiliate it with Arendt's concept of natality, I take it home with me first. My first chapter is about the gap between my personal and professional experience (chapter 1) with discrimination and disability. My experience came first as a parent of a non-neurotypical child and, later, of a neurotypical child. With these experiences came all of the ambivalence and insecurity of no longer clearly identifying within ableist culture while also new to disability advocacy frameworks. This insecurity was trumped, clear to my mind, by a caution: if there is "nothing about us, without us," that I could easily still appropriate the work of disability advocates with my unpacked ableist intentions. I had given this (my) problem a name: the "interloper problem."

In the theoretical framework of the philosopher Emmanuel Levinas, my naming the feeling of ambiguity as an "interloper problem" originates with his idea of the condition of *trespass*, as in: "I came to the party uninvited." In the Levinasian model, the "other" intrudes upon the *jouissance* of self; a selfhood that is socially and culturally preserved as ideally ablebodied. In my case, my "standing"—as ablebodied—literally and metaphorically, is an intrusion among those at the margins of this hyper-individualized idea of self; but, the ablebodied interloper can also be a threat to the world of those who have been resisting ableism in everyday, labor-intensive and invisible ways. I have also worked carefully to hearken the calls made by Disability Advocates, as in the case, for example, of how #CrippingTheMighty, became an effort to resist the click-bait content of an online blog, *The Mighty*. From advocate, Savannah Logsdon-Breakstone:

> *The Mighty* is basically disability content aggregation . . . [with] problematic- and possibly more damaging-content . . . [being] the warrior mommy blogger content. Beyond the fact that it centers parents over disabled perspectives, it frequently is focused on bemoaning how hard it is to parent a child with a disability and on throwing "pity parties" for parents. This is a dangerous narrative, as it normalizes negative and even aggressive narratives of parent- ing, which can end in tragic outcomes for the children of the parents that buy into it.
>
> Additionally it is the pathologizing and/or othering of the disabled child, down to the minutia of their lives. Under this framework, being respectful of the humanity and even the privacy of the child is ignored, and intimate details end up being published. Things that the parent would never post about themselves or about their non-disabled kids become public knowledge.[48]

Responding to and maintaining responsibility for my position of ablebodied privilege, I resist interloping and do my best to *listen*—to "hearken"—and attend to the language and conversations especially as they offer ways of critically addressing ableism.

This difficulty of parenting and the danger of becoming an interloper was complicated by my profession as a philosopher.[49] Professionally, the practice is to seek critique through argument and position-taking. Personally, I find argumentation to be masking aggression; rather, academically, I prefer and have argued for "problem-posing" and bridge-building methodologies in the work of constructing theory.[50] I much rather prefer to seek out the paradox and *aporia* that has no resolve and no clear account. As Judith Butler reads Levinas, to "chart ambivalence" is to humanize and resist dehumanization; to make room for the precariousness of life.[51]

Charting this ambivalence beyond my own experience, analyzing the intellectual, political, and cultural mechanisms of diagnosis [chapter 2] and diagnostics, questioning how diagnoses can disable by constructing and concretizing ableist ideologies and intentions, I will attempt to reclaim the work of diagnostic thinking in ordinary, everyday ways following the calls in Disability Studies scholarship for cultural and social paradigm shifts.[52] Diagnoses and diagnostic thinking raise a conceptual framework problem I think most relevant to a confrontation with ableism, in setting it out of the context of opinions against opinions, what Charles Mills calls a "doxastic environment,"[53] which easily promotes privileged bias and ignorance. In a doxastic environment, ignorance is not innocent.[54] In order that we address these demands to qualify knowledge when it "presents itself unblushingly," I will be reframing the dialectical significance of diagnostic thinking along with a demand for nuance and tension in all diagnostic claims.

Following philosophers already working at the intersection of philosophy and Disability Studies scholarship, like Shelley Tremain,[55] I trace the boundaries and fault-lines of ableist thinking through narrative and critique in effort to resist the embodiment of them in the practice of a dialogue. The chapter on intersectionality [chapter 3] is devoted to this effort and takes up Tremain's demand for more thorough inclusion of disability, here in particular as also a partial intersectional analysis. Influenced by Chandra Talpade Mohanty's *Feminism Without Borders: Decolonizing Theory, Practicing Solidarity* (2003), in which one chapter serves as a dialogical interlude with Biddy Martin, I coauthor an interrogation of ableism and its analogous and intersectional relation to other social and political oppressions with philosopher, Devonya Havis, and with writer and activist, Lydia X. Z. Brown.

HOW IS ABLEISM TO BE CONFRONTED?

The only way I can answer this question is nonviolently; I must comport this theoretical confrontation without the passive aggression of an "argument for argument's sake." Instead, this confrontation is posited *discursively*—confrontation as open-ended discourse—first, out of respect for those who bear witness to the reality of what has passed and ought not have transpired, and second, for the sake of challenging those mechanisms of cruelty and oppression that have been engendered by ableist ideology.

The innovations in critical Disability Studies and theories on the social construction of disability have been an immense resource to me intellectually. Within the emerging,[56] interdisciplinary field of Disability Studies, as a humanistic study, what would be the basic conditions for non-ableist discourse? What is required for a full, philosophical confrontation with ableist thinking in both scale and scope?

Firstly, as Tobin Siebers puts it, "ideology is unacceptable" (2008, 22) which I take to more precisely mean, *all ideology* that preserves some form of ableism.[57] Second, and equally important, Robert McRuer in *Crip Theory* states that there is an "ineluctable [inescapable] *impossibility* . . . *of an ablebodied identity*,"[58] or, on this same point, David Mitchell states that "*the able body has no definitional core* (it poses as transparently average or normal), [such that] the disabled body surfaces as anybody capable of being narrated as outside the norm" (2000, 49).[59] Our ideologies, our stories, our cultural history and social reification as they uncritically celebrate normative ability need to be challenged and overturned. In this way, there is much to be done. This is what "disorder to difference" implies: A sociocultural transition that can ask (require? demand?) each of us to participate with more mindfulness than thoughtlessness, or as Paulo Freire might say, *conscientiously.*

In order to better command the ethical imperative for developing a heightened sensitivity to the potential aggression of my own ableist projections, I have needed to become more "acutely aware of my own lack of self-awareness."[60] The theoretical language that has given me the courage to engage the wide scale and scope of ableism—to travel the borderlands between worlds of experience—is through Butler's ontological definition of precariousness [chapter 4]. More radical than other approaches to addressing ableism that I have encountered so far is this working concept of precarity, as the uneven distribution of the ontological situation of precariousness; it is "a way of thinking connections, of claiming kinship and relations. . . . Precariousness is a place for thinking the ethical because it begins with the Other, rather than with the self."[61] The vulnerability of precarity can excite fear and violence when it is recognized and denied. Precariousness can be exposed for some and exploited by others in an uneven distribution of sociopolitical precarity. It is the existential vulnerability of precariousness that can undo the stasis of selfhood, a basic sense of being in (and belonging to) the world. The existential fact of this condition is also denied when we claim independence from all others. Butler, more honestly, describes how we each depend on anonymous others for our existence and without whom none of us would subsist.[62]

Following Butler, revelations of precariousness also manifest as political and social *threat*; leading to defensiveness and aggression. It could also be an opening to the possibility for more conscientious, nonviolent response. Here, the project for me is to take on something more personal as it is at the same time philosophical; thinking through the mode of intellectual and aggressive self-defense and emotional denial of ableist biases *wherever they may be.* In working toward a mode of honest address, remaining open to the fact of existential precariousness, the demand remains for revealing *vulnerability,* without also rendering any others vulnerable or more vulnerable than they might already be, opting only for the most nonaggressive and open-ended approach.

Out of the lack in the discourse over the public good of *accessibility* and *inclusion* and out of a desire to think of the world reformulated in radically new and creative ways, I extend this address of ableism by exploring the use and function of the prosthesis [chapter 5] as an ambivalence between disabled and ablebodied experiences worth charting. The concept of prosthesis, like that of diagnosis, is a "going back to the Greeks"—a methodologically familiar approach in phenomenology—yet, this is not to return to former conceptions; rather, it is an attempt at a continued reinvigoration of meaning out from the current states of ableist indifference and insensitivity. Taking instruction from the principled work of Universal Design (UD)[63] that maximizes accessibility and inclusion, I build here its companion philosophical defense. Theoretical construction of *habitability* is the concert space,[64] intersecting a plurality of perspectives, localized events that make it possible to imagine that one does not need to directly know one another in order to recognize and respond to one another's need while concomitantly prohibiting the disabling effects. Thinking of it as a sort of "eco-phenomenological" approach, it is an attempt to bracket all of the institutionalized suspicions over the everyday actions and intentions of individuals for the sake of imagining a world with the sufficient tools for democratically-inclined introspection and communication.

Arendt, when asked how to defeat totalitarianism, if in fact it is as pervasive and terrorizing as she describes it, hinted that totalitarian ideology has within it the tools of its own self-destruction (1973, 478). In this way, each part has a critical relationship to the whole. As I will argue in the epilogue, stating perhaps what needs to be said: that the possibility of non-ableist thinking implies that there ought not to be conceived any built "disposable parts." A declaration against all institutionalized and inherited forms of *dismemberment*—materially and non-materially—is required, especially as it is the *modus operandi* of all ableist ideologies.

Chapter 1

Experience

When I arrived at the June 2013 meeting of the Society for Disability Studies (SDS) Conference in Orlando, Florida,[1] I had not quite imagined what my role might have to mean as an ally, first identifying as an ablebodied feminist philosopher and also as a straight and cisgender, white, (newly) middle-class mother of two.[2] As Jay Dolmage in *Disability Rhetoric* states it (2014, 22), citing Tobin Siebers:

> As Siebers writes of the "ideology of ability," we (through vehicles like philosophy and rhetoric) have constructed ability as the key feature of what constitutes being human. . . . Ableism renders disability as abject, invisible, disposable, less than human, while ablebodiedness is represented as at once ideal, normal, and the mean or default.

What I learned was the degree to which I could be surprised and humbled as well as triggered in the context of these new experiences that challenged my latent ableist assumptions.[3] This process of realization included the mix of shame and despair that comes with the depth and radicality of a personal paradigm shift; on the order of an emotional earthquake, my own assumptions created tectonic-plate-like frictions of discomfort and non-resolution. There was no "clear conscience" to be found as I navigated this conference—having been to many other academic conferences in which accessibility was not a priority—and what was most central here: the able-bodied was not the norm.

Accommodation meant something other than what I had assumed. I was asked to reassess my own planning strategies against what was typical preparation for attending a conference: committing to only wearing scent-free personal-care products,[4] large-font copies always on hand, sound and

1

light adjustments before a presentation, the availability of Communication Access Realtime Translation (CART),[5] sign-interpreters, plus, available for attendees, a quiet room, later a dance, with service animals always visible and accommodated as well. I found that my habit of walking into an auditorium space or lecture hall was itself problematic. I would usually prefer to sit on the aisle or in the back of the room thinking I was *unassuming*; but, in this setting, with several people entering the space utilizing wheelchairs, I instead found myself *too assuming*: I had unintentionally taken up the more accessible spaces in the room.

At the same time, I was delighted to find normativity in the nonnormative,[6] activating my imagination for what is possible and what can be made politically and aesthetically real despite recent other experiences of being alienated, rendered suspicious or blameworthy by other communities, including academic ones. The content of the work in and outside of the conference was a practiced and liberating environment of speech and body acceptance. Realizing myself as kind of like an interloper meant also feeling fraught with anxiety and guilt, so being among the Disability Studies (DS) community was privately quite disorienting. This psychological conflict added complexity to the interloper problem: what kind of person—who can identify with normative and sociocultural privileges not only "shows up," but worse—hides out among marginalized or minoritized communities for their own gain? This was a concern that, as I became aware of it, I had to keep thinking through in order to remain less rather than more assuming and if I intended to be honest ("keep it real") about my ablebodiedness.[7]

This disorientation in a professional, academic setting was ironically the more familiar thing to me in my personal life: while this was a space not centered on the movement and promotion of the neurotypical and ablebodied, this is how I had been already reconfiguring my home as I learned how to better parent my non-neurotypical kindergartener. My home had been configured to "fit" her in all the ways she was wonderfully unique and made demands in unexpected ways. I knew that my private spaces were different than most others, because, once we were out of these familial spaces, much like what is already true outside of the DS spaces,[8] there were too many ways in which the world did not easily suit her, rarely accommodating in the specific ways in which she needed supports, and would also judge and reject her as well as us by proxy.

I also had been inducted into the Early Intervention and the Special Education system, perhaps still hoping that she would "grow out of it." But being conflicted with these normative desires and already heavily invested in creating alternative supports for a non-neurotypical loved one in a hostile neurotypical world, this may have been right preparation because I had been riddled with soul-searching, gut-wrenching uncertainties about how best to represent and promote her place in the outside world while privately maintaining her care, including teaching her basic self-care.[9] My literacy in the complex operation and identification of ableist discourse might have been woefully underdeveloped, but my experiences were dense, latent and ready for unpacking.[10]

WHO DO WE BLAME FOR ABLEISM?

With my induction into the Special Education system, already quite segregated and deviated from the paths and experiences of neighborhood parents with children in General Education,[11] I had experienced many ableist assumptions from unexpected places. The parent-blaming was palpable and even came from within my own extended family. It was often difficult to make it simple and clear to others: *there was nothing wrong with my daughter*, even though she wasn't like other children and needed constant, contextualized support.[12] The constancy of these "tests for normalcy" led me to often internalize the microgestures of judgmental stares, sighs, audible *tsks*, or, if they felt comfortable enough, full-on interrogations about what I was or was not doing right or wrong—on planes, on trains, in theaters, at the park, the store, etc., ironically, especially at events or spaces designed for the enjoyment of *other children*.

How was I to respond to these negative perceptions, assumptions, and dismissals of my child? How was I to respond to the suspicious tone directed toward me in my role as her parent? How was I to make her invisible condition visible without exposing her in order to deflect my own discomfort and frustration?[13] Although I have these questions, feeling confronted too often in situations like this about how to respond, I *have no clear advice*. What I can do is outline how, in those moments, the situation had me debating between a few different options:

- To be a bit defensive to the obliviousness in stating the obvious, as in, "I am so glad you noticed that my daughter is not typical."
- To respond minimally with little affect.
- To educate and inform, as a "teacher" knows how to do, to model, and to quip with a "silver-lining" comment against whatever negative tone or import came with the questions and/or comments of the curious.

My child's father would usually use resource option two, while I would tend toward option three—but either way, we found it exhausting. (We then, when we could, discussed privately *and* at length how we wanted to respond with the first option.)

That is the personal side to these questions. Professionally, questions of responsiveness in particular came to mind: asking myself about my "response"—*What do I say? What do I do?* This is akin to asking about my particular responsibility—where it *ought* to go and how it *ought* to be issued—and for that matter—to whom, when? In thinking about this problem—when I am confronted by an ableist society—I realize that I can start by taking responsibility for my own ableist tendencies as best I can.

The Individual Educational Plan (IEP) meeting earlier that same Spring of 2013 was quite the summation of what had been a challenging year for my daughter (and our family) navigating Special Education. The real "induction" included this moment—more like a hazing—when my daughter's Special Education teacher handed out this graph during our annual IEP meeting, one that was not previewed until that moment (Figure 1.1).

Comparing her with a peer, this Special Education teacher represented my daughter with the large black bar indicating a "daily average" of interfering behaviors against the gray bar of a "peer" (and later indicated that the peer was another student from her "enclosed" Special Education class), and, notably, in the last of the comparisons, the peer behavior was recorded as negligible. These noted behaviors include:

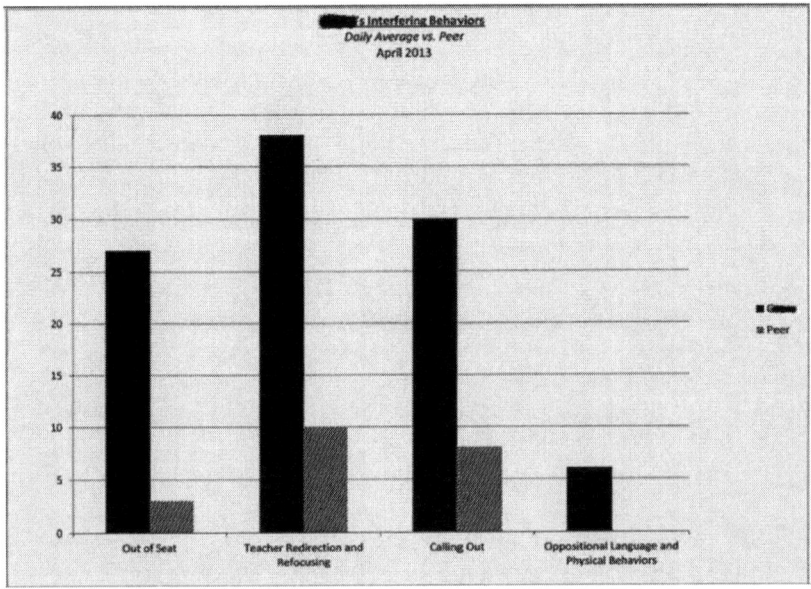

Figure 1.1 Teacher-generated Bar Graph Distributed at an Individual Educational Plan (IEP) Annual Meeting Regarding the Activities of a Kindergarten Student in a Self-enclosed Special Education Class (2013).

- Out of seat
- Teacher Redirection and Refocusing
- Calling out
- Oppositional Language and Physical Behaviors.

As you can imagine, this led to a spirited debate in the meeting and a loss of good faith—a meeting that went on for two-and-a-half hours more and without resolution.[14] I have been known in mixed company to refer to it as an IEP "shit-show."[15] The parent in me was horrified because this is exactly what I would hope would NOT be the interpretation of my child by peers, much less by service providers or educators. The professor in me, who had been teaching Philosophy of Education for quite a few years at this point, conscientiously fell back on a mantra I have come to rely on in my classroom: teacher-blaming is as unjustifiable as parent-blaming. *If we parent-blame, teacher-blame or even student-blame, we will not know how to improve our practice or our pedagogy.*[16] All the same, I was quite aware of how close I was to thinking some form of blameworthiness was required.

It was during this time that I organized events on Autism Education (rather than Autism Awareness)[17] at the same time my child was being personally called out for all of her "interfering [read: bad] behavior," trying to navigate the borderlands between the upcoming changes in the DSM (Diagnostic and Statistical Manual of Mental Disorders) from the fourth to fifth edition (which included no more Asperger's and Pervasive Developmental Disorder—Not Otherwise Specified [PDD-NOS] categories of diagnosis).[18] I had forged ahead with the limited hope for a future in which social, emotional, behavioral, and learning differences meant something *other than* segregation and alienation.

I had some sense that the reading of neurological and behavioral differences should not be so cavalierly treated as *deficits*. It was then that I learned that the puzzle piece as a symbol for Autism is *sabotaging* a critical understanding of the lives and dignity of autistic persons. Now, a puzzle piece (that does not "fit" a puzzle; rather, emphasizing the marginality of someone who is "too" unique) is awareness that does not interrogate; it might only be a superficial acceptance that masks possibility for the self-critical labor of engaged understanding. Simply stated, that pervasive blue puzzle piece or multicolored puzzle ribbons avoid difficult discourse and rides roughshod over the lives and perspectives of those who need to lead the discussion.[19]

As an educator, teaching future educators, I saw also students who announced their desire to learn about "differentiated learning" but limited to Special Education and "Special Needs" contexts, with the most articulate part of their desire being that they "only wished to help people." More often, when we would work through DS literature, unpacking ableist biases, students only really desired to serve themselves better and in more ablebodied ways (and sometimes, they would even admit they were interested in study-ing disability interventions because there is "good money" in speech therapy, occupational and physical therapy, nursing, etc.). The medicalization of dis-ability was pervasive in these assumptions and desires, difficult to challenge with students hearing a DS approach for the first time. It seemed like it was my word against a culture that diagnoses and fixes everything, and with con-stant appeal to economic viability and "success." The greatest drive in their resistance to DS literature—and what I now read as contributing to the depth of their ableist anxieties—was the fear of being not employable, underem-ployed, or of becoming unemployed, despite being educated.[20]

Thinking about the disabling and ableist features of education in a sup-posedly democratic society, this philosophical outlook was perceived as interference to progress in building their academic skill and professional development, disorienting and suspending the comfortable assumptions to which our culture and their educational goals made more readily available. I realized, both for myself and for my students, through problem-posing peda-gogy that "dialectical thinking" is "critical thinking."[21] So, I collected and cultivated exercises that could assist me in generating that dialogical learning. I needed tools to actively challenge privately held ableist biases, so important for getting to the more complex and political ableist ideologies, exacerbated by the commonplace literacy of medicalized disability in the context of a neoliberal economy, given to society at large. DS, for students in this context, was "too expensive" to study.

One exercise was a thought experiment borrowed from Linda Ware in "Writing, Identity and the Other: Dare We Do Disability Studies?" (2001), in which she problem-poses a veteran teacher and asks him to write about his first memories of disability. Tom, in thinking about this, with very little background in DS, in his journey of what she calls "self-discovery," sponta-neously recalls growing up with his twin brother who was physically disabled (115–116). To this she states, "His growing understanding about the cultural and material conditions of disability reminded me of the historian Douglas Baynton, who asserts, that 'disability is everywhere in history, once you begin looking for it, but conspicuously absent in the histories we write.'"[22] In effect, as much as there is a perceived distance between ablebodied and disabled experiences, this small thought experiment made disability intimate and not foreign; it brought disability in a close, intelligible proximity.

Ware's task became a springboard for me to think about how instructive thinking and reexamining first memories can be. As we examine first memo-ries, it is required that it be complemented by an emotional inventory:[23]

- How did I feel at the time of the experience? How did I react to these feelings?

- How did others appear to respond or react to the situation? How did I feel about these responses or reactions?
- How do those feelings deviate from how I feel about them now? How do I feel about those others as I think of their responses or reactions?
- How are these experiences informing my fears and anticipations about disabilities?
- How should I rethink these fears and anticipations about disabilities?

I usually model my own homework, for myself and for my students. In my case, I describe my first memory of a girl I grew up with and, from some memory of my interactions with her, I now realize in adulthood not only that she was autistic, but also that she was a magnet to playground bullies and general peer indifference. I don't remember participating in the bullying—which is not to say that I did or didn't (which is more about selective memory)—but only with a clear memory of everyone identifying her as "retarded": a word that is one of the most derogatory of ableist slurs.[24] With this thought experiment, I imagine that there was very *little chance* that I didn't participate, knowing myself as always interested in peer acceptance, always wanting to participate and seek friendship with those I admired.

This desire to "fit in" was one that I had to actively attend to and modify as I grew up. In my adult life, it became important to inhibit this desire to fit in based on peer pressure, because it had often exposed me to emotionally abusive relationships or contributed to a self-sabotage of my creativity and need for independence. What I had also discovered with this exercise was something more novel: my deep fear of being called "retarded,"[25] coupled with other concepts that felt synonymous, like "weird" and "stupid." These anxiety-triggers were only made more transparent to me in the context of an emotional inventory. And without some basic literacy in the history of how ableist slurs can emerge,[26] one might think themselves quite clever to appropriate language that does not belong to them, and which, with ableist assumptions and attitudes, feel comfortable to name others as they see fit. Particularly problematic is the lack of emotional maturity and general insensitivity to encourage currency in ableist slurs in order to have a good punchline.[27]

This exercise has, critically and more self-reflectively, also given me context for some of the *less defensible* affective qualities of my parenting style—what I worry about, how I react, and how permissive I can be—as the "needy" parent. In being honest and thinking through this experiment, I realized how these deeply affective ableist phobias can diminish my relationship with my daughter *as her own self-yet-to-be-determined* and not as simply in my charge. I have found myself too worried about how others might name her: peers, other parents, and especially when we are out in public. These anxieties are the reactive fallout of a deeper unpacked problem for me; that, as much as my daughter looks "ablebodied," she is not neurotypical. Because we live in a society that has many names for and ideas about the non-neurotypical, I can almost hear them and see them as they seem to be perceived deficits, even though they may be unspoken, unsaid.

In the wake of the first "shit-show" IEP meeting (and there have been more and worse since), when I am frustrated by the manipulations, mischaracterizations, dismissals, and rejections by the Special Education bureaucracy (or, as Arendt might characterize it, the banality of administration),[28] I have learned to ask myself: *Is this about me or about her? Is it about my ego or is it about advocating for her—her needs, her supports?* This is a *minding* and *reminding* exercise that I must do and can be some of the toughest work of parenting, especially if I am to be her ally: that I don't project my own ableist bullshit onto her.

Tobin Siebers' analysis of ableism became a key support for navigating a new script for my role of parent-as-first-ally, an alternative role to my problem of also being a possible "interloper." In this way, I admit my academic training betrays me. Philosophers have done poorly on the question of thinking through disability.[29] I think Shelley Tremain is one of the best voices that can "out" the problem, while unveiling the deeply rooted biases of my profession:

> When feminist and non-feminist bioethicists and philosophers make the reductive assumption and assertion that any and all work that pertains to disability is in some sense biomedical or bioethical in nature—even when this work primarily addresses evidently metaphysical and epistemological concerns and questions—they variously sequester (feminist and non-feminist) philosophy of disability in the realm of "applied ethics," depoliticize and re-medicalize disability in ways that facilitate its continued omission from complex, intersectional feminist philosophical analyses and, furthermore, collaborate with the institutionalized, discursive, and structural ableism of the discipline and profession of philosophy according to which philosophical analyses of disability are "not really" (i.e., not "hard," not "core," not "rigorous") philosophy. In another context, Tommie Shelby has likewise pointed out that African American philosophy is diminished and delegitimized in a related way within the discipline of philosophy. In *We Who Are Dark: The Philosophical Foundations of Black Solidarity*, Shelby (2005) writes: "Within the broader discipline of philosophy as practised in the United States, African American philosophy is still largely marginalized. Many philosophers regard it as not real philosophy at all."[30]

To which she adds in 2014:

> In the six months since I published the *DSQ* article [cited above], little in philosophy has changed: The APA has taken no noticeable measures to include

vital information missing from its website, nor has it redesigned the inaccessible website itself, nor has it acted in any significant way upon any of the other criticisms or recommendations that I make in the article; the conceptual and organizational frameworks of PhilPapers and PhilJobs have not been modified, but rather continue to respectively marginalize and obscure research and teaching in the area of philosophy of disability, for the most part classifying work on disability in medical terms and ignoring its political character; some philosophy blogs continue to generate discursive practices that degrade disabled people and discount disabled philosophers and philosophy of disability; and most mainstream feminist philosophers continue to conceptualize and write about feminism and diversity in terms that limit their scope to gender alone, or to gender, race, and sexuality, or to gender, race, and class, producing "intersectional" analyses that essentially boil down to considerations of (binary) gender to which race and sexuality or race and class are rather haphazardly added and in whose terms disability is nowhere to be found.[31]

It seems that when there is systematic neglect to consider disability beyond personal encounters or experiences, then really, I would think no one escapes the question of responsibility in addressing ableism, independent of particular acts and ideological commitments. The more accessible approach has been the appeal to blameworthiness; an approach, I find, that does not provide enough discourse on how best to address the scale and scope of ableism. The "blame game" is just an easier way to callous oneself psychologically and emotionally from others who may have a greater demand not only on our everyday assumptions and generalized perceptions, but also in the ways it is a game that concretely systematizes an indifference to others.

An approach that would also demand that indifference be considered unacceptable, with a comportment of ethical non-indifference,[32] begins with what Charlton means in *Nothing About Us Without Us* (2000) when he cites phenomenologist and feminist philosopher, Sandra Bartky: "In *Femininity and Domination* [1990], . . . Bartky describes the power of raised consciousness" [Charlton quoting Bartky][33]:

The scales fall from our eyes. We are no longer required to struggle against unreal enemies, to put others' interests ahead of our own, or to hate ourselves. We begin to understand why we have such depreciated images of ourselves . . . Understanding, even beginning to understand this, makes it possible to change. Coming to see things differently, we are able to make out possibilities for liberating collective action and for unprecedented personal growth.

To this, Charlton adds, "it is not possible to definitively explain the changes Bartky describes" (115–116).

This is the beginning of raised consciousness by my account: one no longer finds themselves indifferent to the accounts by others made "alien" by an ableist society as well as accounting-for-others with new possibilities on the horizon,[34] vigilant in this accountability, especially when disability comes into frame or "onto the scene."[35]

In reflecting and returning to the events of the shit-show IEP meeting, I thought to analyze what was the source of the stress and anxiety I had developed from this experience. As a philosopher, I wanted to understand what the heart of the problem here could be—the systemic conditions that would permit a possibly well-intended teacher to present "data" to a parent in that setting and in that context. The terminology of "interfering behaviors" stood out as a source of analytic difficulty. Even the specific markers the teacher chose, like "out of seat" and "calling out" are typical behaviors of an autistic student, keeping in mind that this was an enclosed special education classroom that arguably had no comparative "peer" as indicated in the chart. I say arguably because this is one of the reasons why we stayed so long in the meeting. I began to think that if these behaviors are categorized as "interfering," then it is out of a failure of understanding disability generally and of educational philosophy particularly.

I realized that by pointing out these behaviors, this teacher had only referenced the obvious: non-neurotypical children do not have typical behavior, and cannot "pass" for typical, sometimes and most remarkably because of their nontypical behaviors. Here, the "interference" was not coming from her; the interference was in the expectations of normalness, the management of behavior, and the armchair pathologizing of children as well or poorly "behaved." The goal of "self-regulation"—language regularly issued by Special Education professionals—seemed to be motivated by the assumption that by tracking these "interfering behaviors," we are somehow protecting my daughter from self-destructiveness or, as a worse assumption, "helping her" as if contributing to her educational progress. Yet, if we suspend these normative expectations, this tracking and identification was inherently stigmatizing and could instead be a means for dehumanizing her, in real time, especially who she *could be, will be, and want to be* in identifying herself.

In this case, the goal of "self-regulation" had taken on a mythological quality in the context of my daughter's educative goals and became more complicated by the fact that we (as a family) "flirt" with normalcy: my daughter does many "typical" things and looks like a typical child for her age and gender, likes and takes interest in "typical things," just not in typical ways. What is in her future and whether she will have what she needs to subsist, this feeds my fears and expectations as a parent: so, then I must ask, what (the hell) does the goal of self-regulation really mean? Is it fair to anyone to have "self-regulation" imposed on them as also a sociopolitical expectation?[36]

Beyond the unpacking of privilege, as ally and as parent, I must suspend all normative expectation (akin to the *epochē*—the suspension of the ontic, everyday attitude—to put it in the language of phenomenology). In this context, philosophically, in order to reveal an existentially ethical relation with another, as "my child," as an "other-not me" who is not an extension of myself, needs a sustained and persistent *humanization*. Thinking honestly, there is no way to ideologically address what I have described as the "unmanageable but imaginable risk"[37] of raising a disabled child, or even a nondisabled child; rather, it is only through theoretically addressing (and, I think, that is preconditioned by first *emotionally* addressing) the conditions that deny precariousness and actively disable differences. With this thinking, we might also begin to do what we need to address and redress this kind of "unmanageable" (not to be domesticated?) risk of having to provide sustained resource and care despite the ableist demands and conditions that render all efforts unsustainable.

CAN PARENTS BE ALLIES?

In reviewing my experience, reconsidering the function of intention—and how actions, particularly *re*-actions, are thought about—in the context of the emotive qualities of expectation and desire with particular attention for what is rendered abject, there is possibility in reorganizing the relationships between, as Nel Noddings might describe it, the *one-caring* and the *one cared-for*.[38] The first step in addressing ableism in order to become an ally is to reckon with one's own "ableist anxiety." From Siebers:

> Asch and Rousso argue that psychoanalytic literature often maintains that disability itself causes such undesirable characteristics [as narcissism]. Studies of face-to-face interaction between nondisabled and disabled individuals tend to support these findings. They show that ablebodied people focus in face-to-face encounters more on their own anxiety than on the feelings of the person with the disability, and that their acceptance of disability lessens as narcissistic regression increases (2008, 43).[39]

In the context of addressing the pervasiveness of ableism, we could question the degree that the bias of ablebodied privilege has been made internal to the meaning of parenting, as well as ask for a more critical engagement with ableist expectations in the work of parenting. This critical engagement is not to engage parent-blaming or that some of us might parent children "better" than others. Rather, I would like to offer alternatives for parenting modeled from the situation of disability: when the child one has in one's charge is not ablebodied in traditional, normatively recognized ways.

So, regarding the question of allyship, approaching it from the perspective of disability, shouldn't all parents be allies to their children generally? Shouldn't all parents avoid the tendency for "narcissistic regression"? How might a parent—any parent—who desires independence or self-sufficiency for their child also become an obstacle to this possibility in their own ableist assumptions or biases?[40]

An example of challenging unexamined ableist thinking with DS literature, applicable to *all parents* as a possible source of bias regardless of their connection to disability experience, is to question what seems to be part of a greater ableist bias, that of an "acquiescence bias." Dan Goodley and Mark Rapley describe how acquiescence in people with intellectual disabilities is produced: in which, from a small range of "right" answers, an interviewer validates the answer to questions by an interviewee only when it conforms to the options of possible right answers. The interviewer that maintains an interview schedule and pursues these specific answers can produce a situation of *deficit*: in which the interviewee is unable to respond independently; instead, they say, "in the face of the demands of the interviewer, change their position . . . until the trouble that is brought about by these demands is resolved." They add context to the acquiescence bias in that, "The consequence of the widespread and uncritical acceptance of the notion that people with 'intellectual disabilities' are, essentially, incapable of 'validly' reporting on their own subjectivity is that they are thereby silenced" (130–131). Simply stated, the effect of the demands made by an authority over someone in their charge creates a situation of bad faith[41] through the force of acquiescence, or as Freire might problematize it, in the way they are trying to domesticate reality (2009, 54).

How do all parents and caretakers play a role in the production of this bias? Such that they are in the position of the interviewer and the child as the interviewee, with a schedule of questions or concerns that, "above all else," needs to be maintained? How often has there only been one "satisfactory" answer to which the child has no choice but to acquiesce, effectively responding only in the way that the caretaker cares to listen?

Allyship then, I suggest, would be a resource to think about how to be a more critically engaged parent, open to abandoning the need for normative expectation and inhibiting the projection of one's ableist expectations on children with which they might have the greatest influence—the one who is "mine but not me" (and I would extend this question of engagement to all caretakers: the nontraditional parent, the legal guardian, the grandparent, the adoptive auntie or uncle, etc.).

So, it is important to ask: how much of parenting, or any caretaking generally speaking, must also be an "unpacking of privilege"? How best to unpack one's ableisms? I would argue that there needs to be an ethical defense for this kind of specific work—the real labor that goes into emotional and affective self-critique. Assumed to be one of the joys of parenting, the typical emotional investment in "my child's future" is contented with uncritical projection and wish fulfillment. On the other hand, parenting a nontypical child is to navigate an ableist system, already working at a marginal position socially and politically, if not also economically, having had already suspended any affective attachment to typical and normative expectations.

Yet, as the discussion has been going recently, the concept of "allyship" has gotten some pushback as it is presently employed and has diminished in significance: from political conscience-raising to political correctness. This, from Mia McKenzie, is from a blog post titled, "No more allies," particularly in response to the "Tim Wise scandal":[42]

> I'm kinda over the term "ally." [Because of] the constant cookie-seeking of people who just can't do the right thing unless they are sure they're gonna get some kind of credit for it, I'm done. Allyship is not supposed to look like this, folks. It's not supposed to be about you. It's not supposed to be about your feelings. It's not supposed to be a way of glorifying yourself at the expense of the folks you claim to be an ally to. It's not supposed to be a *performance.*

These suspicions are fair but I am not willing to abandon the concept of allyship just yet. I think it is worth expanding the ethical demand for thoughtful, critical role-taking but to a different context, one less historically specific to one more openly philosophical.[43]

This question of adoptive and less ableist engagement is an interruptive one; it is meant to substantially shift thinking and attitude, as an effort toward a conscientious form of dissent from ableist ideology and attitudes, and, especially, narcissistic regressions. I argue that this openness to the interruption is *ethically required.*[44] Parent-as-first-ally is an opportunity to think futurally and imagine changes in ableist norms so that the world our children inherit will also be more habitable in pluralistic ways. Politicizing caretaking roles as a necessary and conscientious allyship can challenge the ways in which ableism functions through a set of highly personalized, commercialized, and normative expectations of caretaking. Elsewhere I argue the need for ethical and existential *griefwork,*[45] a labor not appreciated by and in an ableist society; a work that is philosophically defined as an *ergon*—a concerted effort, a work of unpacking—that, as emotional labor, is ethically required and morally valuable.

Unfortunately, autism parenting comes with lots of cookies, flags, stickers, and signs that—if it is read critically for its ableism—is more an announcement of the grief, loss and guilt parents feel over not having a "normal" child that could be fixed or cured. While challenging this guilt and grief *honestly* and without regressions to ableist affections, we need to keep asking: *who is the narcissist here?* And, in other words, we need to really ask: *is it possible to parent without wanting a cookie?*[46]

HOW MIGHT WE "TEST" FOR ABLEIST BIASES?

Or, first, I should ask, *why* should we test for ableist bias? In his TED talk, "Our Buggy Moral Code," Dan Ariely describes a situation in the hospital in which, as a patient in the burn unit, he would plead with the nurses to change the method by which they removed and replaced his daily bandages. The nurses would move quickly, creating intense pain on a regular basis for extended periods of time. He would ask if they would go slower, but they believed their method was the best method. Ariely, reflecting on his experience, goes on to study this phenomenon, and concludes that this situation emerges out of a mistaken trust in our "intuitions." The problem he discovered in his research many years later is that:

> . . . at the end of this process, what I learned was that the nurses were wrong. Here were wonderful people with good intentions and plenty of experience, and nevertheless they were getting things wrong predictably all the time. It turns out that because we don't encode duration in the way that we encode intensity, I would have had less pain if the duration would have been longer and the intensity was lower. It turns out it would have been better to start with my face, which was much more painful, and move toward my legs, giving me a trend of improvement over time—that would have been also less painful. And it also turns out that it would have been good to give me breaks in the middle to kind of recuperate from the pain. All of these would have been great things to do, and my nurses had no idea.[47]

Ariely's work was to test this generally—how people make irrational decisions, how they might find themselves "cheating a little" (calling it the "fudge factor"), and that these decisions are based on group norms and influenced according to social environment. We could assume that nurses would rather be allies to their patients, even if they are not necessarily the primary advocates for them. Yet, for all good intention, the professional and personal bias disempowered the patient. What is important with Ariely's lesson for my purposes is how he addresses the outcome of his studies: he argues that we need to test "strong intuitions" because of the way in which the influences and justifications can produce material, social, and political harm.[48]

I offer another thought experiment. If, as McKenzie states it, "it is not about you, not supposed to be about your feelings" because of the way egoism renders claims of allyship inauthentic, then I propose a particular kind of "unpacking" or "thinking through" that addresses emotional content. This exercise does not have the goal of catharsis or is guaranteed to come with some kind of personal therapeutic effect—it is not mere psychological exercise. This is particularly directed to the caretaker who remains personally defensive over their caretaking style (and have the privilege to do so); this thought experiment is simply a way in which one can be more honest with oneself—about how much we intend to do and end up doing that it still "about me" and in defense of "my feelings."

Take the concept: "to help." We, quite often, who are in the caretaking position—professionals and not just parents—ask (or insist), *"Can I help you, please?"* or will say, (repeatedly) *"Let me help you."* This is assumed to be a polite thing to do; part of living in a civil society. It is encouraged, although gendered language, an easily identified rhetorical token: to be *helpful*, a *"helper,"* and wanting to *"help."* Yet, there are many times a day, thinking it benign, that people with visible disabilities are given "help" whether they want it or not. Recently, there has been a rash of inspiration porn videos posted online in which ablebodied people are praised for helping visibly disabled people.[49] Rachel Cohen-Rottenberg discusses the problem of being viewed as a "help object":

> I always feel very conflicted about moments in which people offer me unneeded assistance. I appreciate any attempt at kindness, and I empathize with the impulse to help. I am one of those people whose default approach to nearly everything is, "How can I help you?" and the desire to help runs very deep in me. We live in a harsh and competitive culture, and many people have a deep hunger to do a kindness, to extend themselves to connect with others from a place of giving.
>
> So I understand the goodness of the intention, but I also understand the ways in which it can become patronizing and intrusive. In this case, whatever good intentions were involved, those intentions flipped very quickly from an offer of kindness to a way for the other person to feel good about helping me, with the result that she became unhappy when I refused her assistance.
>
> As a help object, I was not treated with the presumption that I knew what I needed and was acting on it.[50]

How is this not fundamentally ableist despite all "good intention," already utilizing our authority over those we care for, much less for strangers we think "need help"? When I am offered help, am I not required in some ways to acquiesce? Worse, this can be taken for a more overt context of egoic narcissism (if not also aggression) when ableist intentions are added to the ableist language, for example, when one person suggests to another, *"You really need help."*

So, against this, there needs to be a testing out for a kind of *caretaker prescience*—an insight and foresight for when to assist and advocate, and when to "stand down" (or, even STFU),[51] discreetly making space and time for another's self-advocacy and self-determination. I often tell my students to replace the word, *"help"* (because you only help when the other is in need), with the word, *"assist."* When you offer "assistance," there is no implied obligation to have to accept assistance by the one to which it is extended. Even the most powerful and enabled CEOs/COOs/CFOs in our society, even ones who "lean in" and who encourage others to "lean in,"[52] have *assistants* and find themselves in *need of assistance.*[53]

I need to anticipate the world with, and yet against, the expectations that I have inherited alongside the ones that dehumanize and disable the unique existing individual (in every case), that, as Levinas might say, in that it is also always existentially vulnerable to suffering and inhumanity. In anticipation, there needs to be a kind of *sense*—what I am calling a *prescience*—born out of the "heavy-lifting" of thinking in the mode of affective self-critique. The *prescient parent* could be an anticipatory and conscientious ally to the child who is *not me* but *is mine.*

The biological bearing of children does not grant them their humanity, and can, instead, reinforce the disabling and dehumanizing mechanisms that work "without notice" because they are so familiar and normal every day.[54] Anti-ableist allyship, more than advocacy related to specific disabilities, when linked to the work of caretaking, could productively constitute active resistance to ableist affections, in ways that can appropriately recognize it as site-specific and labor-intensive. The work of intimate and real-time caretaking now could work against the intergenerational tides of accrued ableism, not as the place of first abuse and manipulations;[55] meant to better politicize while depersonalizing assistive caretaking labors. Even with prescience, we need to still philosophically question the intelligibility of standards and expectations of parenting full stop and treat the project of "having a child" as a site of new and existentially significant possibilities.[56]

WHAT DOES IT MEAN TO ENGAGE IN "AFFECTIVE SELF-CRITIQUE"?

Dealing with the emotional content of experience, I think, is extremely labor intensive. To be responsible for one's feelings—in particular, to check one's desires, fears and expectations—is a critical but necessary and morally viable position. I would say that many people do not necessarily have to (and therefore, *just don't*) check their fears and desires, especially in conditions of privilege. These fears and desires can serve to feed the imagination and sustain a normative future.

When you have a child that falls into the category of disabled, the effect on one's imagination can be traumatizing. I borrow from feminist phenomenologist Sandra Bartky's description of "ontological shock." It was a way of describing how I felt once my daughter was diagnosed. Bartky describes a two-fold or "double ontological shock" this way, as: "first, the realization that what is really happening is quite different than what appears to be happening, and second, the frequent inability to tell what is really happening at all" (1990, 18). Butler might argue that this is the point in which a defensive preservation emerges—an aggression—from the vulnerability that normalcy can cover over; and anger over the precariousness of one's condition even though, with my daughter's diagnosis, nothing "really" had changed.

Levinasian ethics offers a procreative aesthetic in thinking through what affective self-critique could mean and how it might *feel*. Like my previous idea of the *prescient* caretaker, this too is a state of sensitivity directed to others in the world, in such a way that the needs and desires of the *self* (in its usual dominant and defensive *attitude*) now becomes *suspended*. The possible ethical imperatives emerge because of a fundamentally aesthetic possibility—an affection—for alterity. Levinas describes this affectivity best when it regards the death of another, it is a "departure without return, a departure 'with no forwarding address.' Death—as the death of the other [*autrui*]—cannot be separated from this dramatic character" (2000, 9).[57]

The aesthetic possibility of self-critique is borne from an ethics of alterity; the radical openness to another renders the self disposed and dispossessed. When Levinas describes the death of a proximal other, he describes this disposition as it is *inconsolable*, its radical sensitivity:

> is emotion *par excellence*, affection or being affected *par excellence* . . . as if humanity were not consumed or exhausted by measurement, as if there were an excess in death. It is a simple passage, a simple departure—and yet source of emotion contrary to every effort at consolation (*ibid*).

This is an ethics defending a possible ethical aesthetics in which the possibilities are opened up in the radical "sensitivity to others as they pass (and are in passing)." This is not a generalized sensitivity but one awakened by the *proximal* other (the "neighbor who passes by" and not necessarily a "loved one").[58]

I use this idea of sensitivity carefully because there sometimes comes a gender assumption in this: if "sensitivity" is attached to also being considered *effeminate* while indifference or insensitivity is thought more *masculine*, then this ethics is not defensible but instead reduced to the bias, and gets trivialized as a gendered disposition, (as in, "it is the stuff of women; don't waste your time"). We can suspend that gender-bias here as well, treating these dismiss-als about the ethical and epistemological importance about "sensitivity" as rooted in a deeper and very suspicious cultural misogyny.[59] In that way, there is no further need to consider this as a viable association. My defense of this idea of a non-gendered sensitivity will continue in the chapter on prosthesis [ch. 5].

I want to instead invest in an idea that includes a range of engendered "pos-sibles" which means that we need whole new "starting points"—beginning with the Arendtian sense of natality[60]—to manifest real challenges to ableism. This interest and investment follows Rosemarie Garland-Thomson's call for a transformation of feminist theory as it can be integrated with DS. This is through what I term "receptive affections," as a style of ethical comportment to which I give a range of possible employment:

- The *minimum* would be an openness to the other as a kind of "recep-tive affection," to not be averse to the foreign and nonnormative, but an approach more like an "awakening" and "vigilance." The "affection" is with what Levinas calls *non-indifference*, as the quality of "desire, as a 'tendency' distinct from erotic tendencies" (2000, 112) and is without "the model of fulfillment," a position of an "impoverished knowledge" (114). From the minimum, this could spring-board into an active subject-position of non-indifference in relation to alterity.
- The *maximum* given to self-critique is having a receptive affection for the possibility of *ethical* substitution; what Levinas calls, "the one-for-the-other." It is identity only insofar as it is "the identity of the assigned of him [*sic*] who is responsible and cannot be replaced" (157). Levinas attributes to this "I" position of "*altered affection*" (if you permit the phrasing) as disappointed—an appointment and an election not subject to my will or ego—in part, because it makes the static comforts of selfhood *vulnerable* in its obligation to the other. One takes the other into their concern, takes care for the other in the sense of taking it "upon oneself" [*susception*]. This taking-on is not to be ontically understood as a burden, but existentially is still a "tearing away" [*arrachement*] from a comfortable subject-state (158–159).

This ethical sensitivity is modeled from the idea of neurodiversity as well, correcting the assumption that non-neurotypical brains, those with significant nonnormative cognitive and neurological differences, despite assumed mea-sures about "delays," or "intelligence," are less human (or, worse, assumed to be less morally obligating than sentient animals);[61] here, we treat those in general proximity with the same sensitivity as we would anyone we cared deeply and intimately about, utilizing at least the minimal ethical demand described above.

These demands also emerge from my personal experience. I have been thinking about my own personal work of affective self-critique as my daughter reflects my emotional states. Her sensitivities to her environment often have me renegotiating my assumptions—what I tolerate, what makes me anxious, what frustrates me—and in my biased underestimating of her, have often been held up to me as an emotional "mirror," reflected in her responses to me without filter: *she will reflect to me my attitudes and amplify them.* In amplifying them, I recognize that she depends on me for my vigilance of her, also being vigilant of me. I found that this is true in other stories, particularly about how impactful negative effects can be transmitted, including the ways in which one might internalize the indifference and insensitivity of ableist words and actions. From Rudy Simone, author of *Aspergirls*:[62]

> Aspergirls do not thrive under scrutiny, if it has just the slightest bit of hostility in it. Whether from our peers or teachers, if we are looked at with an unfriendly, intimidating, or threatening eye, we fold. Alone, we are talented, graceful, witty, and smart, but under such circumstances we curl up like hedgehogs. We're sensitive emotionally as we are physically (2010, 31).

We mistake this sensitivity when we pathologize it, make it the subject of psychological and neurological research, associating it with sensory data and nonnormative brain function, as in the case of the study: "Diminished Sensitivity to Sad Facial Expressions in High Functioning Autism Spectrum Disorders is Associated with Symptomatology and Adaptive Functioning."[63]

Affective self-critique is a sensitivity modeled instead on this openness— this existential vulnerability—of non-neurotypical sensitivities. This is also to uplift and defend this nonnormative conditionality—what might be, for now, understood as a disabled identity—as also free of the scrutiny and suspicion thoroughly encouraged (even if unintentionally) by ableist ideology and neoliberal cultural values.

In writing for a functional, non-ableist theory, I set aside privilege for non-neurotypical sensitivities over and against the normative research that measures for speculation about the mind and its operations, (particularly in preventing their "loss") as well as suspending any sensationalism over and objectification of non-neurotypical ("freakish"[64]) idiosyncrasies. This work is neither to aggregate knowledge about the plurality of disability nor is it purely for the sake of personal, professional, or political advantage; rather, it is to confront and overturn the many ways in which *ableist thinking* has been organized and stylized as *permissible*, if not also *fashionable.* From these experiences, I ask questions in order to direct a discomfort with implicit ableism wherever it resides, (but with "me first"), at the same time, also to ferret out the most problematic ableist phobias and attitudes without inflicting further harms.[65]

Chapter 2

Diagnosis

HOW DO DIAGNOSES DISABLE?[1]

Diagnoses name bodies and conditions; a diagnosis can excite concern, solicitude, grief, pity, and fear. This kind of naming, and the event of handing over a diagnostic label—when one has been diagnosed—is of important significance to me personally and professionally, but I argue that it is also underdeveloped in the context of Disability Studies. Personally, I have experienced and share in the experience of being "handed over" a diagnosis of a life-threatening condition during pregnancy and also of a genetic predisposition with a prognosis that future pregnancies are life-threatening (Scuro 2017), but, in my case, I had not experienced the diagnosis of a clinical disability. With this, the more personally profound diagnosis handed over to me was of my daughter by doctors and then educational administrators of Autism. In the "handing over" of a diagnosis, whether it be a disease or disorder, I found to be laden with power and judgment and, more importantly, *uncontested ableism.*

According to *The Oxford Classical Dictionary*, diagnosis [διάγνωσις] is an idea with a long-standing affiliation with ancient medical literature as a way to think how best to "avoid hopeless cases," especially because it is intimately tied to prognosis [πρόγνωσις] in the Hippocratic treatises. According to J. T. Valance's entry on diagnosis, "In post-Hippocratic medicine, the cognitive mechanisms of diagnostic practice—in particular the validity of inferential forms of diagnosis—came under scrutiny," and came to include questions like, "How far can [diagnostic] interpretation go without the aid of theory?" and "Can diagnosis proceed transparently without the interposition of an interpretive framework?"[2] It seems to me, if we take seriously the demand made in this project—to *address*, *resist*, and *confront* ableism—then

21

the question of diagnostics becomes a site of interpretation and inference that needs urgent attention, particularly in its brute authority to make prognostications about "worthy" and "unworthy lives."³

Charlton, in *Nothing About Us Without Us* (2000), accurately describes the phenomenon of being given a diagnosis, in the way that:

> Wilhelm Reich refers to as "bio-energetic shrinking" . . . in which a person goes to a physical, noticeably different in demeanor, announces that the "patient" has cancer. The person immediately feels sick (sometimes referred to as a sinking feeling) and shrinks. *They become less, although there is nothing different from moments before, when the person felt healthy and full. The psychosocial manifestation of this phenomenon unifies all disabilities* . . . (7, my emphasis).

The phenomenon was equally disorienting in dealing with the diagnosis of my child as "PDD-NOS" at the age of two. In my particular experience, when my daughter was diagnosed with what is called a "disorder," everything changed for me when, in fact, nothing had really changed about her or for her with the diagnosis. For all of my professional knowledge as an educator and philosopher, I found myself at a loss for language, and found myself questioning my authority as a parent and as an academic.

For my purposes here, beyond my personal response of "getting diagnosed" or being "handed over a diagnosis," I would like to reinterpret the phenomenon of being "handed over" and "handing over" a diagnosis as a *transmission of affect* following Teresa Brennan's work. She sets up her Affect Theory as a "new paradigm" and states that, "What is at stake [in the transmission of affect] is . . . the means by which social interaction shapes biology. My affect, if it comes across to you, alters your anatomical makeup for good or ill" (Brennan 2004, 74). Brennan opens up her project by asking her reader, have you ever "felt the atmosphere?" This atmosphere can "get into" an individual transforming the biological—and perhaps, I would also suggest, the neurological. As she puts it, "whether grief, anxiety or anger," these are energetic states that are social in origin yet have biological and physical effects (3).

Judith Butler also holds to an affect theory in that "social feelings" coupled with nationalism or media perception are "communicated from elsewhere" (2010, 50), and, especially in a climate of righteous individualism and its corresponding permissible aggressions, "gives power to their version of the subject" rendering the "subject's own destructiveness *righteous* and its own destructibility *unthinkable*" (47). With the question of which lives are sustainable and which are less so (42), ableist affections embedded in medical, educational and service institutions might require a specific form of deregulation,⁴ especially when these particular kinds of affections are of the *normate* and for the sake of the *normate*.⁵ Butler implies that "This view has implications for rethinking gender, disability, and racialization, to name a few of the social processes that depend upon the reproduction of bodily norms" (52).

There are many patient/parent/caretaker narratives that show the world-shattering alteration of person and perspective with being given a "diagnosis," yet, in other ways, nothing is to be done once the diagnosis is "handed over." I want to share two particular parent narratives that I find rich with tension and meaning.[6] From Lisa Quinones-Fontanez's blog post, "Five Years After an Autism Diagnosis (Part 1)":[7]

> In a few days we will celebrate our five year autism anniversary. I say celebrate because when I think of Norrin five years ago and I look at him now—I see a completely different kid. I have a lot to be grateful for. I have so much to hope for. But on the day Norrin was diagnosed with autism—May 19, 2008—I couldn't see any of that. Many people have read my blog posts and written to me asking how I came to be "okay" with autism. But I wasn't always okay with it. Acceptance was a process for me. Any parent who has heard the words, "your child has autism" remembers everything they felt that day.
>
> On the day Norrin was diagnosed with Autistic Disorder and Global . . . Developmental Delay, I felt my heart break.
>
> Even though I tried to prepare myself, there was that small big part of me that wanted to hear that Norrin was "typical" and that there was no need to worry.
>
> On the day Norrin was diagnosed, I put my arm around Joseph in an attempt to comfort him and I thought of our wedding day. Everyone told us that we were perfect together. And then I remembered the moments after Norrin was first born: I immediately looked his wrinkled little body over, counted his fingers and toes and thinking that he was absolutely perfect. And there we were, this seemingly perfect couple being told that our child was not.

This reflects the *narrative* that dominates Western (particularly American) discourse over the value of having and raising children. This anxiety over the imperatives of ablebodiness—the loss of an imaginary "perfection" *and* a way of thinking about others, including one's own children—has its cultural *currency* and is a permissible naivety that gets handed down from one generation to the next.

This is a mode of thinking and a deflective attitude that does not come "from nowhere"; it is pervasive and one in which everyone is "under threat" of not meeting the perfect demand of ablebodiedness. To continue her narration:

> We were handed a twenty-page evaluation, detailing all the things Norrin couldn't do, all the milestones he had yet to reach. . . . I hated reading the evaluations: on paper Norrin sounded horrible. Nowhere in the evaluation did it talk

about his dimpled smile or the sound of his laugh. Nowhere did it describe how his big brown eyes sparkled when he was happy.

Joseph and I cried in the car, neither one of us really able to comfort the other. Both of us thinking of all the things we could've done to prevent autism.

Everyone kept telling me, "God doesn't give us anything we can't handle." But autism and raising a child with a disability wasn't something I wanted to handle.

On the day Norrin was diagnosed, I called up my best friend to tell her the news. After a few minutes, I asked how she was doing. She was seven months pregnant and excited about her baby shower. While I was happy for her, I couldn't feel happy with her. Her pregnancy, her happiness and hope only reminded me of my loss.

On the day Norrin was diagnosed with autism, I cried myself to sleep. And I cried for many nights after that.[8]

Coupled with another example, in which Kate Movius, a parent featured in Andrew Solomon's book, *Far From The Tree* (2012), describes the time after being handed over the Autism diagnosis, as "a fugue state":

Since the day of my son Aidan's autism diagnosis six months earlier . . . we navigated an unknown path together—one completely different from the neat, linear developmental stages portrayed in my dog-eared copy of *What To Expect: The Toddler Years*. Instead of refereeing playground spats and Duck Duck Goose rules, we faced a barrage of assessments, therapists, and stupefying bureaucracy. While other moms on the playground traded stories of their children's hilarious ways with words, I was trying to come to terms with the possibility that my child would never speak a sentence.

This new way of life as a family caregiver meant complete withdrawal from the one I had built for Aidan, based upon . . . well . . . what every other mom was doing. After the diagnosis, there were no more playgroup outings or birthday parties. Instead, our days were filled with clinic and in-home therapy sessions. According to the doctor who diagnosed Aidan, we were in a mad race against time. "The window will close for him at five years old," she told us matter-of-factly at his appointment. Looking back on this, I realize this statement was not only completely off the mark (there is no five-year cut-off for progress) but it cruelly lorded over our lives for years. We raced through our days, trying to make that deadline, which in the end, didn't apply whatsoever to my child. I like to think at the time, though, Aidan must have been immensely relieved . . . [he] had been trying to tell me for several months before his diagnosis, that he was on his own path, one which veered sharply away from the Rest of The World and their terrain of playgrounds, parties and milestones.

. . . And when I meet a parent whose child has recently received a diagnosis, I borrow a quote passed along to me by my friend, Rosie, all those years ago: "Welcome to the club."[9]

In these parent narratives, public and open to scrutiny,[10] is the story of the *break*: where deeply packed, normative emotional, personal, philosophical expectations now reside in complete suspension. It is the lack of resource in response, which in the wake of this loss of expectation, is grief and despair that makes a positive perception of this experience *impossible*, delaying any possibility of acceptance. It is a *raw deal* as well because *even when* there is an acceptance of the situation (that is, *if* there is acceptance), it is still shaded with the legacy of these perceived grievances, perhaps also the negative *effects* of having resentment and guilt for the gap in time for which ableist expectations "cruelly lorded over our lives."

Rereading these more "ordinary" narratives of "being handed over" an autism diagnosis, I want to associate diagnostic thinking as part of the "invisible care labor" that Eva Kittay describes in her "Notes from the Battlefield" (2009),[11] specifically the "invisible care labor that is done by people with disabilities and their families" (606, 607). This labor is both emotional and intellectual (613–615). Kittay reconfigures how professional work is tied to personal life and demonstrates how both the personal and philosophical is never apolitical (624). By reciting her exchange with Jeff McMahan and Peter Singer (621–622) over the moral and political value of "physically and cognitively disabled persons," she shows how irresponsible and arrogant the attitudes were of these philosophical "authorities," stating, that there is a real "psychological cost" in engaging these debates with those who assumed they could objectively judge the value of persons based on how they have been diagnosed.

Kittay also recites a similar emotional and affective response to the one's I've previously recalled in the parent narratives—she describes it as a kind of nausea (621)—when hearing, reading, or thinking about her daughter being casually compared in moral status to an animal:

> [The] impact . . . is devastating. How can I begin to tell you what it feels like to read texts in which one's child is compared in all seriousness, and with philosophical authority, to a dog, pig, rat, and most flatteringly, a chimp; how corrosive these comparisons are . . .
>
> What are the specific challenges facing someone in my position? There are essentially two. The first is to overcome the anger and revulsion that one feels when encountering the view that one's disabled child . . . is less worthy of dignity, of life, of concern. . . . [and when] return[ing] to my daughter, Sesha, find[ing] myself trying to analyze the features that [distinguishes her from these comparisons], . . . I would simultaneously shrink in disgust from such reflections (610, 612).

With Kittay, I want to argue that if a medical or educational or administrative authority is in a position to hand over a diagnosis and is at the same time a "disablist" in that they rivet the diagnosis to the individual, then, dare we say *they have "written them off,"* written their families and the labor of care off? If so, I then could argue that the work of diagnosis rests on a real and consequence-bearing *"conceptual fallacy"* (616, my emphasis).

The political and social support systems often come by way of educational institutions. The rights or services available come with how a public education system can interpret differences categorically. The greater difficulty emerges when there is the assumption that these services are provided in a "neutral" state: as if without ableist bias already motivating the categories and as if these "special" services do not already come alongside the biases that organize hierarchies of privilege in terms of race, class, nationality, gender, "accent, and phenotype." As Annamma, Connor, and Ferri argue through a DisCrit lens,[12] "We believe . . . that racism and ableism are normalizing processes that are interconnected and collusive" (2013, 5).

The collusive quality of normalizing processes must be understood through better modes of explanation than ones that perpetuate racialized, gendered and classed stereotype, and, for my purposes, expected ability. Case in point: the way in which environmental racism emerges in concert with a certain kind of assumption about the nature of how communities are made and sustained. A collusion of environmental racism and ableism is fully manifested when it comes to a situation like the water crisis in Flint, Michigan:

> As Flint residents deal with the consequences of poisoned water, lawmakers, activists, and locals are already predicting what the crisis means for the future of the city.
>
> Mayor Karen Weaver has pointed out that the disaster could devastate the juvenile justice system in the future.
>
> "This damage to children is irreversible and can cause effects to a child's IQ, which will result in learning disabilities . . . and an increase in the juvenile justice system," she said, when a state of emergency over lead levels was declared in December [2015].[13]

If we are asking about ableist tendencies, to directly think through this situation is seemingly impossible, compounded by the desire for causal explanation when only correlations are available.[14] More problematically, clearly, the more prominent public concern is an ideological one, for "the future of the city," not as much for triaging the situation for those most affected and for addressing the most harmful and disabling features of the crisis.[15]

WHAT IS THE PHILOSOPHICAL
SIGNIFICANCE OF DIAGNOSIS?

Anita Silvers, in reviewing Elizabeth Barnes' *The Minority Body*,[16] discusses the difficulty of taking a diagnostic label indicative of a disability from a negative ("injurious to one's interest," "distressing" or "unfavorable") to a "neutral feature" (Oct 2016, 845), and moves to a larger question of significance without necessarily invoking it in the context of ableist bias (without asking about ableism per se):

> There is . . . a practical problem—more propitiously characterized, perhaps as a challenge—for philosophers about what the understanding of "disability" should be. . . . We have effective tools for analyzing and thereby unpacking ideas, and powerful philosophical rules for reconstituting deconstructed concepts in clearer and fairer form. What should guide philosophers when attention is called to the role of definitively negative constructions of disability? (847).

Yet, the philosopher's toolkit (what I will rename in a later chapter as *prostheses*)—and Silvers is keen to point this out—has "verged on dogmatism" (848) and has tended to provide "little defense against the disorientation that seems to overcome nondisabled people when they try to imagine living with a disability" (849).[17]

As a mother and in defense of her daughter in her "dual role" as also a philosopher, Kittay was compelled to offer specific ways to challenge other professional philosophers who threatened the "humanness" of her daughter against any kind of dehumanizing "moral demotion" (609, 613), even though it is incredibly labor-intensive to have to "manage the[se] disablist[s]" (612). Kittay asserts that "No child is simply the parent's own private matter" (623) and so I want to reframe this question raised by Silvers: What should guide philosophers in thinking through ableist biases if disability and caretaking is neither a private matter nor ought be framed by and subjected to dogmatism and imagination?

In doing this work, Kittay narrates the case of a significantly cognitively disabled man who wept profoundly upon the hearing of his father's death to give an important counterexample to disablist dehumanization. She challenges the disablist assumptions of Singer's and McMahan's thinking in this way: if one can form profound attachments in surprising ways,[18] then these intimate experiences of affection bear humanity *in person* and *in their particular person*. She also evidences her position in that, with a privileged intimacy she gets to see in her daughter, "what is hidden from those who are not privileged enough to see [Sesha] when she opens up to another," concluding that it is just "hubris to presume to know" (619). She restates her thesis—in that *the reception and transfer of affection is humanizing work*—when she concludes, "Such [affectionate] recognition . . . effectively settles the case in favor of the moral personhood of people with severe cognitive disabilities" (620).

Looking to Plato as a starting point, as it is my training in phenomenology to do so, I wanted to better tease out how diagnostic thinking is a (just another) mode of thinking, at least according to the original philosophical usage. It does turn out that Plato uses the concept *dianoia* to represent thought (as opposed to *eidos*, translated as the formal ideas), but not *dia-gnosis*. *Dia* means "apart" and *gnoskein* is a "learning," together, as diagnosis, can be plainly translated as "discernment." Although Greek is the origin of the word, it has been treated as synonymous to *cognitio* in the Latin.[19] The *gnosis*, of dia-*gnosis* is related to the Greek idea of *noesis*, or insight, and, here, I want to develop the idea of "insightfulness" that comes with diagnostic thinking, rather than in the way it might be used in Christian "Gnosticism" or as informing a kind of religious mysticism.

Gnosis is also unlike *episteme,* the latter as being the root concept for *epistemology*—the study of knowledge—because, although the work of diagnosis references how knowledge informs experience, as a form of thinking, seems to come closer to what becomes Plato's later philosophical method: the work of developing hypotheses and cataloguing the more *elenctic*-generated definitions through dialectic, (particularly in later dialogues). This dialectical work involves "[the] 'collecting' things generically and then dividing them by a series of dichotomies into species" (SEP, ¶¶11–12).[20] This method of epistemic "knowledge-building" in the generating and sorting of hypotheses is adapted by Aristotle when constructing his biological taxonomies of genus and species. Plato, over the course of the dialogues, did not seem to give great philosophical value to the exercise of generating hypotheses,[21] only for the fact that they were often of more rhetorical benefit than a philosophical one.

In the *Republic,* according to Sara Brill (2005), Plato expresses some sympathy between medical judgment and political judgment, what she describes as a "confluence" of medical knowledge with a political constitution—between health and virtue (298). The "cultivation of self-diagnostic capacity," (Brill names an "odd formulation by Plato") belongs to the "excellent doctor," assuming that the doctor has a kind of "epistemic privilege" by having had "possession of these diseases" of diagnostic concern (299–300, 312 nt. 7); likewise, the philosopher too must make determinations "on the basis of a play between the visible and the *intelligible*" (304).

I would argue that for Plato, *dianoetic* (deductive) reasoning regards more commonplace hypotheses derived from opinions [*doxa*]. Opinions are just that, products of our experiences—diagnostic products of the sensory world—yet, as opinions, should have no bearing when it comes to the veracity of thought. *Dianoia*—rooted in what we might call today "the cognitive," as *noesis*, or as intelligible products of the "mind" [*nous*]—is a concept I want to adapt into this special kind of mental activity of thinking in relation of parts to wholes. Or, in other words, it becomes important here to circumscribe the kind of thinking activity that produces diagnoses and prognostications from the work that is mere opinion and conjecture.[22]

Also in Plato's *Republic*, Socrates cites *dianoia* "as the most vigorous of all powers" when comparing it dialectally to the powers of sight and hearing (477c-d), he distinguishes *dianoia* from opinion [*doxa*] in this way:

> In a power I see no color or shape or anything of the sort such as I see in many other things to which I look when I distinguish one thing from another for myself. . . . [*Dianoetic*] Knowledge is presumably dependent on *what is*, to know *of what is, that it is* and *how it is* . . . [while] opinion, we say, opines (478a, my emphasis).

Here, I read from Plato that diagnosis (as *dianoetic* activity) could also be a cognitive power "more vigorous" than even sight and hearing because it can name "what is from what is not" independent of the experiences which determine the objects of sight and hearing.[23]

Diaeresis is another interesting term used in medicine to indicate the cognitive work of dividing or separating "parts normally united," or as even a more practical exercise indicating the "surgical separation of parts." This kind of cognitive activity is dialectical for Plato as well; and can generate knowledge that is much different than the *heuristic* knowledge of trial and error. But *diaeresis* is unlike philosophical dialectic, generating knowledge gained from the parsing out of parts from wholes for its own sake. Plato mocks the diaeretic method because he identifies it with sophistry and empty argumentation.[24]

Brill argues that it is the need for quiddity—the "what-it-is" with the work of the inquiry asking "what is it?"—that "brings the medical art [*techne*] into kinship with philosophy insofar as both the doctor and the philosopher are actively engaged in inquiring into what things are." This affinity is true particularly in the performative dimension of diagnosis, where "what it is" is a named, diagnosed disease, (306–307). Although one might think that this is "the event" of diagnostic thinking, it is important to note its dialectical dimension. The diagnosing of a disease is not the only "goal"; rather, diagnostic thinking not only is dependent on rational discourse, but also needs a contextualized, active dialectic directed toward *healing* and *action* (307).

FROM WHERE DOES A "DISORDER" COME?

Brill finds that Plato sets up the philosopher as the best to "thematize" the *eros* that "inclines the masses to madness"—an *eros* that is similar to the *eros* of the tyrant. It is not that the philosopher does not know this *eros*; rather, the philosopher, like the excellent doctor, engages critical distance and self-knowledge (2005, 300–301):

The philosopher emerges as distinct from the tyrant not in absence of powerful desire, but in his comportment toward his desire inasmuch as the philosopher emerges as figure both immersed in *eros* and aware of himself [*sic*] as so immersed.

If we argue that the "madness of the masses" is not yet a medicalized concept, one also given to the tyrant, could we not align this Platonic account of "madness" as what is known today as the stuff of ableist narcissism? Could it be that the philosopher (and perhaps very good doctors) could immunize themselves against ableist tendencies—tendencies given to tyrants and the masses, narcissists, and the normate?

In thinking about this, I want to broaden the meaning of diagnosis and have it be recognizable in a new—more everyday and ethical—way. I've separated out the thinking from the products of thought in this mode, noted in the flow-chart (Figure 2.1). I have divided two components that are contained in all diagnoses: Diagnostic Thinking from the "Products of Diagnosis"—diagnoses proper—connected with a directional arrow from the former to the latter. Under the right column, "products," I have three subcategories: "ordinary (disablist) understanding," the sociocultural assumptions about disorders, and the third, "individuals given diagnoses." Between these three subheadings is a rotation arrow, indicating how there is an interrelation between all three often not clearly mapped or organized.

On the left, under Diagnostic Thinking, I have as the most dominant subcategory, Expert Diagnosticians, overlapping the subcategory, "everyday judgments." The Expert Diagnosticians directly inform and "hand over" diagnoses to individuals (indicated by an arrow from the left subset to the right subset), indirectly influencing everyday understanding and sociocultural assumptions. One final subset under Diagnostic Thinking is the one pointing to the Expert Diagnosticians: Diagnostic Training. Some of these arrows do not point in both directions, in fact, the directionality of diagnostic thinking moves from training to expertise, that I argue, overrides any everyday diagnostic judgments or self-diagnostic thinking from informing (or perhaps challenging) how Expert Diagnosticians do the work [*ergon*] of naming, opining, and prognosticating without scrutiny.

With this graphic, I want to challenge the epistemological assumptions of what diagnostic thinking and diagnoses enable or disable, especially when the diagnostic training only assumes the work of *diaeresis* without dialectical relation. In other words, Expert Diagnosticians can fuel disablist attitudes and sociocultural assumptions, (and although there is a bidirectional arrow in my graphic because I do not want to dismiss those ways in which bidirectional influence is not impossible), those usually in a position to "hand over a diagnosis" are only tasked with sorting and placing cases into the taxonomy of known disorders and disabilities.

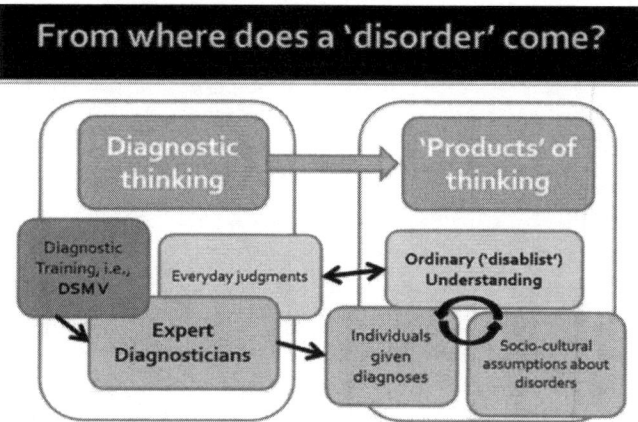

Figure 2.1 *From Where Does a Disorder Come?* Flowchart Indicating Pathways of Diagnostic Thinking—Its Process and Products.

I want to support this argument with how Geoffrey R. Norman, Professor of Clinical Epidemiology and Biostatistics at McMaster University in "The Epistemology of Clinical Reason: Perspectives from Philosophy, Psychology and Neuroscience" (2000), describes how a diagnostician is trained and how they are taught to think of the idea of a diagnosable disease. He states that it is from one of two ways:

- From a nominalist perspective, in which disease is "a collection of abnormalities that appear to arise together."
- With an essentialist view, in which "signs and symptoms arise from pathological processes that can be identified and hopefully rectified" (129).

To me, it seems, there is good reason to favor the nominalist perspective because it invites *dialectical* relation with the patient, the prognosis, and, generally, the assumptions about what could be concluded once a diagnosis has been "handed over." If one takes a nominalist perspective, there can be value in the affective transmission insofar as the alternative, the essentialist perspective, does not invite dialectic; rather, the latter connotation invites *curative* language. The essentialist perspective could make the "riveting" of a diagnosis a reality for that individual to which they are somatically attached, and therefore, the diagnosis becomes disabling.

With either perspective, the issue remains: by reading the lives, voices, and bodies of individuals through symptomology, deficit language gets attached by the handing over of diagnoses—created by the interrelation of the diagnostician and the diagnosed—biasing the expectations and outcomes of these exchanges. That said, Norman admits when he philosophizes on disease, including going through a generic catalogue of philosophy that includes

Plato, Descartes and Wittgenstein: "it is awfully difficult to devise an explicit rule to aid in distinguishing between diseases and non-diseases." The overarching assumption is: *if something is wrong, shouldn't you fix it?* And you can't fix it if you don't know what-it-is.

How does this theory, with already a long-standing history of bias, assist in explaining the phenomena of "being diagnosed" or being "handed over" a diagnosis? Returning to Brennan on this point, she states, "By affect, I mean *the physiological shift accompanying a judgment*" (2004, 5).[25] Because I am finding the ordinary language limited here, I want to try and organize the verb from the nouns—the activities from their products. Semantically, diagnostics and diagnoses can signal an *opinion*, (as in "I need a second opinion for this diagnosis"), a *knowledge* (as in "now I know what is wrong with me"), and as *judgment*, (as in, with this diagnosis, you have something *"wrong"* with you. Read: You have been named with this disease, disorder, or disability).

In this context, we also might have to break from the synonymy between diseases and disorders for just that reason. As a power, diagnostic thinking generates a knowledge independent of the experiences themselves, yet is a way to "hang together experiences" into a working knowledge beyond the "educated guess." With this incredible gap between the descriptive and prescriptive potency of a diagnosis, more questions come to the fore:

- How are symptoms read as symptoms from experience and material conditions?
- How are symptoms hung together and "collected"?
- In what context can a diagnosis be attained and delivered?
- What are the outcomes of a diagnosis (normative, political, psychological)?

Arguably, in practice, in situations in which a clinician might give a diagnosis, it is easily nothing more than hubris, especially if it is handed over in an essentialist way. Diagnosis that is not engaging the ambiguities of diagnostic thinking and practice, will yield, to use the phrase from Plato, merely *an opinion that does nothing more than opine.*

WHAT MIGHT BE THE ABLEIST IMPLICATIONS OF BEING "HANDED OVER" A DIAGNOSIS?

Diagnoses are historically, socially, politically, economically, and philosophically loaded. They have been notoriously and heteronormatively gender-laden, as argued by Ehrenich and English in *Complaints and Disorders: The Sexual Politics of Sickness* (1973). They cite one that was of particular interest to me:

[If] a woman should choose to devote herself to intellectual or other "unwomanly" pursuits, she could hardly hope to escape the domination of her uterus and ovaries. . . . This was not mere textbook rhetoric. In their actual medical practices, doctors found uterine and ovarian "disorders" behind almost every female complaint, from headaches to sore throats and indigestion (29).

These kinds of sexist, misogynist, somatophobic, racist judgments are affective as energetic; as energetic, judgments can "enhance or deplete" (Brennan 2004, 6). Brennan takes care to distinguish *affect* from *feeling* in that while feelings are self-contained, affects are transferred socially and environmentally (7). The displaced energy in the reception of the diagnosis and the indifference and even patronizing, dehumanizing way in which the diagnosis may be handed over have affective consequences that devastate.

As an exercise, I have tried to break down into "moments" what leads to the subjection of one's thinking—in that they *yield dialectically*—over to an expert clinician in event of "being handed over a diagnosis":

- First Moment: Nonspecific sensations, feelings or observations that lead to a tentative self-diagnosis[26] or "ordinary" diagnosis. One begins to think: *something is wrong.*
- Second Moment: A slippage into patient-narrative begins: *When should I go to the doctor? Which doctor do I go to? Will it be something or nothing?*
- Third Moment: Diagnostic tests begin. From undressing to prostration, to following instruction of the physicians and nurses (and even receptionists),[27] as well as answering sets of both familiar and strange questions. In doing so, *we submit the possibilities of our own diagnostic thinking over to the expert diagnostician.*

While these moments are not comprehensive of all experience, they are only to yield a hypothesis of narrative that allows me to inquire into the phenomenon of diagnosis further: When do we submit to the expert? Why is it that diagnostic authority *rests* with a doctor or clinician? If we can confront the ways in which we have become deeply affected by ableist attitudes and ideas, then we could also free up the ways that this ableism is passed on—clinicians to clients, doctors to patients, teachers to students, parents to children. As George Estrich says in his "Open Letter to Medical Students":[28] "The tendency to equate diagnosis with personality has roots in medical history, and ultimately in the history of Western thinking about race."

In my case, when my daughter would not respond to her name when she was about two years old, my family and I started to wonder if she had an issue with her hearing. When the test yielded "nothing" and she was "normal," it triggered an uneasy feeling that "something is (still) wrong" and permitted us to pursue further tests and seek out a diagnosis, at the same time, subjecting her to further diagnostic testing. I experienced similar nausea and slipped into a kind of fugue state as described earlier (and better) by other parents. This willingness to submit to external and expert authority was furthered as I too read the different diagnostic reports from doctors, social workers, psychologists, educators, with the negative characterizations and attaching the "deficits" to my child in relation to developmental milestones. The most difficult problem with the service-providers and teachers, handing over their own (sometimes conflicting) educational diagnoses of my daughter was the *lack of prognosis* alongside of these reports. No one seemed to know what to say would be the outcome of her "pervasive developmental disorder."

According to Ashley Taylor in "Addressing Ableism in Schooling and Society? The Capabilities Approach and Students with Disabilities," the dominance of "ableist preferences" are quite problematic in an educational context [quoting Thomas Hehir]:

> From an ableist perspective, the devaluation of disability results in societal attitudes that uncritically assert that it is better for a child to walk than roll, speak than sign, read print than read Braille, spell independently than use a spell-check, and hang out with nondisabled kids as opposed to other disabled kids, etc. In short, in the eyes of many educators and society, it is preferable for disabled students to do things in the same manner as nondisabled kids.[29]

With Taylor adding that:

> These ableist preferences in functioning lead schools to expressly or tacitly steer disabled children into developing functionings that resemble what is deemed "normal" or "typical." Hehir argues that this raises ethical as well as practical questions, as in many cases much class time is spent trying to change the disability—normalize functioning—rather than focusing on academic learning, possibly compounding educational deficits that children experience (2012, 118).[30]

We are handed and hand over diagnoses in many ways that alienate and isolate experiences from the sharing of experience in possibly dialectical and more non-ableist affective transmissions, especially as the health and human services professions move toward greater and greater economic efficiency. For example, O'Malley, Cook, et al., (Oct 2005) wax philosophical in discussing the work of medical coding as it is related to the paying out of health insurance benefits:

> Nosology (the systematic classification of diseases) has always fascinated the sick and their would-be healers. Western societies developed an interest in nosology in the seventeenth and eighteenth centuries when they began to track

the causes of sickness and death among their citizens. In the twentieth century, when medical insurance programs made payers other than patients responsible for medical care, nosology became a matter of great interest to those public and private payers.

In their Discussion, the authors state:

> The process of assigning ICD codes is complicated. The many steps and participants in the process introduce numerous opportunities for error. . . . [Codes] are likely to be most accurate under the following conditions: the disease has a clear definition with observable signs and symptoms, highly qualified physicians document information on the patient, experienced coders with full access to information assign the codes, and the codes are not new. . . . Little consideration is given to the process leading to the physician's diagnosis. Certainly the quality of the gold standard varies based on disease factors (type, knowledge, and progression) and physician factors (experience with the disease and knowledge of diagnostic tools for the disease). Further research examining which factors influence the quality of the physician's diagnosis and the extent to which these factors affect the gold standard is greatly needed.

With the presumption of a "gold standard" in diagnostic coding, I genuinely ask: this handing over and receiving diagnosis is *to what end*? If the Western cultural "goal-set" of medical diagnostics is to diagnose accurately and efficiently, then how does this play out for the reception of diagnosis?

- When *accuracy* is a goal: If this is how medical doctors and health care professionals are trained and if sets of symptoms do not accurately fit within the range of known diagnostic categories, we could understand that one could get in the intellectual habit of assuming that if "nothing fits" then there is "nothing to diagnose."
- If *efficiency* is translated as "speed" with which the diagnosis is delivered, there is assumed lack of maximized benefit to the patient/client/caretaker, and perhaps a betrayal of diagnostic training, if the handing over of diagnosis a "takes too long" (and, to snark on this point, time is [the same as] money!).[31]

These goals, from the start and at the point of medical training, carry the assumption only of the current body of knowledge of diseases, disorders, and diagnoses. Add to that the issues of diagnostic practice once diagnostic training is complete; diagnoses now conform to a system of insurance and service codes of which requires its own specialized knowledge and literacy.[32] I would argue that this model of diagnostics—as a way of thinking and making judgments about patients, symptomology, narratives of nonnormative experience, etc., is a harbor for the dual biases of *nondiagnosis* (as in, "there is nothing wrong with you") and *misdiagnosis*, the latter of which can create situations of great harm and precarity.

Compounding the problem of misdiagnosis is the way there may be a lack of research and specificity in the presumed knowledge of causes and effects of disorders, diseases and generally-speaking, limited by the current categories that define disablement. One example of how dangerous misdiagnosis can be, Nika Beamon in "Medical Misdiagnosis Nearly Killed Me," narrates her experience for *The Huffington Post*:

> I suffer from a rare autoimmune disease called igG4 related systemic disorder and it mimics many other conditions. Early on, at least, the doctors I saw couldn't see [past] my color when trying to figure out what ailed me. I was evaluated and tested for sickle cell, lupus, multiple sclerosis and sarcoidosis multiple times even though all evidence showed I didn't have those conditions; yet, their common conditions for my ethnicity. Of course, in hindsight, I know I didn't provide each, individual doctor with my complete medical history and I didn't insist on getting more than a few minutes of their time. I also didn't do a lot of research on my own to show them that their assertions about me could be wrong.
>
> Amazingly, I went along with whatever crazy treatment my doctors came up with for years even though my body was rapidly deteriorating. I rebuilt my stomach twice, had dozens of biopsies, took hundreds of pills and took what I call a hospital tour. In the meantime, I suffered two Tia strokes, lost my hair, gained 80 pounds and couldn't keep my eyes open pass [sic.] 9 o'clock most nights.
>
> It was a life and death battle and I vowed, should I survive, I'd educate myself on my own condition and body; I'd learn to read the test results, image reports, and articles about advancements so I no longer blindly follow the advice of doctors. And, I did just that. . . . But, the years of misdiagnosis have taken their toll. Chronic inflammation of my joints has twisted my spine, spread apart vertebrae and the s1 joint, permanently damaged my liver, and left me taking pills for the rest of my life.[33]

Add to this narrative other complexities of how bias can operate against better judgment; for example, Larry Johnson, in "Treat emergency, not disability" argues that "Assumptions [about disability] can be wrong and sometimes very dangerous." In his case, "What brought me to the emergency room was not my blindness. But, sometimes when a person has a visible disability like blindness or is in a wheelchair, it's what doctors, nurses, or ER technicians will focus on first."[34]

There is much that would compel medical and service professionals to work in favor of this goal-set of accuracy and efficiency, little to arrest the practice under these kinds of demands, slipping into an assumed (and even *benevolent*) exercise of power and judgment by one over others.[35] Diagnoses give narrative to these ableist operations of power, normalizing diagnostic authority and, in effect, furthers ableist biases, *despite* the fact that not all diagnosticians are disableists per se.

These biases bring with them the affective preference for both normalcy and somatophobic typicality as if equivalent to "health." Diagnostic training also has a long-standing preference for visible over latent symptomologies, with little time or opportunity to cultivate dialogue and inquiry about what the goal and content of diagnostic thinking is supposed to be and what it is supposed to do—*in word and in deed.*

The cultural-social need to "name"—for naming what is unnamed—is a desire that I would argue excites ableism, encourages disablist attitudes and forfeits ordinary, everyday and individualized decision-making. Following David Pfeiffer, in "The Philosophical Foundations of Disability Studies" (2002):[36]

> Any ontology which presents the world of experience as inferior to a world of divine law will lead to the oppression of people with disabilities. Any ontology which emphasizes ableism and normality dooms people with disabilities to destruction. Any ontology which presents an epistemology based on authority and conformity results in the death of people with disabilities.

The excitability of ableist ideology in this desire to name, for example, can be seen in the language of "epidemic" when speaking of autism, particularly by representatives of Autism Speaks.[37] As Jenell Johnson states it, in "Negotiating Autism in an Epidemic of Discourse," citing Richard Grinker, the word "epidemic" implies "danger and incites fear, calling up associations with plagues . . . threatening the ones you love. With autism, the label of 'epidemic' sounds both frightening and tragic."[38] Johnson goes on to add, "Epidemics, in other words, are as much about meanings as they are about measurements. The word 'epidemic' conjures a public body that must be protected at the expense of the bodies it pushes to the margins—harbingers of a tragic future that must be avoided" (2013).

In an effort to locate and package experience into consumable and commodified values, the diagnostic label should not ease the call for responsibility to *nuance* (via Tobin Siebers)[39] and encourages an affective indifference to the *tensions* (via Ferguson and Nusbaum)[40] necessary for challenging ableist biases. In order to continue my addressing of ableism, including the method I've called a "philosophical exorcism," I transformed the excitability of ableist affects into a set of thought questions. This was a template I used to frame a (not necessarily therapeutic, but knowledge-bearing, knowledge-generating) story-telling exercise:[41]

- In what ways have you experienced a life-changing diagnosis? What were the affective qualities of the experience? Were you diagnosed in an ableist or non-ableist way?
- Do you have a diagnosis that you can publically and emotionally identify with? Does identifying with a diagnosis add to your dignity? What is the 'invisible care labor' is involved in being able to identify and take ownership of your diagnostic label?
- Have you been a position to diagnose someone in a life-changing way? In what ways did this impact you? Were you able to engage any of the nuance or tension in the handing over the diagnosis?
- How might you have submitted your own diagnostic thinking over to an expert diagnostician? Have you ever been told "nothing is wrong with you" or been misdiagnosed? Has this experience disabled you in any way?

There needs to be more narratives of being handed over and of handing over a diagnosis that contain these nuances: especially attentive to the ambivalence for naming disorders and sensitive to the depth of affect in its being handed over, while avoiding the foreignness of impersonal clinical diagnoses devoid of dialectical considerations.

My final thought on the problemata of diagnosis is that we could recall nuance and sustain tensions in at least three ways:

1. Permission for and announcing of the ambivalences that exist in all diagnostic categories, treating the "naming" of and handing over of a diagnosis as always already *tentative*;
2. Acknowledging and assessing the significant *depth of affect* in the handing over of diagnosis in both ordinary and specialized contexts; avoiding indifference in principle and in practice;
3. Because impersonal, clinical diagnoses actively and ontologically construct disability, one must engage in *conscientious practices* that will not rivet specific diagnoses to individuals in ways that are alienating, disempowering and destructive.

To this last point, I want to support it with a testimony. From "Reclaiming the Dignity Lost in a Diagnosis," Cas Faulds writes:[42]

> As an autistic person, I have multiple facets to my identity—just like everyone does. One of those facets is that I am also a parent. My son is autistic, and I know what it is like to sit with professionals and be told how limited your child is. I know what it is like to receive a diagnostic report that includes horribly negative words about deficits, and I know what it is like to have to explain that to other people in your child's life including teachers and family members.

So, based on that, I would like to offer some advice to parents who have gone through this process that I wish someone had given me when I was there.

Take the diagnostic report, full of the language of the pathology paradigm, and reword it to reflect the neurodiversity paradigm.

From a report:

> *X appears to have impairments in communication and social interactions. In addition, he was reported to have several restricted and repetitive behaviors. Specifically, he was noted to have difficulties engaging in a social conversation, high pitched vocal tone, impairments in use of eye contact, difficulties socializing and interacting with other children, and limited emotional reciprocity. He also collects rocks, has an inflexible adherence to routines, displays heightened sensitivities to light and loud noises, and finds it hard to cope with changes to his daily routine.*

No, that doesn't say anything positive at all!
So, how can I reword this to say something positive?

> *X has differences in his communication style and social interactions. He prefers to engage in behaviors that are comfortable for him. Specifically, these include conversations that remain on topic and relevant to him. He prefers not to make eye contact because it is uncomfortable for him, and he prefers interacting with children who are older or younger than him, rather than only interacting with his age mates who can be less predictable. He loves collecting rocks because he is interested in the different shapes and substances that rocks are composed of. X prefers predictability in his daily routine, and enjoys being in sensory friendly environments.*

Why should you do this? Why go to the effort of rewriting a professional report? Because you are going to have to introduce your child to teachers and therapists and you're going to have to do that more than once. When you do, you want to do that from a place of strength rather than a place of weakness. You want to highlight your child's unique potential rather than place limitations on them, and you don't want to have to confront all those negative words every time you do this. This way, you have the words you need to ensure that your child receives the support that he/she needs without trading in his/her dignity.

More than just about the supply of new, better, more "positive" words and names, the underlying imperative from Faulds' rationale is key: there is an ethical obligation to rethink and even rewrite the significance of diagnoses—the products of diagnostic thinking. First and foremost, this must be an obligation instructed in the training of diagnosticians, but then continually and consistently reintroduced and rethought, so that it can be a practice that operates in specifically non-ableist ways, to reduce the intrinsic harms of disablisms everywhere—intentional or not—for the sake of ensuring dignity.

Chapter 3

Intersectionality

A dialogue with Devonya N. Havis and Lydia X. Z. Brown

Intersectionality!!!

– Alice Wong, founder of the Disability Visibility Project,[1]
[my emphasis].

Figure 3.1   Photograph of Alice Wong via Tele-Robot with President Obama at the White House. Photocredit: Pete Souza/The White House.

HOW IS INTERSECTIONALITY IMPORTANT
FOR ADDRESSING ABLEISM?

In the conclusion to *Dangerous Discourses of Disability, Subjectivity and Sexuality*, Margrit Shildrick argues for "thinking differently" about disability and to "explore the fluidity of all forms of categorization" (2009, 170). Shildrick argues that, "The key to new scholarship is critique . . . as a risky enterprise that subjects all the conventions to new and potentially disruptive analysis" (16). Using Queer and Deleulzian theories, Shildrick also argues that Critical Disability Studies approaches are an "ethical necessity—a responsibility to otherness—that leaves no-one behind" (177).

Add to Shildrick's demand for new and disruptive scholarship Alice Wong's declaration, "Intersectionality!!!" and together they offer a twofold injunction: one ethical and one ideological. In thinking about ableism and in attempting to define it, I have found that the insistence on intersectional approaches becomes a necessary part of the work, especially as it supplements and challenges the traditional points of intersection—race/class/gender—and as they operate by more than just analogy. Simply stated: ableism *is like* racism and sexism and yet it *really, really is not*, thoroughly complicating the conditions of racism, sexism and the like.

Although there may seem to be nothing particularly unique about Wong's exclamation,[2] I purposely couple it with the image of her on a visit to the White House (from a different post), which philosophically provides an important reading of the novelty of the situation: *who* is making the exclamation, and *how* it is stated as an exclamation. To the first point, Wong, in making herself present in the Oval Office, exemplifies the injunction at the heart of Disability Social Justice, *"nothing about us, without us,"* and, although there are staffers and forefathers (note the painting on the wall) "watching" in the background, this also makes present a question that registers the borderlands of the visible and invisible, presence and absence, the foreign made more familiar respectively, interrogating who counts and who is accounted for. Again, from Shildrick: "The responsibility for enquiry and analysis falls . . . not on disabled people alone but on all those who participate in the relevant structures" (15).[3] This differential is in a face-to-face relation, as a kind of confrontation, present in a place of power—symbolically and actually—made more honest.

To the second point, Wong treats the work of challenging ableism as including an exclamation for intersectional analyses, intersectional study—because it implies an injunction, a claim. I read this injunction—this exclamation made by Wong—as stating that *one needs more intersectionality not less.* It is not just a politically salient claim, but that it begs the question of moral context of both implicit and explicit biases. It is especially on this second point, that Wong, through the novelty of a communicative and robotic prosthetic, can have a "face-to-face" exchange with the seat of power; she is materializing what is both necessary and possible in attending to intersections: *that power must defer to what is beyond its own influence as well as lend itself open to altering the boundaries of its preconceived ideas.*[4]

As perhaps an introduction to intersectionality, I find Iris Marion Young's "Five Faces of Oppression" a useful starting point. Young writes about how these five points can become functional personally, socially, and politically as they might manifest as racism and sexism. I also find that these five "face[t]s" have explanatory power for homophobia and heteronormativity as well: 1) violence, 2) exploitation, 3) marginalization, 4) powerlessness, and 5) cultural imperialism.[5]

When Young articulates that oppression operates structurally, despite best intentions of individual persons, it is out of this "family of concepts and conditions" (2014, 4):

[O]ppression refers to the vast and deep injustices some groups suffer as a consequence of often unconscious assumptions and reactions of well-meaning people in ordinary interactions, media and cultural stereotypes, and structural features of bureaucratic hierarchies and market mechanisms—in short the normal processes of everyday life (5–6).

Philosophers and moral theorists have been limited in their account of the conditions by which systematic oppression can be possible (8–9). Citing Heidegger, Young challenges that way we are "thrown" (our "thrown-ness") into social groups and social affinities that can reinforce and segregate privileged groups from oppressed groups, without any transformational move toward social justice (10, 12), despite being primarily interdependent.

As much as there is an analogy between the operations of racism and sexism with ableism, this analogy is quite limited. This would be the goal of the following dialogue with Devonya Havis and Lydia Brown in addressing ableism: *What are the limitations in the analogy of racism and sexism with ableism?* In other words, how is ableism a unique form of oppression and marginalization, separate from racism and sexism, yet compounded by contexts that are racist and sexist, classist, homophobic, etc.? It may also be worth asking, in a philosophical vein, whether ideological (and perhaps even political) conservatism and neoliberalism, works against intersectional approaches such that narrow boundaries are policed rather than radicalized and transgressed.[6]

Rosemarie Garland-Thomson outlines what must be the case for a feminist disability theory as a critical theory, and I follow suit here: "1) that representation structures reality, 2) that margins define the center, 3) that gender (or disability) is a way of signifying relationships of power, 4) that human identity is multiple and unstable, and 5) that all analysis and evaluation has political implication" (2011, 18). This is one of the ways we can see intersectionality work as both analogy but then also a conflation and compounding of the situation, particularly, as "Subjugated bodies are pictured as either deficient or as profligate" (21); this can be true in parallel as it engages race, class, gender and disability but then also compounded—a conflation and compounding—as it marginalizes those who are non-white, poor, queer, and disabled. Add to this the *invisibility* of some disabilities, like chronic pain, neurological differences, with the need for a basic defense of place and person in a culture already finding the body abject,[7] and the world is constructed as essentially *uninhabitable* in any sustained way; we might then need to read these complexities more thoroughly with a feminist and disability critical theory. Critical Race Theory and challenges to globalizing capital must also be part of any theory construction if it is to also have richer political implications, as Garland-Thomson suggests.

There is no specific defense of "political correctness" here in the dialogue that follows. From Butler's Preface to *Precarious Life*:

> Dissent and debate depend upon the inclusion of those who maintain critical views . . . [to] charge those who voice critical views with treason, terror-sympathizing, . . . moral relativism, . . . juvenile behavior . . . anachronistic Leftism, is to seek to destroy the credibility not of the views that are held, but of the persons who hold them. . . . [Quelling dissent means] a certain psychological terrorization as their effect . . . It is precisely because one does not want to lose one's status as a viable speaking being that one does not say what one thinks (2004, xix–xx).

The complexity of this psychologically terrorizing effect is not fully accounted for here. The trolling and harassment that is possible when dissent and critique comes from underrepresented and non-privileged groups and persons, especially when it is toward people who identify as disabled, People of Color (PoC), genderfluid, non-neurotypical, etc., is psychologically and personally terrorizing for those who experience it.[8] This kind of terror is only unthinkable for those who don't directly experience it, and is dangerous when this is attached to a political conservatism or nationalism.[9] *The fact that it is and happens without any generalized concern* ought to be enough to demand all our attention.[10]

There is a kind of "low hum"[11] terrorization in the ways ableism intersects with other oppressions. If it is the case that racism, through microaggressions, can cause PTSD,[12] and if this also intersects with conditions of educational segregation and poverty,[13] to the degree that it also has been shown that as long as "African American students continue to be three times as likely to be labeled mentally ~~retarded~~, two times as likely to be labeled emotionally disturbed, and one and a half times as likely to be labeled learning disabled, compared to white peers,"[14] then, absolutely, there is *much work* to be done challenging ableism via intersectional analyses. As Annamma, Connor, and Ferri state it (2013), "Given the ways that race has figured so prominently in special education status, we would argue that it would be nothing short of irresponsible to leave race out of dis/ability related research" (4).

It is worth introducing my interlocutors in this chapter. Devonya Havis [DH (she/her)] is a philosopher that has worked with great care describing and defining the context of race in relation to identity, particularly auditory identity. An Associate Professor of Philosophy at Canisius College in Buffalo, NY, Dr. Havis' publications include "'Now, How You Sound': Considering a Different Philosophical Praxis" in the feminist philosophy journal, *Hypatia*, in its Special Issue on Interstitiality. She also has published, "Blackness Beyond Witness" in *Philosophy and Social Criticism*, and "'Seeing Black' through Michel Foucault's Eyes: 'Stand Your Ground' Laws as An Anchorage Point for State-Sponsored Racism," a chapter in the anthology, *Pursuing Trayvon Martin: Historical Contexts and Contemporary Manifestations of Racial Dynamics* (2013). She was also a "Featured Philosop-Her" on Meena Krishnamurthy's blog profiling women philosophers.[15] She is currently working on a book titled, *Creating a Black Vernacular Philosophy*. Devonya also teaches to promote social justice. This interest is especially evident in the Immersion East Side (Buffalo, NY) Ignatian Seminar that she has co-designed and co-directed for the last five years. The immersion is designed to engage students with the unique rites, rituals, cultural practices, and perseverance of Buffalo's East Side residents who operate in the context of numerous structural, social, and political impediments. The seminar, not only explores these realities but also celebrates the historical Black capacity to "create" even in the midst of a desert. Havis has also been involved with *Partnership for The Public Good* and *The Prison Visiting Project Western New York Auxiliary*.

Lydia Brown [LB (they/them)] is a queer, east Asian[16] autistic disability justice activist, organizer, and advocate, dedicated to intersectional social justice. They are a recent graduate from Georgetown University in Washington, DC, and are currently attending law school at Northeastern University in Boston while teaching a course they designed on disability and social movements at Tufts University. Lydia authors the blog *Autistic Hoya*, and from 2015–2017, served as chairperson of the Massachusetts Developmental Disabilities Council. They have worked with the Autism Women's Network to curate the first-ever anthology by autistic people of color, titled *All the Weight of Our Dreams*, and their publications include the chapter, "'You Don't Feel Like a Freak Anymore': Representing Disability, Madness, and Trauma in Litchfield Penitentiary," in *Feminist Perspectives on Orange Is the New Black: Thirteen Critical Essays* (2016), and the chapter, "Ableist Shame and Disruptive Bodies: Survivorship at the Intersection of Queer, Trans, and Disabled Existence," in *Religion, Disability, and Interpersonal Violence* (2017). They have also published "Autism Isn't Speaking: Autistic Subversion in Media & Public Policy" in the Disability Studies (DS) reader *Barriers & Belonging: Personal Narratives of Disability* (2017), as well as work in *The Asian American Literary Review* (Fall/Winter 2016), *QDA: A Queer Disability Anthology* (2015), *Torture in Healthcare Settings* (2013), and the radical disability anthology *Criptiques* (2014). Lydia co-founded the Washington Metro Disabled Students Collective while an undergraduate student, and co-created a Disability Justice Caucus in law school. *Pacific Standard Magazine* named them one of the "Top 30 Thinkers under 30," and in 2013, Lydia was honored as a Champion of Change by the White House for their disability rights advocacy.

As we discuss the following questions, it becomes important to communicate to you, our readers, that these concerns about intersectionality are *partial but important* to put forth. Following Falguni Sheth's "Interstitiality: Making Space for Migration, Diaspora, and Racial Complexity" (2014, 77):

> [I]nterstitiality builds on . . . intersectionality. In recent years, new issues, themes and subject populations have captured our attention, raising questions about how to account for subjects, who in the context of prevailing cultural, racial, or ethnic discourses *present similarly*, but whose cultural, social, or political commitments may not only differ but conflict—while accounting for those subjects who *present dissimilarly*, but who perceive themselves as having shared political and social interests and commitments.

The dialogue that follows should be understood as only an *initiation*, and while we build onto the work already done on intersectionality, so too we also might still need to work toward interstitiality, with continued attention to the more urgent and pressing complications that come with this work. Kristie Dotson is instructive on this point (2014, 12 [emphasis added]):

> The term *interstices* is often defined as "spaces between closely related things." The preposition "between" is a close approximation for an interstitial space, but it is not perfect. A more accurate preposition, though rarely used today, is "*betwixt*." Interstices refer to positions betwixt closely related locations, ideas,

positions, and the like. Being located "betwixt" two locations, for example, is to be neither wholly separate, nor wholly part of two closely related, though, some would say, thoroughly demarcated areas. Though "betwixt" has often been deployed to indicate indecision, here it refers more closely to undecidability. It is not that interstices are rife with indecision, as if the people populating them are in a constant state of "not having decided." Rather, interstices are rife with distinctly undecidable conflicts. That is to say, *interstices are often demarcated spheres where hard and fast decisions carry unacceptable losses of life and health.*

Any intersectional approach will require a certain amount of attentive openness and open-endedness to what and who resides "betwixt" and yet is unacceptably unaccounted for; with this, it must be a willingness to engage the political and ethical implications of biases, now with the included additional commitment to destabilize ableist operations.

WHAT IS YOUR EXPERIENCE OF ABLEISM/DISABLEISM?

JS: First and foremost, for me, my experience came as mother to a child who has been diagnosed with a disability and that I could not explain the depth of discrimination I was encountering. It sometimes was sneaky and implicit—as in the stares and dirty looks that came my way and her way—and how it also operated along race/class/gender lines of discrimination of which I was already more familiar. I was sensitive to the way in which assumptions about who we were and what my child was able or not able to do operated on microlevels—particularly in the microaggressions and microgestures—as in the condescending look of a Girl Scout Troop organizer who decided that the troop was better off *without* than *with* my daughter.[17] What became more obvious was the complexity of challenging ableism when I refused to keep looking through the narrow lens of white privilege.

Part of the context for this first question is that I've been using ableism as the broad term for the bias and disableism as the more defensive posture of ableist attitudes and thinking. Eva Kittay[18] seems to use it in that way: as certain people might remain uncritical or even defensive of ableist ideology, then we might say they are *disablist* in their rhetoric and/or attitudes. I've been using the terms similarly to the way racism is the general term, and then from that might say certain people are racist because of the way they promulgate and defend racist ideas and attitudes.

LB: For a long time, I actually have had a different understanding of the word disableism. I haven't used the word "disableism" in general, because I understood it as centering abled people as opposed to disabled people. Lisa Egan[19] who identifies as disabled and gay, argues that ableism as a term privileges abled people and instead people should use the term disableism. I've felt the opposite, that ableism as a term reflects its meaning. Specifically, ableism is a system that values and idealizes abled people and the able-normative body as superior and more worthy than the disabled body. The term disableism actually moves toward individualizing disability again, and locating the problem of disability in the disabled body rather than the narrative of compulsory ablenormativity.

More recently, I have begun to take a different turn in my understanding of the terms *ableism* and *disableism*, especially as I've reflected on the fact that proponents of both terms make the same claim that is their dispreferred term that really centers abled people over disabled people. I now posit that ableism and disableism are not so much competing terms for the same concept, but rather, that *ableism* might describe the value system of ablenormativity which privileges the supposedly neurotypical and ablebodied, while *disableism* might describe the violent oppression targeting people whose bodyminds are deemed deviant and thus disabled. In other words, ableism is to heterosexism what disableism is to queerantagonism, and both terms convey valuable linguistic interpretation of our lived experiences. In my daily use, I still use *ableism* more frequently, as it is the more common term in the United States where I live.

JS: I think it is important to have this as part of our dialogue. The limits of some of the ways these words function or get used need to be discussed. I know, for example, Devonya had preferred the concept of interstitiality to the idea of intersectionality, so too I want you, Lydia, to be able to challenge the use of a term like disableism. I do like the idea that how a word is being used or who is using the word could be part of this discussion.

LB: My thoughts on language do depend a lot on what word we are talking about. There are plenty of words that I use that other people don't use and vice versa for very valid reasons. Whether we are talking about scholarship or activism, when we start treating language as a litmus test or as an absolute—either it must be this way, or it must be that way—if you use this language you must be a "good" activist, a "good" scholar, on the "right" side; if you use that language, you are a "bad" activist, a "bad" scholar, and you're on the wrong side and we can't trust you, then we are missing a lot. That mentality is also deeply ableist, classist, and racist. Instead, if we talk about a plurality of bodies and minds, and if we really believe in challenging ablenormativity, and acknowledging that there are infinite ways of existing and that those experiences can exist at the same time without contradicting or negating any others—it can be *both/and*,[20] it does not have to be *either/or*—then we also have to acknowledge multiplicity in the kind of language and terms that we use to negotiate our realities.

Thus, if a term might have a salient and important meaning for one person's experiences or for people in that person's social circle, then it is okay. It doesn't negate the feelings or the experiences of another person or group for whom that term means nothing, and even if that term has a lot of baggage, even negative baggage, it is recodifying. It can be *both/and*. The term "queer" is a perfect example of that. There are many people for whom that word carries an enormous amount of baggage from past and current violence and trauma, both personal and collective. And there are others among us for whom that baggage does not go away, but our primary relationship to that term is one of empowerment, self-identification, and enabling access to a collective of people who have like experiences. Linguistic violence and empowerment do not have to be mutually exclusive.

Most importantly, I want to emphasize that we don't have to deal with language issues by ignoring them or not acknowledging them out of politeness, putting it in a footnote out of a false sense that they are "beneath" us or irrelevant to activism, or talking about them only from one's perspective treated as canonically right at the exclusion of any other possibilities; rather, it can be *both/and*.

JS: I think we need to work past the issues of "political correctness," and particularly academic political correctness, in support of this point you've made. The indifference that I've seen philosophers have had to requests made by DS scholars and disabled scholars, for accommodation or for consideration of language, has a lot to do with the quality of the dialogue, and that these questions have been dialectically excluded. The outright discrimination and shaming of academics in ways that are patently ableist has been, for me, quite disturbing.[21] There have been quite a number of recent cases of outright harassment and bullying of academics—even doxxing[22]—that amplified anti-black racism, transphobia, and transmisogyny but those critiques seem to miss the ableist underpinnings of these aggressions.[23] It then does become about who we listen to; who we think is worth attending to; and who "creates" baggage, as you describe it, and better understanding what that might mean. Our experiences can shape the way in which we communicate and certain words do have a way of informing and perhaps challenging deeply entrenched value-laden ideologies. In this way, the complexity of the use of "queer" still holds as a good example. More importantly, how we talk about things, the context by which we use certain terms, can have real, material effects.

DH: I struggle with labeling things as well. In particular, my life has been a constant roll of experiences for which the labels ultimately fail or the labels, while sometimes useful, also demarcate zones of necessary contestation. In some cases, this problem emerges because what the labels represent or symbolize do not make problematic how the labels, themselves, are a function of complex—often unacknowledged—processes of social construction. Hence, what a term "means" in the popular imaginary often represents and operationalizes everyday violence that depends upon unquestioned assumptions and everyday practices that have been and continue to be normalized.[24]

There is an awkwardness, for me, with these terms that stem from my desire to unpack, contextualize, historicize, and expose the power dynamics at work in the language used—as well as the casual ways the language used and referenced functions to frame every day encounters into what is "acceptable" and/or "tolerable." Lydia alludes to these issues when problematizing the use of the ableism/disablist terms. All this is to say that I have felt very inexpert in using certain terms. There are times when I have acted toward terms that denote relationships to "disability" much like the white person who does not want to use the incorrect racial or ethnic term lest she offend. My husband's catastrophic stroke that left him without expressive spoken language and with significantly diminished use of his entire right side forced me yet again to confront "terms" and their meanings.

Not only was I dealing with the trauma of radical changes in the way our family operated, I also found myself again considering what it means to be labeled "disabled." While our family has and had previously contended with a number of conditions that could be labeled "disabilities," I had been reluctant to describe our experiences with that term. Perhaps, one could call it a kind of "passing." To me it was a different kind of passing than racial passing because the aim was to insulate the family from additional assault and vulnerability. To draw upon Jen's references to Young, such "passing" as insulation was an ongoing way to mitigate the faces of violence, exploitation, marginalization, and cultural imperialism that are even present when one inhabits a racialized body.

Moving away from simply framing things as normal/abnormal has long been a concern for me. I think such a departure is what is also at stake in the inquiry about the terms ableism and disableism. I also think that the imbedded notions of what can and does "pass" as normative, raise for me the ways that certain kinds of passing are defensive rather than uncomplicated associations with normality. It is the case that there are also costs associated with all passing. There may be some insulation but there is also a great deal of unacknowledged labor connected to the extra work required to function in a world calibrated to a certain notion of "normality." Unaccounted for are the material, everyday effects associated with the "failures" covered over in this defensive "passing." It is also the case that the inability to "pass" materially affects one's life.

When one is Black with Black/Brown children and family, there are always concerns about not drawing more attention because of a particular label. It was not simply a family matter but was also a question of what it meant institutionally. These were concerns not simply about our preferences, but concerns associated with which of the needed services my husband would ultimately be eligible to receive. Moreover, there is a concern with who or what entity has the authority to render labels—to assign terms. So, this idea of defensive passing is not a way of championing the normative constructions, it is a way of mitigating forces that already presume the normative and therefore is nonnormative.

My husband, EJ, prior to his stroke had been diagnosed with Multiple Sclerosis (MS). This condition, while it posed certain challenges, did not—in our case—significantly alter our everyday routines. As a family, we negotiated our everyday terrain without major shifts. This came to an abrupt halt after the stroke. EJ could no longer function as the Chief Financial Officer for the Buffalo Economic Renaissance Corporation, a public/private local governmental entity with significant reporting demands. The entity was also in the process of a reorganization that he was managing. EJ had a schematic, generalist's frame for organizing and analyzing business practices. He was great at developing processes that structured solutions and seeing how various operations were interrelated. He was well-respected and liked for his contributions. He was also very active in other ventures beyond his "day job." He worked to help develop a community-based business incubator, was engaged with a group seeking to create a Buffalo African American museum, and remained active in a Boston-based real estate development venture. So, one of the major effects of the stroke is that it disrupted all these anticipated possibilities. There was the frustration, not only about the significant physical changes, but also about the failure of things to "pay off'—much unfinished business and the end of certain expectations. He had all this sweat equity in numerous projects. Yet, I look around and think, "these projects are great but not a bone for retirement." We were really holding on and counting on continuing progress. I am now beginning to get that even though there is unfinished business that he needs to get to, it is possible that EJ may never be able to get to it. Much of my framing has shifted to "He can do these things" which is very different from my initial shock that took the form of: *Oh shit, this is totally different.*

EJ's circumstance has also made me think, yet again, about the extent to which one "outs" oneself. I didn't really acknowledge the notion that I was internalizing ableism or disableism, nor did I spend a lot of time focused on the ways we were rewarded for managing to function that may have seemed "normal" to those outside the family. When you no longer pass, or events in your life draw attention to the failure to pass, then there is a different appreciation for how one perceives disability and the benefit of having been assumed to have been "ablebodied." I raise this because of the MS and other family conditions through which we have negotiated.

JS: The grief is very difficult, especially when there is an affective experience of *loss*—especially loss of perceived capacities and expectations, or in what had been an ablebodied (albeit a *passing*) identity. And I think that is where a lot of the work comes from: being able to see possibility again in a way that if you don't contend with that grief—and it is contending with that grief part, really realizing that there is possibility despite a loss here– and, in your case, it is not necessarily a loss of/for him but there is that loss of possibility that you had invested in that makes this the stuff of grief. That is what makes acceptance so important: if you can get to that acceptance, there's a lot of joy that comes with that. There's a lot of joy that comes with saying this is how it is, this is what it is. In your case, I think this is the case. You had accepted it. And that's what I found so impressive is because your relationship with EJ sounded, at least from my end and as also your friend, when you would talk about it and everything, sounded so stable. And I think you had created that for yourself.

DH: Yes, there is the grieving. But, I am not sure that the joy comes from a kind of resignation or acceptance. I guess I want to deeply trouble the ways that we so easily move to frames that establish what represents normativity and/or stability. From my standpoint, this kind of contestation was an intentional feature of my relationship with EJ. From the outset, we wanted to challenge much of the way things have been framed as normal/abnormal. In retrospect, I might argue that this was at the heart of our marriage vows. It was not a relationship designed to "fix" the other person. It was not so much that we didn't want to change or that change would not happen. Rather, it was a realization that it was and is not the partner's job to craft the kind of change that the other person needs to undertake. Right? So, we committed to growth and an openness to supporting the kinds of things the other person viewed as important and needed to aid that growth—not as a kind of imposition.

I think we were somehow aware of Michel Foucault's admonition about the positive aspects of power. He notes that it is not simply by prohibition but also by means of enticements and rewards that power operates. What this has meant to me is that we often neglect how the things we are encouraged to do and the modes we are encouraged to inhabit are also effects generated in and through our positionality within networks of power. Hence, narratives of freedom and even progress can reinforce experiences of oppression even while we presume we are "freely" choosing something. Our very characterization of norms and the "normal" must therefore be interrogated because the very framework under which we operate imports in certain coercive power elements that may remain unacknowledged.

Hence, even our processes of self-crafting and self-envisioning may move us to take up what is normative and not really what works for our lives. I think EJ and I were always sensitive to the way normalization closed off other possibilities. And, we didn't want to do that. The aim was to leave room for ongoing development that included critical engagement with norms and normativity—an ideal goal. The real challenges to one's ideals often arise when pressed with everyday demands. Such demands began to arise when our youngest daughter was identified as having speech difficulties early in her development. We noticed that she was super frustrated when communicating and many times, we could not decipher what she was saying. Early Intervention came in and worked with her on speech which improved her ability to be understood. What remained unclear in this process was that early speech difficulty is often a predictor of difficulty with developing the ability to read.

Over time and after much testing, we learned that she processes things differently. This meant that the usual teaching methods were not effective for getting her to read. This is its own challenge on many levels. One is not wanting one's child to begin to think of herself as less intelligent. Another is feeling like a failure in helping one's child develop an essential life skill as her peers move forward; and yet another is wondering how to be supportive in helping her navigate terrain that is unfamiliar. Then, there is the way that race and gender play into parental concerns about how one's child will be characterized by the educational system—even when one is using class privilege to "buy" one's way out of certain narratives by sending the kids to private school. Very complicated stuff that draws upon the ways that "literacy" can really be a threat to "vernacular" sensibilities. While education is important, it is also crucial to recognize that the traditional forms of education often exclude and minimize the significance of intergroup knowledge.

Moreover, as the Black parent of Black children, I have grave concerns about how institutions interpret and use information about Black children. There is a long, disturbing educational history throughout which Black children have been mislabeled, maltreated, and mis-educated in ways justified by tests and/or presumptions about their intelligence.

JS: In my case, the gender bias became a real difficulty—a complexity in not only my care of and for my daughter, but in her defense and representation as well as for her self-esteem, her own self-identification and desires. She also had difficulty early on, but as time went on, as she got further along in school, expressed difficulty staying in enclosed classes—"Special Ed"—not only as she became aware of what that segregation represented, but because she was in (and spent most of her day) with boys and all she wanted to do was be with typical and peer girls. The Special Education classes were often mixed with younger and older (mostly male) peers as well. At first there was no question by the teachers and administrators that this was an appropriate setting for her. And she started to make it very clear to me if she stayed in that classes like this, she felt like she was being left back and excluded in ways that almost *physiologically* grated on her. And this is her *right*[25]—to be with other children in the grade—what is termed "the least restrictive environment." Her enclosed class had children with all kinds of issues—learning, psychological, and emotional—kind of a "catch all" room of students with Individual Educational Plans (IEPs) that could not be integrated "yet" into general education settings. Often, I'd wonder, *who is this really for?* Her or them?

Mind you, she was already struggling developmentally in her social interactions. She wanted so much to be with girls of her own age and then when she was with them—in unstructured interactions—the peer aged girls would exclude her from their group, or worse, make her just "clean up after them" in their "club" during recess. Although she could not respond typically to these interactions, she intuitively knew what was happening.[26] She is intensely emotionally sensitive, even absorbing and reflecting the emotions of others in an unfiltered way, and she would—mostly after the fact—communicate these experiences to me in pieces.[27]

DH: Oh wow! And the fact that that she could see that though. . . . Her perceptiveness is clear despite having to endure the negative experiences.

JS: I had to decode it out of what she was saying. It was coming as a resistance. And gender difference was playing a significant role in her self-perception here because her social interactions with peer-aged boys were not successful and her interactions with girls that she wanted to be around were also not successful. She is a really sociable kid and here she was being "set up" to fail and felt very left out. Feeling left out was a real trigger for her as well.[28]

DH: So, the language to communicate what was going on in a way that you could understand it was the rub. Again, this involves presumptions about "norms." Resistance is seen as an obstacle when in this case it had much to do with communication and attempts to create a more tolerable space. My daughter exercised many "resistances" as well.

JS: Yes, she was really throwing out lots of signals until I put it together and I realized—"Oh, that's what she said." I was devastated when I realized how long she had been functioning and trying to integrate without that support and being so often misunderstood, even by me. She was *so relieved* when I made it very clear that I understood what she was trying to do and would argue at every turn to represent that to her teachers, to her school. She recently got to attend her own IEP program meeting—she couldn't stand that there were meetings in which we were talking about her—and she was *so happy* to speak for herself.

DH: This was part of her enthusiasm.

We were lucky that we had already chosen a school that was not overly committed to norms for norms' sake. Those surrounding my daughter talked to her about her brain just working differently, not better or worse, *just differently*. And that she was having a little more trouble learning to read and so there needed to be a different strategy for smart kids whose brains worked differently.

JS: What I think is really important is that, with my daughter too, how much I've internalized what I think she should be doing based on what I was taught I should be able to do. One of the key components in this book—in mapping out the scale and scope of ableism—is the intergenerational transfer of ableism: how parents pass on their ableism to their children, and, in turn, those children internalize it, identify with it, transfer it into social and psychological currency, etc.

DH: Yes, this is a critical point and it has much to do with self-perception and confidence in the world. Also, it is about how we think we are being rated as good/bad parents. Negotiating this territory has also triggered for me the things that I relied upon to feel safe as a kid. My ability to crawl into a book or to think critically made me feel safe. So, it is scary if my kid does not also gravitate toward or share those abilities. How will she be safe? Disentangling my baggage from my daughter's concerns was crucial for me. This also involved navigating through what I learned from my mother. It turns out that my mother is also dyslexic and she always felt "stupid" because of the challenges she faced. My mother's experiences were the subtext of my own school experiences and of a way of dealing with children that was not interventionist. When I was in school, it was the case that if kids were smart enough to figure out how to cope, despite something that might be labeled a disability now, they would be characterized as not working hard enough, lazy, avoidant, or contrary. In effect, the individual and not the existing structures are to blame. I think my family has a great deal of this intergenerational ableism and shame. I hear much of this judgment in the background of things my mother says about her childhood experiences and in some ways she wants to approach the difficulties I encountered as a child and in dealing with her grandchildren.

On the other hand, my dad has had a greater tolerance for developmental progress and differences. In discussing my children, he has always been less inclined toward intervention even though he is a clinical psychologist. My sense is that some of the reluctance comes from his experiences during childhood. Formal testing through the educational system got him mislabeled as "retarded." What was not included in the school analysis was the fact that the society was rural, segregated, and southern. The interpretation and use of the test had much to do with the fact that my father was a black person growing up black, in the rural south picking cotton, and about the cultural differences and expectations that go into IQ exams.

In many ways, his experiences make clear the dangers associated with testing in classed, gendered, and racialized social structures. My suspicions about normalization have been earned. My dad is one of the smartest people I know. He is self-taught in many areas. He has gone on to earn a PhD and is a deeply ethical human being. These things are not measurable or conceivable based upon a test and its subsequent interpretation.

JS: That's the thing—and how ableist it is to think that people are *smart* or *stupid*; that is linked affectively to a *long history* of ableist slurs. I mean, that's that line I draw especially with autistic behaviors because usually what my daughter is saying is quite sharp and interesting, but it's how she's saying it that most people have no literacy for how to listen, no cultural supports except by drawing from their discomforts. And it's *not* really *less ableist* when people think, "Oh, it's not that she's stupid, she's just got mental issues." . . . It's a lot of push to say people's brains for the most part are wired very differently and uniquely—that explaining difference through neurodiversity against most people's pop- and pseudo-psychological assumptions is also going to mean more labor-intensive advocacy.

DH: There are different kinds of intelligence that we have become accustomed to discounting. And yet, there are all kinds of intelligences. I was recently having a discussion with my kids about "intelligence." They were expressing their frustration with a person at their school who gets labeled as "smart." The person they were discussing has repeatedly done well by strictly academic measures and is a familiar type of overachiever who skipped a grade. She makes A's in all classes and has certain kinds of intelligence. My kids said, "But mom, everything is planned out. It's all in a box. *how is that smartness?*" As a way of helping them explore the issue, I brought up Simone de Beauvoir in *The Ethics of Ambiguity*.[29] In that text, Beauvoir discusses the problem of fleeing one's own freedom. She argues that those who thematize their lives or work the world into a singular narrative theme pursue a kind of certainty that makes them not open to the ambiguities that are required when one is fully engaged with living. Beauvoir's observations offered a model for engaging them in conversation about how what counts as "smart" or "together" has been represented. It was a model for helping them explain some of the discomfort they were having with celebrating someone who put life into boxes.

I think using this sense of "inauthenticity" works to raise questions about how we are living and where we place value. They resonated with the idea that working one's entire life into a particular theme could be limiting and "inauthentic." They could understand how one can simply *become the theme* and stop actually living because the sense of living that is valued involves simply living out and realizing one's existence according to the theme. I was trying to talk to them about the way such themes generate a narrow framework through which people live their lives. Thematizing can also generate the narrow frameworks through which one can easily say this or that is "smart" without really addressing things in a wider perspective. In this framework, one can take a narrow set of skills that may not well-equip one to fully live or successfully engage the world outside of school settings. The way Beauvoir might describe this conundrum that my kids and I were discussing is that it is a *narrowing*, by living life according to a theme, rather than increasing one's freedom, and really prevents one from pursuing freedom instead, it demonstrates a flight from one's freedom.

It was interesting that it finally came to me when watching Pinocchio. And Pinocchio walks to school by himself and when my daughter saw this and she goes, "Where are his grownups?" Like, *how is he going to school without his grownups?* And for her there was a sense that we were there to keep them safe and she could not imagine a world where there aren't grownups who keep you safe and then you wouldn't end up a donkey at a carnival having to try to figure out how to get home. I mean, it was inconceivable that Pinocchio would get there because my daughter couldn't even get out of the gate with the start that was presumed for Pinocchio. I mean, that wasn't her experience.

And there's the challenge of not limiting your child by your issues. I mean, I struggled a lot with this. Sort of my perceptions of race, my perceptions of what's going on. And they just have a very different sense of the world then because of whatever "craziness"[30] that was part of my upbringing that I had.

HOW DO YOU IDENTIFY YOURSELF AND YOUR WORK IN RELATION TO DISABILITY STUDIES SCHOLARSHIP AND ADVOCACY?

LB: I identify as autistic and disabled, I also identify as asexual, queer, and genderqueer, I am a transnational and transracial east Asian adoptee into a white family in the United States. I also have many privileged experiences—I had an elite college education, I am a US citizen, I am from a mixed-class background and grew up with middle and upper-middle class income and financial resources, and I was socialized around the communication and social norms of whiteness. My work as an activist, organizer, and advocate has primarily focused on violence against disabled people, especially those who are multiply marginalized, like disabled people of color and queer and trans disabled people.

JS: Because I identify as ablebodied, I find that I am very self-conscious in taking on and addressing ableism because I know there is a limitation in the way I will account for disability and I don't want to ride roughshod over the narratives and the scholarship already there. There are ways in which I can identify with the corresponding somatophobia that comes as part of operational ableism[31] in my experiences with pregnancy and miscarriage (Scuro 2017), as well as issues better addressed in Fat Studies scholarship[32]—although I don't personally quite identify as "fat." Teaching courses on Philosophy of the Body and Critical Disability Theory have given me an opportunity to better map the overlaps between ableism and other operational biases. I know that I cannot avoid and neutralize ableist bias myself and that only when the question of ableism is in the context of a dialogue, might my personal or professional or political ableist biases be qualified and corrected.

I find that I've been talking more and more about the work of "excising ableism"—as if an exorcism could be a sort of philosophical methodology—and as if you can get "rid" of it like a kind of demonic possession. I've been also testing out different "thought experiments" that anyone—including me—could try and measure for the degree of internalized assumptions, phobias, anxieties over ablebodiedness and "out" them appropriately. I'm really trying to "un-disguise" ableism. I found using Affect Theory in my Critical Disability class to explain how ableism is manifested and transferred was most helpful for constructing these experiments and tests.

For example, thinking of theory as also the source of critical pedagogical strategies, in one class, composed mostly of students in health-care professions, I polled them regarding what most "disgusts" them, asking them to describe what it is that they react to adversely in their service work. One nurse seemed to be willing to admit: "children with a lot of earwax." I added context to this confession in that, 1) that adverse feeling—the gut reaction to some aspect of their work—is something many people in the service profession have but will not necessarily admit, 2) although in her case it may have had to do with earwax, but that the content could be different for each of us, the important analysis came in the common affective quality of aversion, and 3) that reflecting on this aversion may also free her (and the others by proxy) from giving this particular task to others, from avoiding that which she was adverse to. I suggested to the class that patients/clients/children may actually pick up on this affective aversion, and that if we take it too personally, we cannot improve our professionalism.

What I found though was an additional outcome from the exercise: that by getting into dialogue with herself and opening herself up to the group about her particular affective aversions, another student who worked in family services and support for many years, responded that, despite the reaction to earwax, it is worth investigating the context of the person with this issue. She said, to paraphrase, "children and people who are in someone else's care who have been neglected tend to have issues like that. I would find out if the person is getting the support they need and that it is not a sign of a more systemic issue of care." The nurse responded gratefully that she had not thought about it like that—in the context of class and of care—and now she would not feel comfortable turning away a patient out of her own ableist aversions.

The teaching has allowed me to figure out how to bring my philosophical training into scholarship because there is so little in philosophy that addresses directly these issues of thinking and practice. It was your list of ableist words,[33] Lydia, which I used for another assignment, a Life Writing exercise inspired by Linda Ware's "Dare We Do Disability Studies?" Students had to take one of the terms and "own" it, meditate on how they might have used it, how it is ableist, etc. In that case, we had a whole discussion about "wheelchair bound," a term which I think most people might assume is a neutral characterization of disability, but in fact is quite ableist in that the perception of being "bound" to a wheelchair makes it an *either/or* of wheelchair use. So, if you were to use a wheelchair but also be able to move free of the wheelchair, most of the ablebodied world will police the person as a "fraud" and question their credibility. It is really hard to explain in a climate in which being "wheelchair-bound" is a normative-enough identity that anyone in a wheelchair, who also might not be "bound" to it *loses the right* to using the wheelchair as they see fit, undermining their credibility as a disabled person as well.

In my first chapter, I describe my experience and my need to define the discrimination that I saw in an urgent way. Yet, in this way too, my experiences were limited to my daughter's experiences and recently I have taken to the concern about parents' "oversharing" and in that way sabotaging their children's ability to control their own narratives, tell their own stories, maintain their privacy.[34] My work has been in the scholarship and the teaching. Having had the opportunity to teach classes in DS proper in which I'm working to define ableism such that my students can "own" their particular ableist thinking; this becomes my advocacy.

Considering that Lydia is the one that brought me to this work when they suggested in 2013 that I go to the annual Society for Disability Studies (SDS) meeting, I am so grateful because I don't think I would have engaged this work otherwise.

LB: This is a good question. If you asked me for a general description of the types of work that I do with disability, I often tell people that what I do is straddle and blur lines between policy advocacy, radical scholarship, and community organizing, and that's because I do all of those things. I don't believe these types of work are mutually exclusive.

I also want to be clear that I absolutely don't believe that everybody in a movement can or should do "everything." That assumption is extremely oppressive in multiple ways. It is ableist—many disabled people cannot attend outdoor demonstrations; disabled people may struggle with written language, organizing logistics, or crowded rooms; many venues for activist and scholarly events are totally inaccessible. It is classist—low-income rural people may have extremely limited or no access to transportation to events; low-income people may work multiple jobs and have no time or energy for additional unpaid activist work; low-income people can't afford to go to expensive conferences and workshops. It completely disregards specific dangers to queer and trans people at risk of violent attack, undocumented people in danger of imprisonment and deportation by attending protests, and black and brown people for whom police encounters may well become deadly.

Everybody cannot do everything, but, some people can do certain things and people who can't do those things can do other things. There are specific things that I have done, for example, presenting papers at academic conferences that are definitely in the world of scholarship, or organizing protests or a call-in day to legislators, that are very much community organizing, and writing legislation or sitting down with administrators at my university repeatedly to ask for certain changes in procedure on how to handle disabled students, which is definitely policy advocacy. But I don't see these as different areas of my life or my work. They all come down to the same values that I hold; they are part of the same vision I have for possibilities for which I am committed and care about developing and working toward. They are just specific manifestations of how I can bring those about, what I can do to try to bring that vision into being.

That is generally my answer, but if you ask me more specifically what is my feeling about my current relationship to DS scholarship, funny enough, it would be "one that is at the margins." I say that because, up until a couple of months ago, I didn't have formal degree in anything and I just graduated from college in May 2015. *I did not have a formal degree* and the degree that I now have is in Arabic language. I'm not a scholar in the conventional sense, but many friends and colleagues have described my writing and thinking as *scholarly*.

JS: That was specifically what impressed me about this work and the quality of your work, that you did not have a formal degree but that it was permissible to engage the scholarship anyway. This, I didn't find elsewhere—to bring together the work of advocates, policy makers, and scholars into the DS community, and that it wasn't a strict traditional idea of scholarship. Everyone seemed to be working together in a more humanistic way,[35] more than any other academic setting I had been in. It wasn't about credentials and status that gave you voice and a platform. In some ways, Lydia, you took the platform and there is something so powerful about some of what you have been able to speak to and against. Now that you are going to law school, it seems to me it is like *due* to you—owed to you—so that you are further empowered with those credentials. And this is something you are doing *for you*; especially since you've already made such an impact.

But there is also another point here about the struggle in the context of formal education and the normative expectations of performance—what you have to do, how you should do it.

LB: And that is really about ablenormativity being tied to class and capitalism.

JS: There's this nice thing that Siebers talks about that could allow us as philosophers to add a special kind of insight into the scholarship and context for these experiences: that there's a kind of philosophical realism[36] that needs to be maintained in the work. And being able to say, "You know what, let's call it what it is. Let's name it in a way that stops dancing around it and accept it."

It's also a question of political precarity of exclusion and inaccessibility: a condition that preconceives and prescribes whose lives count more and whose lives are less important as the general attitude, even when it is no one person's specific intention: *Who's less grievable? Who can we get rid of? Who can we keep and who can we dispose of?*

DH: The questions of who's life is valued and who is framed as valuable are important considerations. It is the case that I had already been accustomed to precarity through race and not disability. So, when my husband EJ had a stroke, I was confronted with a different kind of precarity. We entered the emergency room and he was talking. I was confident that medicine would fix him. I thought, "We got to the hospital in time. It's going to stop. It's not going to get any worse." At first he was more functional and able to do certain things but, by the time he was transported to rehab, he was incontinent and he couldn't sit himself up in bed. Hospital transport staff had to put him on a stretcher to transport him to rehab. And he couldn't talk. As I watched the process, I thought: *Oh my God! What does this mean?* I was glad that he was alive because he easily could have died had we not come to the hospital but I was terrified on so many levels. How will we survive economically, spiritually, and as a family? Who will EJ be in this post-stroke life?

And, there was the very difficult fact that his speech was significantly compromised by the stroke. He was cognitively and physically different yet the same person. In all of this, the idea of language and communication has been particularly key. Since he became unable to communicate in "conventional ways," many people viewed and view him very narrowly because he cannot communicate in the expected ways. This also seems to be the case with others who have similar difficulties. They get narrowly viewed because they do not communicate in particular ways which causes us to miss out on what they have to offer.

I have been taught this lesson by both my husband and my daughter, who had early speech difficulties. My husband because of the stroke affecting the area of his brain where the speech center is located who is often discounted because he cannot communicate fluidly. In many cases, he is unable to speak and cannot rapidly participate in conversations. Without the usual forms of spoken language, he is often viewed as far less capable and people talk to me instead of him even when the focus is his health or care. He is aware of what is going on and rightly is upset about how he gets excluded from conversations about his care or preferences. It is particularly pronounced because prior to the stroke, he most valued his ability to effectively communicate through spoken and written language. He is able to communicate in other ways but they are not the usual modes and people do not always have the patience required to discern his communications. He cannot do these things fluidly now; in some cases he is unable to speak. Because of this, I've been thinking a lot more about silent communication.[37]

JS: And there's a disposability in the way in which we treat people with disabilities and impairments like this. Again, your fear, that terror was in the reality that this life—his life and his person, *this* person—is a grievable life. This person, the value of who he is to you, who you need in your life now, he could die. That is precarity for him and for you made real in an unmediated way.

DH: Yes, the stroke brought forth an intense, immediate experience of vulnerability. I was also witnessing and bearing witness to the helplessness of those experiences. The sheer terror that is part of confronting the possibility that things could go awry at any point. Emergency Rooms symbolize and remind me of this basic terror against which one has no recourse. The full impact of the helplessness is a bodily memory of terror, impossibility, and helplessness. I recall looking into EJ's face as the transport staff moved him from the hospital to rehab. I could read the terror on his face as they moved his body and placed him on a stretcher to transport him.

He was alone, unable to effectively communicate, or control his body. I had to meet him at the rehab facility because he was being moved via ambulance. So I was, in practice, sending him off with strangers and there was no way to explain it. These strangers, while well-meaning, were handling him as a mere body. Again, the communication I could read in his eyes spoke of the fear of falling and the terror of not being able to control his body to even get out of bed.

JS: Because he becomes a *body*. He becomes *just a body* at that point, vulnerable to a society who will treat him as nothing but a body.

DH: The terror and vulnerability of being reduced to a mere body without having any ability to defend oneself is a compounded terror for many black folks who are often reduced to bodies—albeit black bodies, not necessarily disabled bodies. So, in EJ's case, being unable to act on behalf of himself and having to rely on others, elicited a terror and vulnerability in its own right. It also tapped into a long-standing history for black men in the United States who have been viewed as disposable bodies. I found myself in the role of caretaker saddled with my own fears of not being able to protect, helplessness in the face of this health crisis, and vulnerabilities in a historical context and in the present because EJ might not be able to communicate his experiences to me. I was deeply concerned about keeping him safe and insuring that he got the best care. When it happened, one of my friends said, "Well, you just have to figure it out when you get to the hospital." One of the things I realized in this process was that if I don't show up *everyday*, they might assume that they can just treat him however they want. So, I had to ensure that he was being attended to. I had to go to the hospital every day . . . and spend some time. I needed to be aware of how he was being treated, the treatment plan, and balance caring for EJ with all my other responsibilities to our kids, work, and dealing with people who wanted to help but who needed direction. I'll never forget, one of my colleagues at this point got upset because I wasn't spending enough time around the department at work. I thought, *I don't think you get it. In a basic and fundamental way, have you asked me about my life?*

JS: And, by asking, be responsive to you in a human way. But that kind of outside demand, when others just don't get it, it is a kind of inhumanity in how they act toward you and the things that they feel comfortable enough to say behind your back or even to your face or, passive aggressively, just within earshot.[38]

DH: Yes, in that way, we need empathy for the different conditions of living. In this one catastrophic health event, everything that I had assumed about my life got turned out. What seemed like a solid foundation was shown to be quite porous and vulnerable. In the aftermath, I had to figure out how to live in a different way that shouldered all the demands of the former life and these new responsibilities that required care. Things were radically different and yet, because I grew up with the expectation that one continued on despite the challenges, I worked to maintain the pre-stroke life and to attend to the new demands. I fell into a form of "passing." In those moments, when I began to experience an extreme amount of dissonance between the effort required to pass and my resources to sustain the effort of passing, I felt a certain deficiency on my part. Despite many friends in my life and field of study who had already dispensed with that kind of passing in a world shaped by ablebodied expectations, I still maintained a barrier. It has been very difficult to accept and embrace certain limitations that challenge my propensity to act "as if." So, it really wasn't until I was unavoidably confronted with ability and disability in an everyday way, that I began to connect with the work of DS and critical DS. I am aware that this work is necessary and unavoidable. There is an interconnection between critical DS and work in critical race and gender studies. The experiences of living have pushed me to lower the mask of passing.

HOW DO YOU DEFINE INTERSECTIONALITY?

LB: Firstly, the term *intersectionality* entered popular and academic discourse after introduction by a black woman, scholar-activist Kimberlé Crenshaw, in response to white feminism that completely ignored how the lives of black women were marked not just by patriarchy or sexism, but also by racism, and in ways that, as black women, neither white women nor black men could share in their experiences.[39]

JS: Yes, Crenshaw's work on intersectionality is foundational.[40] What is also interesting about her work is that she has recently been more cautious about the term. When she was asked why intersectionality still seems to be a difficult term, she stated, "I'm only speculating, but there [are] lots of different reasons. I mean, intersectionality is not easy," she says. "It's not as though the existing frameworks that we have—from our culture, our politics or our law—automatically lead people to being conversant and literate in intersectionality. . . . Intersectionality draws attention to invisibilities that exist in feminism, in anti-racism, in class politics, so obviously it takes a lot of work to consistently challenge ourselves to be attentive to aspects of power that we don't ourselves experience."[41] When intersectionality is taken out of the context of black feminism, it can be another kind of erasure: so that again, we have new forms of "collective forgetting" in which "women of colour are invisible in plain sight."

LB: My understanding of intersectionality is more complicated than the "canned" concept of intersectionality as the connections between race, class, and gender (and specifically, cisgender womanhood). I find that it is more complicated and nuanced and that is how I approach a lot of questions. My own personal baggage is that I've been unfairly labeled the "language police" by many people in the disability advocacy communities for years. I care deeply about language and I'm very linguistically-minded. I absolutely believe language is a powerful tool that shapes and perpetuates our realities, and therefore, the language used in our society does reflect the values that we hold; it can be violent or it can be empowering.

That said, I'm *not* the language-police. . . . Instead, let's think about the complicated ways language affects people's lives, and draw upon people's experiences to give it the power that it has. Likewise, when I talk about intersectionality, I'm thinking about the complications. My understanding of it is that intersectionality is a framework, and not a static thing. It is a framework that challenges us to think about how the whole of someone or some community's experiences or identities shape the things that happen to them, the things that they do, and their relationship to those around them as well as the structures of power that they have to interact within their daily existence.

I also taught two classes in the summer of 2015: one was on disability rights activism and the other was a creative writing class on character development. One thing I talked about—in the writing class actually, not the disability class—was that when talking about identity, we are talking about who somebody is and what identities they have. We are talking about what happens to them, asking: What communities have they been a part of, continue to be a part of? What things have occurred in their life? What have they experienced? What do they do? Whether that is defined as "they are a student," "they are a baker," or "they are a doctor" or defining them by the things that they engage in, "this person is an organizer," or "this one is a singer." . . . Who they are also has to do with community, and communities are constantly in flux, not necessarily *one* thing. A person can belong to and engage in many different communities over the course of their lifetime. So, intersectionality is about thinking how all of those things are *aspects* of somebody: *Who is this person? What is their identity?* Or, *what is this community?* Each one of these aspects influences everything that they do and how others are responding and are relating to them in turn.

Thus, when I introduce myself the way I introduced myself, it was very deliberate. I told you who I am, some of the experiences I've had, and what I do—those are three things. To do this is to say, here are some of my identities, because they "mark" me as belonging to certain categories in society—whether they are privileged categories or marginal ones—and they are specific to me. There are other people who may share the same set of identities as me, which can place us in a baseline for certain kinds of common experiences in society, but then there's the other aspect of this: *What do we experience individually? What have we done and what kind of choices and relationships with others have we had as individuals?*

DH: My encounter with intersectionality as an academic concept is via Crenshaw as well, who wanted to account for the particularity of the discrimination experienced by women who were simultaneously impacted by their race and gender. The issue taken up by Crenshaw was that there was no way in law to remediate the unique form of discrimination that was suffered by the women in question. Their experience was one of both race and gender yet, there was no legal way to speak to the reality of the interconnection of race and gender as they were simultaneously operative. Crenshaw understood that the court saw the attempt to account for this simultaneous type of discrimination as if it were an attempt to get more than their fair share of remediation. The view was that one could pursue discrimination as a woman or as someone who is raced but not both. There was no way within the existing legal framework to understand the specificity of their experience and the complexity of the discrimination. Hence, the concept of intersectionality seeks to give an account of the complexities of multiple, unique, and simultaneous experiences—in this case experiences of discrimination.

When I think of intersectionality, as is my tendency, I think about the things it doesn't do as a theory—as a heuristic—but I also embrace the possibilities that I suspect Crenshaw intended. Mainly, I use it as a place to mark an absence—what's missing—to designate how a failure to attend to this absence diminishes our capacity to understand or even register certain experiences.

I understand the "practical" uses of this conception of intersectionality yet I stumble over the way it works as a theoretical model to represent certain types of experience. I am reluctant to use intersectionality as a catch all for the meeting points of race/class/gender/ability/non-ability because without context, the term also runs the risk of creating yet another limiting conceptual "box." What I do like about the term and conceptual register of intersectionality is that it challenges us to move beyond our own limitations to see unaccounted for possibilities; perhaps, it provides a bridge between our limited experience and the experience of others. I am always suspicious, however, about turning concepts into methodologies. My worry is that the "methodology" runs the risk of allowing the concept to be taken out of its particular contexts of struggle and experience. While intersectionality might be a useful tool for developing coalitions and pointing out places where there are gaps in acknowledgment, I worry that taking it up as methodology might result in reifying existing conceptual limitations in spite of the work it seeks to do.

JS: That's why I start thinking about intersectionality in terms of functional analogies. Ableism is like racism and sexism in that we all must acknowledge it and collect tools to resist it so that it cannot be so easily naturalized and internalized—a critical consciousness in the Freirean sense,[42] or closer to a decolonizing methodology, perhaps. When I say "ableism is everywhere," is not the same as saying everyone is a "disablist." So, part of this work is also distinguishing ableist operations from disableist practices and dispositions; in that sense, I borrow from Kittay when she calls Peter Singer and those who defend ableist ideology as "disablists,"[43] similar to the need to out the "bigot" or "misogynist."[44] I think there needs to be a readiness to challenge the current social and political lexicon as it has historically aggregated racist, sexist, ableist assumptions, but that this requires that each of us address these disableisms outright, as much as we can and as best we can.

I'm thinking here of how, in the recent case of Rachel Dolezal, that she presented such a confusing problematic to race identity and advocacy.[45] As some of us argued against the idea of "transracial" identity,[46] and here you can see the limits of an analogy between race and gender (in that *transgender* does not translate when it comes to race identity), there was some uncritical engagement with the concept of "color-blindness." Intended to challenge the way some people think it is okay to neutralize or not "see race," while others "see race everywhere," the term employs a long-standing assumption that blindness means ignorance. I would argue that the actual condition of color-blindness—especially to the extent that it can count as a disability, excluding some people from roles or jobs because of it or as it can function as another form of inspiration porn[47]—but that it is used as a metaphor to really cover over what I think Charles Mills better describes as "white ignorance":

Imagine an ignorance militant, aggressive, not to be intimidated, an ignorance that is active, dynamic, that refuses to go quietly—not at all confined to the illiterate and uneducated but propagated at the highest levels of the land, indeed presenting itself unblushingly as *knowledge* (2007, 22).

This ignorance has nothing to do with the condition of "blindness," in fact, and, arguably, it has been traditionally those who benefit from white privilege that prefer to claim a position of "color-blindness" and is similar to the use of an assumed appropriate (but completely inappropriate) term for Autistic persons: "mindblindness."[48] I think it is fair to say that these positions show themselves as not only disablist, but also implicitly *racist*, coming from white ignorance.

In 2014 at the Society for Phenomenology and Existentialist Philosophy (SPEP) was a discussion about the definition of intersectionality. Devonya and I were present for that along with other philosophers on the politics of race and gender. What I found very interesting was the suggestion that interstitiality[49] is a better term than intersectionality in thinking about the contexts in which race, gender, and class complicate identity politics. That's when I became aware of Sheth's particular concern and I thought that it was an important provocation to the current practices identified under the heading of intersectionality. If intersectionality had become just a placeholder for politically-correct thinking as well as a concept that functioned more like a stale tool of sociological theory, then—from what I understood—Sheth was able to point out how the silencing of the unique, critical and analytic voices of people of color could be done in the name of intersectionality, instead of being viewed as the primary authors to an urgent conversation, and with a priority for addressing race.

DH: I agree that we need to constantly seek challenges and correctives to the functional concepts we utilize. I also think that black women's thought and work in particular has always already been concerned with the kinds of issues we now describe as intersectional. The life experiences of black women thinkers have, by necessity, forced an encounter with the types of complexities symbolized by intersectionality. These various dimensions have perpetually involved strands of difference that resonate within frameworks of commonality. It is also the case that such thinking is often initiated by thinkers of color and then, when it gets uptake and becomes alien and/or is alienated from those same thinkers of color, their concepts are used by others who do not attend to the contexts and experience that gave rise to the thinking. It is important to attend to difference and to be cognizant of the contexts in which difference announces itself.

Another way to think about these dimensions of difference is musical. The identity of musical notes while different is not driven by an absolute definition. Notes, from a musical standpoint, derive their identities based upon their relationship to other notes. Identity is determined because of relationality. Moreover, differences in identity are required to produce a chord. Built into the experience of a chord is the dissonance produced by difference. The dissonance is a necessary component for a chord's production. And so, the aim cannot be to make all the notes the same, rather the aim in producing the chord is harmony. So, what is included in the idea of harmony is not fixed but something relational within the context of organized sound where the components are not all the same. The chord and harmony have been interesting metaphors for me because I have been seeking non-visual ways to talk about things like race that have been overdetermined by the visual. I think there are ways to understand identity beyond the visual and to explore how identity might also play out in an auditory dimension. The notion of the chord also reiterates the necessity of not working to make everyone the same or variations of the same but instead celebrating the importance of difference. Audre Lorde often encourages the kind of strength and power that emerges when we embrace our differences. In my view, the possibilities opened when considering auditory identity set the stage for understanding what I increasingly refer to as "communities of difference."

JS: On that point, your reading of auditory identity for the way in which it is also a reception and expression of "registers" will be important and useful tool for future work on critical DS.

WHAT ANALOGIES FUNCTION FOR YOU WHEN THINKING OF ABLEISM AS IT IS A BIAS SIMILAR TO RACISM, SEXISM, AND CLASSISM?

LB: I find that analogies are both incredibly useful and incredibly limited, so they must be used carefully. Especially because it can be harmful when you give an analogy and the response is "yeah, it is just like that." But no; *no, it's not.* No two oppressions are ever exactly the same. But what analogies can do, for example, when I'm talking to people who do not understand the concept of ableism or have never been exposed to the concept, an analogy can help somebody get an idea of the kind of concept I'm talking about. So, I do use analogies as an educational tool.

When people ask me about what ableism is, I will typically say, "ableism is an entire way of thinking and doing that treats some kinds of bodies and minds as valuable, as ideal, as desirable, and other kinds of bodies and minds as less valuable, as unwanted, and undesired." Essentially, it is a set of values that treats people considered disabled as inferior, while treating people who are supposedly "normal" and "healthy" as superior. In some ways, it is kind of like how when some people who are queerantagonistic (or homophobic, in more common terms) treat being straight as "ideal" and superior to not being straight. This can influence policy and science, or laws.

What also makes an analogy useful is that it can show a pattern between things as opposed to the specific nature of things. In its specific nature, it will never be identical, but the types of patterns can be helpful. For example, using certain words as "value-neutral," like words that associate "being gay" or "being black" as more general negative terms, but "being white" as neutral. Here is another analogy that I use that has worked very well (but it is not an analogy I would use to teach or to educate) and I used it to help a particular person clarify their thought: It has to do with a friend of mine, Amanda Jaczkowski, a white American, raised in a Christian family, who converted to Islam. She was trying to explain to me—struggling to explain—why she wore the hijab. She said that "although it does not make me more modest, it shows that I'm Muslim." She added, "not that you need to wear the hijab to be Muslim." So, I suggested an analogy to help us both process her thoughts.

Wearing hijab is an outward sign of being Muslim. She was performing "being Muslim" and wanted to be associated with being Muslim, and chooses to wear the hijab so that other people—Muslim or not—can identify her, similarly to how I, as an Autistic person who doesn't instinctually or innately flap my hands or arms—it was never a stim that I developed independently—will deliberately and frequently *choose* to flap, especially in public, in order to call attention to myself, so that other people—whether autistic or not—might identify me as autistic. I use this as an outward sign, [similar to how some Muslim women might choose to wear hijab even in the absence of religious convictions about headcoverings].

JS: That is a good, functional example of instructive analogies because of how heteronormativity organizes bodies and minds into the valuable and desired or the "less valuable" and unwanted similar to ablenormativity. I find I've been using the fear of and suspicion for women's bodies as they are non-sexual, when they are not visible and available as fertile, as not performing their "natural function of reproduction"[50] for the sake of some neoliberal, social good. It has been helpful in explaining intersectionality as it provides sets of analogies. The non-productive, non-sexual bodies of women is threatening to a system that wants only productive, ablebodied people to perform naturalized, domesticated, and gendered tasks. Bodies that are not young, white or exotically nonwhite, and "sexy" are disposable, especially if they age and become infertile. How harmful is that! For me, this has been a very functional analogy with ableism, but then also with ageism and misogyny and misogynoir.

But if we need to use analogies to explain ableism, then we also need to show the limits of the analogy right away. Because, to Lydia's point, they are not the same thing, as in: pregnancy is not a disability but can be analogous to it and intersect with it in very specific and complicated ways.[51]

I think the limitations also have to do with *asymmetry*—a non-transitivity—between the tropes of binaries. We might call out "white supremacy"—and this is where I think scholarship does something different than advocacy—but this, I find, can be limiting to future discourse. In calling out race bias, it is important to recognize the limitations of the analogy and, for example, to think through how it is that one cannot simply "pass as black" despite a long-standing and problematic history of "passing (as white)"[52]—because this also has to do with specifically an anti-black racism.[53]

Also, by another analogy, how the experiences and reception of trans men versus trans women is asymmetrical because this identification is within the larger context of a misogynist culture,[54] further again complicated by misogynoir.[55] So, I shy away from calling out "white supremacy" although I admit that particularly for the ways it closes down future dialogue and excites defensiveness.[56] It may be a trigger for a rhetorical game that I cannot play, and if I try to and fail, may in fact reinforce its coercive political agenda. Which, because I present as white,[57] can in itself be a problematic and ineffectual position to take. That said, I am often gobsmacked by people who claim that white supremacy does not exist or if they interrogate people who do.

So, when we talk about choices in the context of marginalized identities and if this is a functional analogy between racism, ableism, sexism, and the like, then we must maintain the context by which these "choices" emerge. So, as with your friend, being a woman and being Muslim, these are choices that have to do with self-selected representation.

LB: It is about representation and visibility, and this is what Amanda and I were talking about.

JS: Thinking of this question I had really been thinking about the problem of "passing" because Devonya and I had already been discussing this as a site of functioning analogy between race and disability. My interest began with the problem of invisibility to certain kinds of disabilities in the way which we do not necessarily have the "translation" of these experiences into visible symbols of difference and diversity. In this way, I also think gender can sometimes work as a better analogy than race because race can rest on such visible markers as skin color and style of dress, or modes of speech and social association. Gender is something that has a long history of being masked and manipulated into submission, in that way I find there is something of a more instructional analogy in how gender and ableism can operate.

To add to your account of complexity is that, although intersectional analyses can be tolerant of analogies between marginalized identities, that there is also a neglected dis-analogy in the way ableism operates—distinct from how traditional intersectional frameworks might account for identities and corresponding communities. In fact, disability *compounds* and *complicates* those identities and the existential particularities that are already marginalized and even erased by racism, sexism, and classism, not to exclude the erasures through compulsory heteronormativity. I want to add the nuance of locality as well in that geography—locality—can also add a layer of complexity to identity difficult to assess "from the inside." In other words, only by cross-cultural, trans-sociality—or maybe a better term is cosmopolitanism—might there be a way to dialectically engage specifically, historical, temporal, and spatial "regions" of unique intersections in identities and communities. This regional approach to intersectionality may be important in locating and local-izing ways in which "deficits" emerge, not as just part of particular people and experiences, but in order to challenge how ableist attitudes and ideologies emerge and get normalized.

DH: I guess I come at this with a Foucauldian lens. It is not specifically dis-ability as such but also the systemic and structural power dynamics that deter-mine what will count as the "norm" and the processes by which those things that lie outside what is deemed "normal" will be managed and subjected to forms of "correction" designed to enforce performance of the established norms. These power dynamics and their deployment can be explored histori-cally through institutions and in terms of conceptual battles.

Crucial for Foucault is the necessity of examining the processes by which certain practices get established as rational, normal, and desirable. It is cer-tainly the case that histories of racialization, attributions of sex and sex dif-ferences, as well as what is considered "abnormal" have such histories and relationships to deployments of power that privilege certain races, sexes, and a certain sense of what counts as able. In this respect, I think Foucault is use-ful in pointing out the power operative in how particular conceptions of what counts as normal have been naturalized. Foucault clearly sees the construc-tion of the norm and those categories that fall outside of established norms as mechanisms that influence how people are categorized. He goes as far as developing a conception of "racism" against the abnormal. This, for me, has been an instructive way to interrogate categories that we often consider basic or given. Under what conditions and with whose interests in mind do such categories emerge?

IN WHAT WAYS HAS YOUR EXPERIENCE WITH DISABILITY BEEN COMPOUNDED BY GENDER BIAS, RACE BIAS OR CLASS BIAS?

DH: During our early time in Buffalo, EJ had a health episode after which he was diagnosed with MS. After being treated for this acute episode, he said,

"I'm glad it's MS and not a stroke." He was very much in the mode of: "All right, I'm good, let's just keep pressing on." And I think in some ways that's why he didn't attend more to his health and he passed off things as MS which might have been pre-stroke symptoms. This approach to health I am learning is not uncommon for men and is especially pronounced in the behavior of black men who are often reluctant or unable to maintain ongoing care relationships with doctors. Early on I did a lot of nagging but I had come to the point of declaring: "I can't follow this grown man around and make him go to the doctor." In hindsight, I wonder, what if I forced him to go, would that have made a difference? I mean, it may have or it might not have but I ask, "Gee, was that the right boundary to set?"

In our post-stroke world, I wonder and am also aware of the fact that we were both juggling a lot of things. I was in a new job, we were managing our two children, and I took a stance refusing to play parent to my husband with respect to his management of his health. Granted, this was from my perspective. From EJ's perspective, he was the one who was managing me. For many years, he viewed me as the "sick" person that he was taking care of because he was the earner, he is the Harvard MBA. And yes, he is all these things. Even so, I have been the family caretaker in a lot of ways and have not been credited for the amount of effort and work that has gone into this caretaking. It has taken many years for EJ to realize those efforts and early on he would have likely denied my labor. I do think that the invisibility of the kind of labor that women and caretakers assume in families is related to the dynamics of gender, race, class, and disablism. It is no accident that it was my husband who could least see these labors and who felt that he adequately attended to my work—all of my familial and professional work.

JS: . . . there's something very masculine about that.

DH: Sure. I would often make an effort to call him out on these oversights and he would respond, "No, No, you know, I'm pro-women, I'm pro-this." And I would say, but *that's not what I'm talking about.* I was calling attention to the way he was framing the relationship. Namely the idea that he was doing all the heavy labor while I was merely along for the ride. It was difficult to explain that I was doing a heck of a lot of labor too. We went through this push and pull for many years with a great deal of resentment that built up. Even though he would deny it, I think much of the resentment was because of gender roles. As the father and the major earner, he should not have been expected to be on the playground with the kids after school. That should be my role because my work was more flexible and less crucial for our economic survival.

It really was not until our life in Boston imploded when he got pushed out of his company and I got a tenure track job offer in another state that things began to shift. We were at a major crossroad in our relationship. It was only in the context of this major upheaval that he came to appreciate much of my labor. All that said, I also have to acknowledge that my reflections come within a context where my impulse is to push forward despite the obstacles. I have chosen a profession in which black people are underrepresented and black women's numbers are so low that we do not register as statistically significant in data on the profession. In many ways, this prompts me to put my head down and get to work. Embedded in this imperative is a form of internalized disablism where I do not want to make reference to certain "limitations" imposed by my disabilities. I would hardly admit my struggles with anxiety, depression, and ADD to my peers. Aren't I judged enough because of my race and gender? I still wrestle with negotiating these dynamics because I do not think there is a place in professional life where one can enter into such conversations. I do not deny that disability is a part of my individual and familial experiences but I have only begun to explore what that means in a larger context.

JS: But by outing this, you also get to challenge the ableist assumptions built into the work you do. In other words, how you've had to get "dressed" every time. You have had to put on the costuming . . . .

DH: Yes, in black theological terms, one might say I have to explore the Armor of Battle that I assume to greet each day. Increasingly I am more aware that for me to do what other people do requires so much more energy . . .

JS: . . . and resources. That does require more resources and supports in a way that it would be easier to exclude the people who don't and can't do it 'this [assumed proper] way' then it would be to incorporate those people who can do it in another way but with different kinds of supports.

On this point, Siebers discusses the dangers of "disability drag" as "it represses disability and affirms the ideology of disability" (114–115), but more importantly acknowledges that it is politically important that a person in a marginalized position have the option to be able to choose when to "pass" and when not. He states, "Temporary passing is empowering, producing brief moments of freedom from prejudice . . . often found to surround disability" (118). In many ways, the marginalized position already has been coerced to the degree in which that individual may be *tokenized*, "outed" if you will, or simply not able to self-identify in their marginality. In other words, the politics of their visibility might not give them agency already, so other ways in which they can successfully code their identity should be made available in order to compensate for other socially constructed liminalities.

DH: I often wonder what it would be like if I did not expend so much energy managing anxiety or marshalling motivation. Perhaps it would be easier but that is not my life. . . . I would also say that the experience of having to remake myself each day to get out the door makes me far more sensitive to others' experiences. And, I am attuned the fact that I often "pass." It makes me wonder the extent to which some degree of "passing" is invoked to navigate a world where one's categorization determines their access to opportunities and possibilities. It is interesting that Fanon in *Black Skin, White Masks* argues that passing is a more difficult possibility with respect to race. He writes that the Jew must be ferreted out while blackness because it is embodied and epidermalized cannot be evaded.[58] This is particularly interesting to me because while growing up I was taught to recognize certain structural limitations but to press on to overcome those limitations. In many ways, to embracing "limitations" was a way of making excuses. If one was able to "achieve," one was expected to persist for as long as it took. There was no mediation for learning differences and the response to limitation was more persistence. So, a certain kind of passing is imported into presumptions of what is required to succeed. Yet, it is a form of passing that elevates race through success thereby disproving deficiency.

LB: The other part of that is that it's a privilege if you are able to choose whether to pass or not. Some of us do not have the ability to choose. For instance, some of my Autistic friends could never pass for neurotypical in public. It would just not be possible. There may be any number of reasons why someone from a particular marginalized group may not be able to "pass." Not belonging to the dominant group corresponding to the groups exposed to marginality, the ability to pass then becomes a responsibility and a privilege [if you can choose].

JS: Siebers states it as, "Passing is a solo experience for most people" and that the "feelings of relief that accompany coming out as disabled often derive from the discovery that one is no longer alone" (118).

One thing that has struck me as a limit of this kind of analogy-making is, for example, the cases of adult black men who are non-neurotypical, and because they might present themselves in a certain kind of way, and are perceived in the public sphere in a certain kind of way, can be threatened by law enforcement rather than protected. Despite the way in which they could be understood—as say, non-neurotypical, dealing with mental illness, or, as in one case, having a stroke[59]—they are still perceived as a threat. That perceived threat has been the justification for much of the harmful and dangerous way in which PoC[60] have been handled in the face of law enforcement.

LB: Yes,[61] think of [Steven] Eugene Washington,[62] Mohammad Usman Chaudhry,[63] both Autistic men of color (one Black and one Pakistani) killed by the Los Angeles Police Department, and Stephon Edward Watts,[64] a Black autistic teenager killed by police in Illinois, among many other deaf and disabled Black, Brown, and Indigenous people killed by police.

DH: I agree that the perception of threat and insubordination complicates how certain bodies are "read." This is overwhelmingly the case for racialized bodies regardless of gender. Racialized bodies are often presumed to be "non-docile" and in need of intervention to be made docile. For many men of color, their bodies are "read" as threatening while non-male bodies are often read as insubordinate—as engaging in a refusal of the power of authority. In effect, such bodies by their very presence are effectively seen as dangerous. The way this danger functions is something I have been pursuing through Foucault's notion of "the dangerous individual." My sense is that one might be able to map force against these bodies within a framework that sees their management as part of the aim to ensure "public hygiene" and thereby keep society safe. This speaks to the interconnections between race, gender, class, and disability and it raises questions about the categories used to assess people. In some sense, those classified as "abnormal" are—by definition—a threat to the social order.

JS: This is a complex phenomenon that begs for critique. We need to really rethink what disability means when it is defined through the ableist lens we've created. How is it that when someone is in a state of impairment yet they are seen a as danger to society, a threat to persons that justifies lethal harm, as if they present as already willful and ablebodied and you cannot view them any other way, with no compassion, but only with preconceived judgment? Ableist bias has really gone unchallenged; there is too much cultural favor for the idea that authority and credibility comes only through privilege. That the police are "purveyors of all that is good and right in the world" makes such a mistake in the way power and authority over others really works. Even their training does not allow them to perceive a black male as anything other than a potential perp/target.[65] There are so many different things that could explain behavior, many things that could be factored into an exchange, but instead, these become *miscues* that lead to violence and death—like not responding to a law enforcement instruction in the "right" kind of way—in reading the situation as they might be trained to do by an ableist society and system, dangerously misunderstanding the complexity of intersectionality.

Often the work of *compensating* for these misreadings and miscues then again rests with family members, those who really care about that person and know that person, now having to be "on" all the time to also protect those they know and love from a public that would sooner put them away or dispose of them—an ungrievable life—as a life rendered thoroughly precarious.[66]

DH: The way you describe precarity is part of why I find it difficult to argue that we can "be whatever we want to be." In fact, we are trapped and defined by external forces. This means that we are constantly negotiating, contesting, resisting, creating, and recreating who we are in the context of these external forces. It reminds me of a paper I presented on Black women's philosophies. During the question and answer period, someone protested: *Why must the black woman always be the resisting subject?* I thought, she's right but resisting is a reality. As a result, I have done work to demonstrate that being racialized is not simply about resisting those naturalized normativities. There are also rites, rituals, and practices that represent more than the experiences of oppression. These practices speak to unique cultures that are not derivative but that are their own creations. This means that we have to engage these cultural creations and formations, to listen to them, so that we might better understand the broad dimensions of those experiences and how they are theoretically important.

WHAT LITERATURE OR IDEAS DO YOU DRAW FROM WHEN DEALING WITH THE CHALLENGES OF ABLEISM AS IT INTERSECTS WITH OTHER BIASES?

JS: As a mode of analysis, I think that intersectionality offers a critical approach which can also bridge common points of non-traditional intersection.[67] For example, Sami Schalk's "Transing: Resistance to Eugenic Ideology in Nella Larsen's *Passing*" (2015) is an organized analysis around eugenic language in context with the time that Larsen is writing: her novel, *Passing*. Schalk teases out and contextualizes the role of identity and desire in Larsen's *Passing*, knowing that Larsen was surrounded by an ideological environment that promoted "good fighters" and "good breeders" (151), an ideology that excited binaries in terms of race, class, and gendered thinking, manifesting discourses concerning "racial uplift" as well as fears of "race suicide" and "race degeneration," in other words, components of eugenic ideology. Schalk reads Larsen's main character as not victim to this ideology in her "passing" as a white, middle class woman; instead, Schalk reads Larsen's Claire as demonstrating a "transing" identity, exhibiting a resistance to the dominant discourses with a "both/and desire."[68] As she states it, "Clare's constant transing of these central [race, class, sexuality, and gender] binaries and her rejection of their stable social divisions make her impossible to understand for the people around her who—consciously or not—cling to the personal and social stability, consistency, and safety provided by adhering to identity binaries" (156).

DH: Foucault is always an important influence with respect to my thinking and I'm also informed by the text of experiences that I've come to call "black ancestral discourse." There are many resources like Anna Julia Cooper that I did not discover until graduate school. My encounters with this work have demonstrated to me the extent to which many women of color have always had what would now be described as intersectional concerns.

Young adult fiction is also a resource for me. I find it a welcome break from formal philosophy and many novels also deal with important ethical/political concerns. In one YA book series that I have been following, there is an autistic character who has a central role. The role depends on a type of unawareness but also emphasizes the character's unique way of engaging the world. The character's existence is crucial for maintaining the universe and the uniqueness of the character's identity as autistic is important to the story line.[69]

JS: But there is a simple point too in thinking about intersectionality, following Schalk's use of Patricia Hill Collins' concept in describing it as a "philosophical linchpin" of racism and sexism; we must include ableist ideology as an *either/or* thinking (2015, 157 nt. 15) at every turn.

DH: I also draw upon the concept of invisibility from [Ellison's] *Invisible Man*: Here invisibility is simultaneously a hypervisibility. Moreover, the kind of invisibility Ellison engages has an effect upon time. I worry that conceptions of intersectionality do not attend to the temporal dimension. Linkages are somehow frozen in a particular dimension without considerations of how the specific temporal, geographic, and relational contexts affect intersectional dynamics. The seeming paradox of an invisibility that is simultaneously hypervisibility, from my perspective, points to some of this difficulty.

LB: I have learned (and am constantly learning still!) an incredible amount from activists/performers/writers, like Cyrée Jarelle Johnson, Kay Ulanday Barrett, Mia Mingus, Edward Ndopu, Leroy F. Moore, Jr., Chanda Prescod-Weinstein, Darnell Moore, Talila A. Lewis, Kylie Brooks, Ki'tay Davidson, Eli Clare, s.e. smith, Shain M. Neumeier, and Nai Damato.

JS: And you have three passages from some of these authors and activists that come to mind when thinking of this question.

LB: [First] Ki'tay Davidson, a fellow activist who died in December 2014, writes:[70]

Ableism is a result of the commodification of the human experience, or capitalism. That is, capitalism has saturated law and society so intensely that it begins to define "functioning" and "whole" by one's capacity for "economic productivity" (within a system that is already structured to highly benefit those who are resourced, white and male). Notice the correlation between human worth and "wholeness" as defined through strictly capitalist paradigms. Ableism is perpetuating a "normalized" and narrow standard of a valuable human experience; only certain types of functioning, experiencing, producing and living in our society can be esteemed. You and I are worth more than our production. Your body, my body is more than a means to an end. We need to challenge and really talk about who receives dignity and value in society, and to start naming the grotesque nature of ableism. We can and do exist uniquely. Disability is diversity and diversity is beautiful. Does disability have challenges? Ask the person. For me, yes. Am I still worthy of care, dignity and love? Always. Disablement comes from a lack of inclusion, a strict adherence to "normalcy," and the inability to value other types of ways that people move, understand and experience the world.

[Second,] Edward Ndopu and Darnell Moore write:[71]

Ableism renders invisible those bodies not privileged by dominant definitions of ability, those bodies that do not fit the conceptions of gender that we often imagine. We "read" the movement of bodies, the ways people walk, hair styles, and the ways our bodies interact with other bodies in social spaces without ever realizing that all of the aforementioned performances are gendered expressions that center on the privilege of physical movement. We tend to place a lot of emphasis on the body, and one's use of the body, without attending to the fact that for some the use of the body is an impossibility.

[Third, unedited, from] Kay Ulanday Barrett (and this is a direct quote, and for reasons of not wanting to perpetuate racist, classist, and ableist norms of "language," I don't want the grammar "corrected"):[72]

Comrades, loves, & shakers: Int'l workers day is for all of us y'all! Please remember that noone is less or better in the compass of labor because they aren't in "the streets," son. Not all lives/bodies fit the dynamic of productivity & racist cis american scripts of "normal" labor. To my loves achy in bed, to the coughing wheezing aching healing, to homies who can't leave, to the mad brilliance shaken with anxiety, to those with revolutions that have to ascend the physical blocks or barracades of the body, those surviving with chemicals or cleaning in the underbellies, the lonely workers, the ones who can't can't can't organize but sing to themselves, those whose lives are told their work is a waste, shouldn't work but uphold the wizardry of survival as first language, to the loves whose deliberations don't get status in cultural capital but make waves in chosen fam, for those deemed too lazy but forever the crux of all the

little things taken for granted, for homies who coordinate who juggle public
assistance/cops/intimacy with loved ones like a chant, to my poor homies too
imaginative for the comprehension of money, for anyone whose dreams may not
match their pay stubs, for the workers whose hands and spirit are the concoc-
tion of rough tenderness, whose hustle fucks with sterile white picket fences,
those tackling street or multiple gigs that don't balance a clock but create a new
time continuum, for those whose connections or work aren't seen as interview
worthy, those with no nest, those with no back up plan, those who bargain like
breathing air, those who love themselves a break even when they are forced to
workhorse it out, those who bend hours & don't get paid, those whose sweat is
forgotten due to placards or protest etiquette. For spoonies whose simple math
is a critical campaign for living. For the hands that hold you with the ancestor's
loud speakers reminding you to eat/sleep/pray, for the chewed up and burnt
out brunt of people who were mistaken as dispensable. For the slow slow easy,
be easy it'll get done . . . . Or not, in you. For y'all with juggernaut hearts that
feed us & can't log in hours for payment, for those whose worthy isn't a title
or a press release but a constant check in, we work daily breath for each other
and often times, there's no income bracket to capture that wealth. I offer you
gratitude and hope you ease. I offer you my blessed thanks for your efforts.
You deserve health care, dignity, self-determination, laughter, good food and
good love makin'. We all struggle for those things and our beauty is valid. Let's
de-bunk and debate our dependence on american white cis straight ablebodied
dynamics of capital. In bed, in the streets, at the kitchen table, in long lines, in
our dreams, in love songs, our work is on-going, deliberate, our work deserves
dimension, and please remember, long after the contingents and slogans have
raspy throats—we deserve each other.

JS: Ulanday Barrett here reads like a manifesto and worth preserving in full
form.

WHAT ISSUES OR PROBLEMS DO YOU THINK KEEPS ABLEIST BIAS DISTINCTIVE AND INDEPENDENT OF ITS INTERSECTIONS?

DH: One of the things I'm coming to realize is the invisible ways in which
I deal with disability just in myself and the biases that I invoke in my own
self-talk. As I said earlier, my socialization included the propensity to simply
press beyond any limitations and to see failures to press on as a kind of
weakness. This is an internalized barrier to accepting disability in its every
day manifestations—not conceptually but in terms of acknowledging what it
means as a limit. So, what does it mean to be just a "regular" person working
to negotiate the education system or other institutions *and* simultaneously a

person of color? I mean, we have become accustomed to negotiating the terrain given all the crap we encounter. We've had to figure out how to navigate a lot of these situations especially with people who perceive us in a certain way because of race, gender, or presumed class. But, *what if you're without that ability to negotiate?* What if your only coping mechanisms are defensiveness and confrontation which is then perceived as being difficult? Then one gets categorized as a problem. You're *blah, blah, blah . . .?* And you may have very legitimate issues but given the way you have been framed, there is no way to get traction with the issues.

JS: And we have to think about how adults with disabilities are infantilized. They are never free of these systems of instruction.

DH: And intrusion. Of course, that is why I work hard to keep an eye out for EJ while not also hovering over him. I can sometimes end up doing more than I should. But sometimes he needs to have time on his own. That is one of the nice things about being an adult. That one is entitled to time alone and time away from external management.

We don't discuss these needs for those with non-abled bodies. While there are similarities with race, it is not the same as the "problem of race." We need more language and better ways to challenge ableism in ways that bring us into confrontations with our own complicity. It is far more frightening to think of myself as "unable" than to admit complicity in ableism.

JS: Here, this is where I'm pushing for an idea of affective self-critique as predisposing us for the possibility for non-ableist thinking.

DH: In this context, I think about constructive dissonance that might make possible experiences beyond what you think you know. This would be similar to the idea you reference from Mills, and calls attention to the fact that we are more entrenched in ableist ignorance than we might be aware. We hardly have a language . . . and in this case there is no idealism to which we might appeal—we can only make gestures, movements in resistance to the difficulty of ableist ignorance.

I like Audre Lorde on this point:

> The quality of light by which we scrutinize our lives has direct bearing upon the product which we live, and upon the changes we hope to bring about through [living]. It is within this light that we form those ideas by which we pursue our magic and make it realized. We learn to bear the intimacy of scrutiny and to flourish within it as we learn to use the product of that scrutiny for power within our living . . . those fears that rule over lives and form our silences begin to lose their control over us [giving rise to] places of possibility within ourselves.[73]

I follow this in my thinking that poetry is not a luxury. Similarly, I assert that philosophy is not a luxury. It is crucial to developing the important scrutiny that one needs to live. I mean, thinking of Camus, are we going to choose life, or are we going to commit suicide? Let us do so without invoking "hope" as an evasion. I take both Lorde and Camus seriously on the encouragement to live and tarry with the difficulty and challenge of creating a life that does not seek to evade these complexities.

JS: It is on that point exactly that I also really want to give you both a platform to be able to discuss a bit more the issues involving caretakers, and care-taking work. Lydia, I know you were involved in the vigil for people killed by their caretakers.[74]

LB: I have been at a couple of vigils and hosted one. Zoe Gross, of the Autistic Self-Advocacy Network (ASAN), organized the first vigil in March 2012 after the murder of 22-year-old George Hodgins, a white autistic man from a class-privileged family[75] whose mother shot him in the head.[76] I have written and spoken on this issue, and I had articles published in *Tikkun*, ["The Crisis of Disability is Violence: Ableism, Torture, and Murder," (Oct 20, 2014)] and in *The New Idealist* ["The Long Road Ahead for the Autistic Rights Movement" (Jul 9, 2015)],[77] where I talk about these murders.

DH: I have been thinking a lot lately about caretaking. We have been having my daughter work with a child psychologist. We had a meeting to talk about things and she asked me how I was. I am tired and overwhelmed with deadlines. [My friend said to me during this time:] *You realize you have been in crisis—putting one foot in front of the other. You have EJ's stroke, its aftermath, and the push to get tenure . . . even though you may not be in crisis mode, you are tired.* I am the only adult on deck. My children have not been trained to be as independent as I was; not as a value judgment, as a fact of the situation. Assisting and not taking over: here is the "line" one must "walk" as parent and as caretaker.

People count on me to do real stuff and I cannot do all things—it is impossible, as Lydia said, we have limited resources. *What am I giving up to do this?* My friend looked at me one day: *What are you going to do, give up? You can't leave them alone, you can't leave your husband on his own, etc. There is nothing there that you cannot do.* That sense of overwhelming need to meet the demands and needs of my family is an ongoing feature of my roles as parent and caretaker. I feel the pressure of familial and professional responsibilities. And in the shadow of my particular circumstances, I also note black experiences of state-sponsored violence. As a parent, one of my primary responsibilities is protecting my children. This involves working to keep them out of certain circumstances and also making them aware of their particular vulnerability because of their embodiment. It is not lost on me that *Basic Black* (Bates & Hudson, 2005), an etiquette book specifically for black families has a chapter on how to deal with the death of children. This demonstrates how codified racialized violence is for certain families. It underscores the necessity of talking with one's children about how, not if, they have to deal with police encounters. The chapter on death is not in other etiquette books.

I work to do the best I can with what I have. One care-takes because—and this is in my case—I'm obliged to because *I love them*. People will say, "that's so nice of you." But what wouldn't you do for someone you love? The question of not caring or care-taking is unconscionable if one cares and wants them to be okay in the world. How does one maintain integrity without upholding one's commitments? I mean, *how do we really want the world to be?* So, I cannot imagine walking away or farming my loved ones out despite the challenges.

Among the challenges I have had as a caretaker is that medical profession-als would not talk to my husband directly. Doctors would often talk to me about him with him in the room. This was bad and very uncomfortable for the two of us. After all, he is not unaware or unable to understand. He simply cannot communicate in the usual ways. One of the specialists that he came to like spoke directly to him, not me. He felt so much better about the encounter. Profound and subtle differences like these count a great deal.

WHAT COMMUNITIES, TYPES OF DISABILITIES, OR ISSUES THAT AFFECT DISABLED COMMUNITIES DO YOU THINK BECOME MOST MISREPRESENTED AND/OR MISUNDERSTOOD WITHOUT ATTENTION TO INTERSECTIONALITY?

JS: Regarding the question of representation and misrepresentation, Lydia, I know you have already written critiques of Autism Speaks. I have found these criticisms from you and from Autistic self-advocacy groups very provocative, and for good reason, raising fair sets of arguments.[78] Similar criticisms need to be made about other groups that exploit disability for commercial gain, or, for example, how the Wounded Warrior Project could be viewed as an ableist organization, promoting stereotypes, and arbitrarily or inappropriately distributing aid.[79]

LB: One issue I've been wanting to discuss is my concern about *which* autistic people have become prominent either in mainstream discourse, or within the Autistic Rights movements, and *why*. Specifically, virtually all of them are white, white-passing, or able to (and do) choose to identify with whiteness; the majority come from money and education class privileged backgrounds; and even in the Autistic Rights movement, many are men and often heterosexual.

The handful of Autistic people most widely cited, because they have written semi-autobiographical books about Autism, that are popular and mainstreamed, include Temple Grandin, John Elder Robison,[80] Stephen Shore, or Daniel Tammet, who are also all white and all class privileged. If you go into the Autistic Rights movement—and I'm purposely using this term—*nebulously*, the two co-founders of the ASAN,[81] Ari Ne'eman and Scott Michael Robertson, are also straight educated men who are either white or conditionally white-passing. Until recent years, ASAN's board members had been either white or at least conditionally white-passing, with no representation of Black, Latinx, Indigenous, Asian, or Mixed-Race autistic people.[82] The Autism Women's Network, though currently the most racially diverse autistic-led organization, was originally founded by a white woman, Sharon da Vanport. Many popular blogs by autistic people on neurodiversity are by white authors.

I'm happy that the tides are beginning to change, with two Black women, Morénike Giwa Onaiwu and Reyma McCoy McDeid, now serving proudly on ASAN's Board of Directors; AWN's board including several women of color with E. Ashkenazy, Heather Thomas, and Morénike and myself; and individuals like N.I. Nicholson (of the Teselacta Multiverse) and Sara María Acevedo gaining well-deserved rec-ognition within and outside the autistic movement. I would now love to see work by transfeminine and genderqueer people of color like Tracy Garza and Bridget Liang, or queer Black writers like Mickey Valentine/Jay Samantha and Michón Neal and Cyrée Jarelle Johnson, or Indigenous autistic writers like Sloane Cornelius and K.J. at University of Nebraska, Omaha, or younger autistics of color like Manuel Díaz and Leanne Libas, similarly become more elevated and central in autistic movements.

JS: This is why Alice Wong's exclamation of "Intersectionality!!!" is at the start of this chapter as a kind of ethical injunction. When you have communities and this pooling of power and privilege setting the stage and setting the tone for how discourse is created, how discourse informs policy, how this discourse then becomes part of the cultural imagination, then we have to have advocates speaking out at every turn calling out the "white" and "male" as itself a "question mark." I mean if we are talking about this, I think it is good whenever we see a white cis-male representing a community, we should just ask: Why is there a white man (or men) talking about this? Why does he get to speak and who might we (really) need to hear from? Or, in my case, why is it white suburban moms get to represent and engage in the dominant discourse about what is needed for the care and advocacy for children with disabilities?[83] When I think of the anti-vaxx movement, I can't help but also want to reference white ignorance at length.

LB: I've been publicly bitching about this for a long time. Either people ignore it or they say "don't talk about this."

JS: I kind of love that you call it "bitching." Do you think there is something inherently feminizing, and inherently politicizing about this? The field of philosophy has neglected it for so long and the fact that you have to come up with language just to explain or make sense of it—speaking for what has not been said, what has yet to be said, (what I've called "voiced harm"),[84] making ethical demands—comes across as threatening to the status quo. Yet, if we don't build theory in the direction of voiced harm, then we really are just "keeping house."[85] Because you call this "bitching," then I read that as a call and a need for theory. Intersectionality has to be part of the conversation every time and I think you've been able to take that energy and feed it back into the scholarship.

LB: SDS is incredibly white and privileged.

DH: There are racist connotations at work here. Much bound up with the sense of privilege that accompanies the notion that some of us are perceived as taking away something from those who have should have privileges. I think this is also at play when one is cautioned against criticizing movements lest they foment discord. Critical challenges are seen as an impediment to coalition rather than as strengthening overall movements by exploring all stakeholder concerns. As Nina Simone sings, "you don't have to live next to me, just give me my equality." Here she challenges the notion of an "integrationist agenda." She rightly points out that people who are different don't always want to "get in" with everyone else. It could be that those who are different want access to community resources. And, resources—broadly speaking—need to be there. Even a resource like credibility—namely that I could be believed in giving the testimony of my own experiences.

There is a long story of certain people not being allowed to credibly give their own testimony. As Audre Lorde states in her Forward to *Wild Women of The Whirlwind* (1990):

> It's not that we haven't always been here, since there was a here. It is that the letters of our names have been scrambled when they were not totally erased . . . often we have printed our visions upon our children . . . . But our words have been there [as in] . . . Cheryl Clarke's words, "a necessary bread." . . . So that the children of those Black women never drank peaceful lemonade, or lay

at night protected . . . Dee-Dee's three youngest [would be] lined up on the sofa giving them each quarters to yell, "Down with capitalism!"

These daughters' daughters did survive . . . Black women's words are testament that we were there, bridges through one another's realities, tough and tender. Intricate and nourishing.

They will need to know that hatred destroys by silence, by trivialization, by the pretense that nothing we have to say is worth anything simply because we are saying it . . . [by] the arrogant assumption that anyone else knows better than we do which of our words should survive (1990, xi-xiii).

JS: When I attended the Black Disability Studies Caucus and the Queer Caucus meetings at SDS, I could really note the complicated problem of under-representation against a larger context of racialized discrediting and erasure. DS is already underrepresented in Higher Education, in the Health Care Professions, then add to that limitation, people within the DS community being recognizable, privileged authorities. What I found at these Caucuses was an openness to what is possible, and it is not "bitching." It was more like: "we have to start making things possible that right now are not possible." There was also a kind of hope and joy from finding community at these meetings, something quite celebratory and welcoming. That said, I can't imagine that what you have to say, Lydia, is "bitching" in the order of "complaining," as if worthy of dismissal.

LB: But being dismissed actually does happen to me constantly.

JS: Well, I had my students read your essay, "What the Empty Room Means,"[86] and you demonstrate how ableist and easy it is to dismiss people who are advocating for social change and how demoralizing it is to be met instead with indifference, especially when there's nothing in place to make this advocacy urgent.

LB: One of my most recent blog posts was on "How Not to Plan Disability Conferences"[87] because each instance of ableist aggression (I won't give them the courtesy of calling them microaggressions) actually happened to me.

JS: But this is a version of truth-telling in that *it did happen*—not that we have to publicly shame anyone—but this kind of truth-telling is indigenously philosophical. The work of philosophy includes calling bullshit.[88] This particular piece on conference planning did get some currency as well; you were able to provide a cautionary tale. And there is something really liberating (and non-ableist) about the fact that you did not dress it up in euphemistic language[89] and put out there as: "let me tell you how to not run a shit-show."[90]

DH: I agree. It is the case that those who do not inhabit "desired identities" or who are part of communities that have to fight for empowerment do not have access to white privilege in the same ways as other communities. While members of marginalized communities and the communities themselves may develop avenues of empowerment, often people from outside those communities begin to appear and want to benefit from the hard-earned efforts of the community without doing the hard work.

JS: I do think this is something where a lot of what we do comes from the need to cope in a world that has impossible and thoroughly ableist expectations—as if they are neutral and natural economic and political expectations. I think, captured insightfully, Osagyefo Sekou (2014) has argued that this is rooted in a lack of radical critiques of neoliberalism, as well as the lack of real-time challenges of aspirational politics, citing the less popular critiques by bell hooks of Beyoncé and Cornel West of President Obama [emphasis added]:

> Their anti-racist, anti-sexist, anti-transphobic and anti-homophobic sentiments are easily incorporated into the neoliberal project without critiquing neoliberalism. As [Audre Lorde] so eloquently wrote—a now often-quoted refrain—"The Master's Tools Will Never Dismantle the Master's House." Neoliberalism is the master's house and tool. It limits discursive space, subjugates radicality and seduces the othered into defending its existence.

> Nevertheless, economic and ecological catastrophe abound. In order to vacate the premises, contemporary black intellectuals must shed the aspirational politics of individual success and situate ourselves in the broader tradition of black radical thought—never mistaking individual success with collective progress; thin opposition for revolutionary struggle; acknowledging clearly that white patriarchal capitalism and its neoliberal expression is amoral and unstable. The American empire is burning. *We need firefighters—not cheerleaders.*

A lot of what we do we take in and we internalize and we make habit, we build and rebuild it into these cultural and economic systems. I think the results can be very toxic and get passed over and passed on to our kids. So, I have one component of my discussion on precariousness that also has to do with the ecological side of disability construction. I'm thinking of the chemical pollution and how it can directly cause disability by way of "deformation," impairment, development. Add to this populations made vulnerable by other geographical issues: situated alongside political conflict, economic impoverishment, loss of habitat, etc., and the ecological conditions need to be addressed as they are also the outcome of ableist thinking and practices.

Think of the fact that there is a lot of woman-blaming when it comes to something like children born with birth defects.[91] With autism, especially with the anti-vaccination movement and the dietary prescriptions and all that, I feel like much of the interventions have mother-blaming attached to these kinds of "advice," lots of ableist phobia attached to their urgency—there's just *lots of pervasive mother-blaming*.

And at the same time, it's like what I find most frustrating to some degree is there is an assumption that it is also genetic—which might make us "blameless" in the question of autism as a "disorder," but to some degree I'm really suspicious of what it may have to do with environmental factors like air and soil pollution. When it comes to the amount of chemical production alone—so much we do not understand about long-term impact, how much is ingested or how much exposure is toxic—that instead of caution and care for those rendered vulnerable by these forms of production, it is instead heavily guarded with economic, neoliberal interests and (white, Western) ignorance. We might never know if there are any causal connections between industrial production and everyday consumption with how certain physiological and developmental differences manifest as disabilities and disorders.

DH: Which are largely out of our control? And that also call us to further examine the injunction and imperative offered by Lorde in her declaration about the master's tools. She also insists that context and creativity can alter those tools that have been in the "master's" hands.

JS: It's not just out of our control but I think whose control it's in is the lack of understanding of about what we already put out there.

DH: Right. What people are taking in, what we are breathing, what we are consuming. This means that we must re-tool to be more aware of these under-represented concerns.

JS: But even the systems of biological management. The way in which we inhabit the world. It's the problem of the built environment. The world of architecture has created a toxicity that I think makes it very hard for us to sustain our bodies in the model of living that we are supposed to be able *to do* things. Like we are supposed—in a "natural" and "normal" sense—to be able to get married, have kids that are normal and healthy, go to school, become efficient job holders, and all that. And I have realized how much I have been kicked out of that game, but also in many ways still find myself playing it. As Siebers states it, "The compelling issue for minority identity does not turn on the question of whether one group has the more arduous existence but on the fact that every minority group faces social discrimination, violence, and intolerance that *exert toxic and unfair influence* on the ability to live life to the fullest" (30, my emphasis).[92]

ANY CONCLUDING THOUGHTS?

JS: I don't know if it serves much in the way of a concluding thought, but it seems that accessibility audits of public spaces, educational, and service institutions needs to happen more than it does now.[93]

LB: Georgetown University's LGBTQ Resource Center had had a Braille sign on the top of the door frame for years. Unless a particular blind or low-vision person were seven feet tall, I can't imagine how they would be able to read the old sign.

JS: That's funny and not funny at the same time. I do remember that it was difficult to get around the campus of Boston College when I was there—it was beautiful—but not really accessible—and I'm ablebodied! When a space is organized so that it provides a *natural aesthetic*—like a "beautiful campus"—yet, it is not a space that maximizes access; politically speaking, it is a space that becomes part of the accumulated capital of the ablebodied, and therefore is an exclusion to what should be publicly accessible capital. Yet, now these kinds of spaces are not accessible to those who cannot benefit from the experience of that space.

LB: I can also tell you a story and it is one of those stories—a "10 on a scale of 1 to 10" kind of story—that is still worse because it is *not funny at all*. Someone who is a friend of a friend who had multiple disabilities, chronic illnesses, uses a wheelchair, and is deaf, had to go to the hospital. This person chose to go to Georgetown Hospital for reasons unknown to me given the treatment this person has always gotten there. Because of this person's physical disabilities, this person needs to be fed by somebody else—they cannot feed themselves. Physically, a support person would do that for them at home. The person went to the hospital because they had an issue with one of their chronic conditions, and it was very scary because this person is typically sighted. The person became blind out of nowhere. So, thinking "what is going on?" this person goes to the hospital. For three days, the doctors neglected this person, didn't care that they totally went blind, talked to them like they weren't really *there*, and never bothered having anybody feed them. The person that is our mutual friend, who is also multiply disabled, had to go to the hospital in order to manually feed them because the doctors and nurses wouldn't. The person would have died.

JS: One of the things that comes with a lot of these stories, which I found so thought-provoking in defining ableism, is how much, how *deeply* embedded the attitude is that, "You're better off dead than disabled." And so, one of the ways in which you can really tap into the *question* of why ableism is what it is, there's so many ways we do not account for those people who survive disability. So, I'm thinking of this in the sense of "the event." Judith Butler quotes Levinas on this in *Precarious Life*:

> The approach of the face is the most basic mode of responsibility . . . not in front of me . . . but above me; it is the other before death, looking through an exposing death. . . . [The] face is the other who asks me not to let him die alone, as if to do so were to become an accomplice in that death. . . . In the relation of the face I am exposed as a usurper of the place of the other . . . my duty to respond to the other suspends my natural right to self-survival.[94]

So, the *event* of stroke or the event of blindness, signals a shift in where and who one was before relative to now; which means that there's been a *break in the life of that person*, a real difference, regardless if there was familiarity with disabled experience prior to the event or not, and now the attitude of "self-survival" is not possible when the circumstances become unsurvivable without another—especially one who knows "if I let them die alone, I am an accomplice in that death."

DH: This is an interesting line of exploration. It makes some sense of why many people think it is courageous for me to continue to care for my husband. I think that way of thinking is deeply disturbing. It is as if his post-stroke disabilities make him not valuable anymore . . . better off forgotten. I reject that sense that choosing to care for EJ because he is now disabled makes me courageous. The courage is really his and my role is to support. To affirm that he continues to live a grievable life, a life that is valuable. I emphasize this because right after the surgery, EJ could imitate words but he couldn't form them. He had use of both hands and he was actually in better shape than by the time he left the hospital for rehab. By the time he left the hospital, he had degenerated in function and I was just not prepared for that. Because that's not how it is when you see medicine played out on television. If you get there in time, and there's an intervention, then it stops. But in the face of the loss of function not stopping, one cannot simply declare their loved one no longer valuable. Such a declaration, to me, is shameless.

JS: I love that you just resourced the television-version of medical care. Well, yeah, because that's what we have in our imagination—that is, until this kind of "event." This is where those experiences become so important to building knowledge that we don't get from the television version, because the television version is a deception. *It's a setup.* It sets you up to make mistakes about what reality is in the face of the other, in the face of the event.

DH: And it sets you up to believe that if they can fix it, it does not get any worse than the precipitating crisis.

JS: Right. The glory of the doctor. The intervention. "It will be made right."

DH: And neurologists are really all about the science, not about the human. And so, the way they talked to me was about the brain. And I don't know if it's that they don't want to be sued, but they give you the gloomiest possible scenario. So, we went in to do the follow up . . . with the neurosurgeon. It must have been a year after. And the guy walks in and says, "He probably won't read." And I said, *"That's odd because he is reading."* And he says, "Well, yeah, he does have 50 percent of that capacity." And I'm like, *so why would you tell me he's never going to read?* Does he not know what that does to a person? How does that set expectations for you to be engaged in helping someone get back much of the vitality that they've lost? It's not necessarily that they are going to get back the full "able" capacity they had, but to have a quality of life, to have a vitality, to do things that they enjoy. You're basically barring that possibility because you're telling me without knowing this person, only having seen him . . . maybe three or four times . . . what I can expect of life. One often makes decisions in the face of these expectations. So, I would keep asking, *how do you know?* I mean given everything that I had been reading suggested that there was elasticity of the brain. With proper stimulation, brains develop alternative ways to do stuff. And the reality is we don't know what the brain can do. Much of the current discussions of brain injuries indicate that people can develop additional abilities as far as ten years post-trauma. So, I get the impression that we're really in the Middle Ages about what we know about brains and their function.

There's so much we don't know against how much we think we know, and all this is speculation. The literature used to suggest that if you have a stroke and have not gotten function back a year out, one could not expect to get it back. And now they're saying, you make strides for as long as you're living and you're engaged.

JS: You speak to one of the components of my chapter on diagnosis which was the affective quality of being handed over a diagnosis, and how many clinicians resource this kind of dehumanization. They really do depersonalize it to such a point that makes it almost unconscionable about how much they transfer this specific kind of ableist affect to the families who must caretake or advocate as proxy for that person, that then have to take that all in so personally.

DH: And they set you up to devalue your loved one.

So I remember wandering the corridors of the hospital because EJ was in a wheelchair and he was there for two months in this rehab unit. I'll tell you the story of the drama of fighting to keep him there because we had twenty-two stairs before you could get into our apartment. I knew I could not bring him home until he could manage the stairs. The stairway was too narrow to put in a chair lift. So, if he can't get up the stairs, he can't come home. I've got to say, the stubbornness that I really hated during the course of our relationship served him well in rehab. And that's kind of the double edge of these kinds of traits that our kids have—traits that are marvelous and horrific at the same time. The stubbornness gave him a capacity to just persist through the rehab stuff until he could walk again.

JS: Again, these stories become important to a project like this. Not only is this a narrative that shows the crisis of diagnosis as I've argued in the previous chapter, but also, particularly, we have left the work of diagnostic thinking in the hands of the experts, dangerously so.

LB: People do say to me, "I think I'm Autistic but I don't really want to say that because I've never been diagnosed," that is, given a diagnosis by someone with letters after their name. My response is: "Well, it's not up to me to tell you how you should or should not identify," but I don't believe in giving power to the medical-industrial complex and its monopoly over getting to define and determine who counts and who does not count as Autistic, especially because there are class implications caught up in that gatekeeping. . . . It's not an inherently bad thing to want a diagnosis or to get one if you have the means to do so; the problem is treating people with a diagnosis as more authentic or valid than people without one.

JS: Yes, once I started to get into the territory of diagnosis, once I started playing around with the problem of diagnostic thinking when it is only left to trained diagnosticians, this allowed me to challenge how all of us must contend with thinking diagnostically, especially when it comes to the predictors of ability and disability: the effects of diagnosis—prognostications, prognoses, the diagnoses that don't even mean anything—*the diagnostic label says nothing* (right, good, fair or true) *about what the future holds*. The diagnosis can't really determine what is not possible. Yet, when a diagnostician diagnoses, they make all kinds of assumptions about what's going to happen and what should happen, whether it is going to be good or bad, etc. . . . But stories like this are indicative of the fact that a lot of this kind of questioning has not been done—not having been worked through, thought through. What is at the heart of the problem here especially when someone knows something is wrong, but by admitting themselves into the hospital, into a situation where they are supposed to get help, instead are further harmed? These narratives mean there is still a lot of work—a lot of critical thinking—that still needs to be done.

Chapter 4

Precariousness

If certain lives do not qualify as lives or are, from the start, not conceivable as lives within certain epistemological frames, then these lives are never lived nor lost in the full sense.

The precarity of life imposes an obligation upon us.

—Judith Butler, "Precarious Life, Grievable Life"[1]

WHAT IS PRECARITY?

Although there has been recent Disability Studies (DS) scholarship on the idea of precarity,[2] this chapter is dedicated to the work that Judith Butler had produced in the wake of September 11, 2001. This work engages what I want to describe as Butler's "Levinasian turn," in that she, in her recent work, has drawn from Emmanuel Levinas's ethical metaphysics in order to explain certain new sociopolitical phenomena, especially as it manifests with an American exceptionalism. Butler uses *precariousness* as the existential term and so it will be my focus here, and distinguishing it from *precarity* as the sociopolitical manifestation of the existential precondition. This more philosophical concept of precariousness carries ontological weight in that it "levels the playing field" for which bodies and persons can and will, or should and might count. With this distinction, Butler is calling for a "new bodily ontology" (2010, 2).[3]

This phenomenological interrogation into precariousness comes as a deconstruction of social and political assumptions about disability, where the "precarity of life" has come *to bear on some more than others*. My next and final philosophical chapter on prosthesis will be the positive, creative complement to this chapter's more negative exposition of the "first" and elemental fact of existential precariousness: the vulnerability in that *we* each and all *depend on anonymous others* for our existence, our sustenance, and our humanization. Precariousness is the ontologically complicated source of ableist affections and phobias—the fertile ground of ableism in its multiplicity and its multiplication.

With this existential fact of precariousness, the anonymous interdependence by which we each subsist is *inescapable*, yet, in frameworks that determine and value some lives as more grievable than others, precarity is further exercised by the arbitrary privilege of normative ablebodiedness. I am willing to be plain on this point: the most grievable body is also the ideal of "ablebodiedness" represented by white cis-male body, historically constructed as if only *he* has the strength to survive at will, covering up the interdependence on anonymous others. *Here we can think the conjured image of the self-made man.*[4] The preservation and sustainment of these kinds of bodies and their corresponding desires/activities/needs are given priority and value over others, such that, for some, precarity can be *"disposed-of,"* yet, for others, in effect, precarity is *"dispensed-to."* By Butler's account, this distribution of the precariousness and value of a grievable life, over and over again, in Butler's term, frames and "reframes" our "sociality."

This precarity has been historically and culturally determined; built into the world of Western capitalist values of life, work, space, wealth, and property. This neoliberal value system is ideologically compact; therefore, it exercises itself efficiently in material and experiential ways. Butler finds this to be the case as well as she describes what the Western world does as it sets itself to war with others, the "them" relative to an "us," in exercises of nationalism coupled with the assumed justified brutalization of bodies and persons—not "here," not "ours," but elsewhere and "theirs."

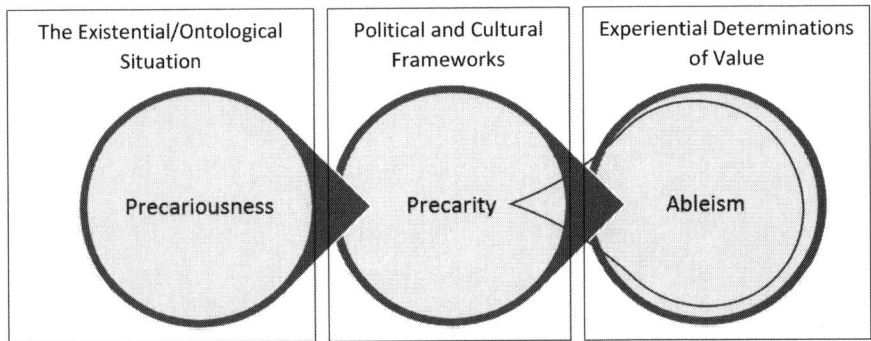

Figure 4.1   Graphic of Existential Precariousness.

What I want to outline here, particularly with this graphic (Figure 4.1) that distinguishes precariousness from precarity, is that as precariousness preconditions states of precarity, these differentials in precarity are the preconditions for the anxiety and aggression at the mere thought of the disabled body (mine, yours, hers, theirs, etc.)—ableism *proper*—and so, should be understood as a *pre-political* problem. There is a "feedback loop" in the way these ableist anxieties and aggressions can then frame and reframe the differential distribution of precarity as it sustains and makes habitable a grievable life.

Yet, in utilizing Butler's definitions, while she remains clear about the distinction between precariousness and precarity in *Frames of War* (2010),[5] she mentions ableism in this context only once. Perhaps Butler does not intend for me to read her this way; but, if the influence of Levinasian ethics is behind her analysis,[6] then precariousness is the site in which ableism emerges out of a primordial, ontological condition and can be assessed *existentially,* and because it cannot quite be understood with more familiar sociopolitical frameworks. So, arguably, instead, this is what is at stake in my "address" of ableism as Butler also describes it:

> The structure of address is important for understanding how moral authority is introduced and sustained if we accept not just that we address others when we speak, but that in some way we come to exist, as it were, in the moment of being addressed, and *something about our existence proves precarious when that address fails* (2004, 130 [my emphasis]).

The overarching concern that I hope to develop in this "thinking about precariousness," as I organize it alongside the problem of precarity and toward prosthesis, is how best to challenge the latent ableist thinking. To restate: *an obligation has been imposed upon us* independent of the historical-cultural fact of disability; we need to treat the phenomenon of ableism with more than what is available through theories about the social construction of disability. The dominant social and political assumptions about disability condition thinking in *unthinkable* ways; so, in existentially accounting for precariousness, there ought to be recognition for the *depth of the demand* cited in Butler's injunction above.

Cora Diamond offers me a possible starting point for how to think through this difficulty, about what remains "unthinkable" and "unsaid":

> The awareness we each have of being a living body, being "alive in the world," carries with it exposure to the bodily sense of vulnerability to death, sheer animal vulnerability, the vulnerability we share with them. This vulnerability is capable of panicking us. To be able to acknowledge it at all, let alone as shared, is wounding . . . [Quoting Simone Weil] "Human thought is unable to acknowledge the reality of affliction" (2008, 74).[7]

This approach I take is an anarchical—perhaps, radical—"equalization" of what has been at the heart of the historically uneven and deficit-oriented understanding of disability; the visibility and reception of any instance of disability can easily become uncritically, unthoughtfully representative of *all human affliction*. Any sign of disability can trigger ableism as if only always *abjection*; the affective response to the bearing of affliction—even if only symbolically—seems to arrest the everyday modes of acting and thinking, the means for ordinary judgment and expectation.[8]

Students have raised interesting and speculative questions when provoked by reading critical disability theory, and in that "state of arrest," they ask: *Won't there always be people with "disabilities"?* Or, *will we ever overcome disability?* I can't help but think these questions do not get to the "real," or rather more philosophically provocative problem of ableism at hand. This line of questioning implies one of two kinds of response:

- An ideological optimism in progress and enlightenment toward a better, greater society, one that will not have disabled people. There is a curious and long-standing *affinity with eugenic ideology* with this kind of ideological optimism, as in "a future with no more Autism." Transhumanist thinking tends toward a similar kind of "neutralization" of all disability through the investment and production of ever-new technological advancement.[9]
- An intellectual nihilism rooted in a naturalistic fallacy: *that it is the way it is*, and this is *the way it will be* (and implicitly, *should be*), so disabled people will always be "there"—as a given, natural condition of human society.[10] This nihilism preserves other inherited cultural and social biases, for instance, there will always be poor people, there will always be pollution, and the earth has always had "climate changes." This makes social justice work quixotic in character and defeats what are sometimes truly righteous causes (and its requisite urgency to act) for change.

These modes of thinking futurally about disability and the meaning of disability, seem to me to have missed a step. There is also a form of deflection[11] embedded in these attitudes of optimism or nihilism, without investigating a more thought-provoking approach. But the current political framework of precarity, as an inheritance of a Western neoliberal system, cannot value the unequivocal intimacy of individual subjectivities and that "affliction" can "come on the scene" at any time.

And our Western sociality—as it is material and experiential—is also *fully ableist*. Even by asking questions about the future, as I did with my students in the exercise described, we do not necessarily avoid the pitfalls of eugenic metaphors and metaphysical essences about the nature of bodies and minds, reminding us of the phobias and attitudes that trigger a long history of segregation and erasure. In this attempt at describing the preconditions for ableism, our existential dependence on anonymous others is shaping cultural and political anxiety about ownership, identity, power and place, in other words, setting up an epistemological and ethical frame for *who* has *what* and *how* and *why* they get to have it. In the context of contemporary, American sociality, this segregation has been surreptitiously practiced *as if* fair and permissible.

What is reflectively of interest at this point is the *reproducibility* of ableist thinking and attitudes that *affectively* frame disability as sites of impairment, deficit, nonnormative and, in plainest language, *negative* by default.[12] As inherited, much of the identification with the anxieties that come from a world that regulates and controls the precarity of persons through our Westernized ideological needs of self-directed identification: say, of "having a diagnosis," or of one's "employability,"[13] while at the same time being educated only for certain kinds of intellectual capacities (or trained in rote strategies),[14] or through the pressure to have ambulatory or cosmetic prostheses,[15] etc. To benefit economically and personally, the "I" *must command* (and *commandeer*) *all that I am*. These are practices and assumptions that get uncritically (and *affectionately*) passed down, affectively framing current and future ableist interrelations.

This *passing down* and *handing over* of ableist attitudes and ideologies (as essential to the forming of one's independent identity) is rich with the latent and active preference for and privileging of ablebodiedness, exercising itself for its own sake. If precariousness cannot be properly recognized in itself—being *existential* and not *experiential* as I am organizing it here with the assistance of Butler—and there is honestly no schema with which to fully capture ableism, then the way to question the latency of ableist inheritances must be in the way we find how precarity has been arbitrarily determined and distributed, for "them," those others, and not near "us," kept out of close proximity to "me."

The philosopher as such has a function here: addressing ableism is not just about disabled persons, their experiences, personal testimonies.[16] In fact, those who have been constituted as the bodies and persons disabled, need liberation more properly from the ways in which ableist ideology gets *riveted* to their situation. I springboard fully into the ethical injunction at hand with Butler's definition of precariousness (2010):

Precariousness is not the effect of a certain strategy, but the generalized condition for any strategy whatsoever. . . . Non-violence thus would seem to require a struggle of the domain of appearance and the senses, asking how best . . . to overcome the differential ways through which grievability is allocated and a life is regarded as a life worth living (181–182).

The distribution of grievability excites conditions in which violence exerts itself as some lives are framed—set up (as in "a set up") in such a way that becomes a more generalized expression of "it is better to be dead than disabled"—and some over others are made more precarious as lives not worth living, not worth saving, not worth salvaging. If, as Butler puts it, "Precariousness implies living socially, that is, the fact that *one's life is always in some sense in the hands of the other*," (1–2 [my emphasis]), the manifestation of precarity, in frameworks that determine the values of some lives as more grievable than others, becomes a place of fracture, framing disability—even symbolically—as exceptional,[17] as special,[18] out and against the desires and interests of ablebodiedness.

Exploiting the gaps in this framework while doing so in ways that are nonviolent and in the promotion of nonviolence, we might need to more fully interrogate the preservation and sustainment of some bodies and activities, especially in the way they arbitrarily signal priority and value of some, by and over others. The ontological/existential discussion of precariousness is the one I intend for this chapter because that is where I could best ask the more philosophical question of how ideologies get *embedded* in everyday thinking and acting, *attached* to bodies and minds, and then extend the discussion to approach a more comprehensive account of ableism, if that is even possible.

A more critical view of ableist sociality is possible if we attend to the narrated and under-narrated experiences of marginalization and debilitation; as in, the stories of when families cannot bear the "weight" of disabled children by being rendered economically and emotionally precarious, so they institutionalize,[19] abuse or abandon disabled children, in effect, accelerating the precariousness for disabled and disadvantaged bodies, displacing it away from the family members in the form of privilege;[20] as if to escape the entanglements with affliction, even if only symbolically. It is also a sociality manifested with the ambitions of urban and suburban development on the outskirts of wealth-generating cities, built with the intention for only certain bodies to inhabit and feel the power of self-direction, clear-cutting land for building the "American dream" particularly as homeownership,[21] and, at the same time framing the demand for ghettoized housing and mass incarceration toward invisible margins,[22] situating precarity in those who are already precarious, now rendered further dependent and disabled.

The context by which my line of questioning becomes confrontational with ableism as such still begs for more philosophical depth: that we need to question what has become of the value of space, of time, as well as of ethical interrelation. Ableism needs primary address with those who intentionally create and further render those who are disabled as "less-than," with those who embody ideological and *intentional* ableist preferences, or who actively and defensively segregate themselves from those who do not identify or cannot identify as ablebodied: distinguishing these practices and characteristics as *disablist*. This is an aggression added to the injustices of ableist sociality: *to defend* one's membership as the preservation of privilege, by identifying with and uncritically disposing oneself to ablebodiedness as if also ontologically the most natural and preferable condition.

For now, the point to which we must continually return to and is an important aspect of this project as critique is that *when nondisabled persons speculate upon the lives and experiences of people with disabilities, it is disablism at work*. It is a speculative activity that can be pornographic[23] and makes more precarious those who do not fall within the range of the normate—to use Rosemarie Garland-Thomson's term (2011, 23)—and, in turn, also actively *preserves* and *polices* the *corpus* of this normate.

So, if ableism is everywhere, as I have asserted it in my prologue, then we might find it attached to all kinds of bodies and minds, even in those people and the institutions that are not intentionally disablist: even in the groups formed in the name of disability rights and advocacy, in the good intentions of special education service providers, in the assumed benevolence of kind-hearted strangers, etc. Precariousness, therefore, is the necessary next step in thinking-through and addressing ableism, the step before we return to any discussion of disability.

The kind of phenomenological reading of "sociality" conditioned on an ontological precariousness, as I am describing here and that I think Butler is also referencing, originates with Levinasian ethical theory. Quoting Levinas directly:

> The Desire for Others—sociality—arises in a being who lacks nothing, or more exactly, arises beyond all that could be lacking or satisfying to him [*sic*]. . . . The relation with Others challenges me, empties me of myself and keeps emptying me by showing me ever new resources. I did not know I was so rich, but I don't have the right to keep anything anymore. Is the Desire for Others appetite or generosity? (2003, 29–30).

But I take caution: this kind of abstract thinking masks ablebodied privilege in that does not return to what Siebers insists upon, "a philosophical realism":

> Philosophical realists recognize both the social construction of identity and that identities constitute theories . . . about the world in which we live. Realism defines objects of knowledge not as natural entities but as social facts that exist in human society as part of a causal network. In other words, realists take the cognitive value of social constructions seriously, viewing them as points of departure for further research into the status of knowledge claims. . . . There are few cases that exemplify this epistemology better than the disability experience (2008, 126–127).[24]

In the context of a philosophical analysis, I can be accused of blurring carefully determined boundaries here by attending to precarity as an existential phenomenon rooted in precariousness, and on that point, I need to acknowledge any masking of what is ablebodied privilege. To be clear in the context of this approach: *We are not all disabled; we do not all equally know disability as it is a product of ideological and institutional discrimination and marginalization.*

It is also again important to note that within advocacy communities there is great concern over who best represents disability and who merely interlopes.[25] I do not find it theoretically sufficient to fall back on Temporarily Able-Bodied thinking (in that: aren't we [the ablebodied, that is] just all "Temporarily Able-bodied"?).[26] I instead ask (a point I will return to in the next chapter) about what produces the need for prostheses—equipment and devices (material and nonmaterial) that alleviate the ways in which precarity manifests as deficit, as disabling?

To that I would add, it is a brutalism that also renders the natural world in a state of precarity in that our dependence on anonymous others is not limited to our sociality but extended to our "ecologicality,"[27] especially when the world is not engaged for its ecological possibilities, but only its economic ones. Economic ideology infects institutions ideologically and not in ways that accommodate a diversified, inclusive, and socialized pluralism. The institutionalization of non-ecological and predominantly economic affectations domesticates bodies and minds, and, importantly, at a very early age.

Cas Faulds, an autistic parent of an autistic child, states a point that is worth emphasizing:

> As an autistic person, I wish that my parents had accepted me for being me, rather than trying so hard to make me into their version of me. Their efforts to make me into their version of me were unsuccessful but it did result in me feeling as though there were things wrong with me.[28]

What I find articulated here is twofold: first, Faulds invokes what I think is the danger of all parent-blaming (which is also to say, the dangers of parent-blaming/teacher-blaming/student-blaming)[29] in that it does not and *cannot* address but only *excites* ableism. Faulds is in a position where the personal experience of "feeling like something is wrong with me" is limited because the political and cultural frameworks have already gone to "war" and defended normative neurological function. In this way, her parents are in the paradoxical position without being conscious of the biases at work: both in defense of their child but also having themselves inherited and needing to displace their ableist anxieties of a cultural and political system of intolerance and nonacceptance. Arguably, as much as they may be to blame for affectively modeling their child into a frame that is familiar and "normative," there is a certain blamelessness in their defensiveness as product of the affective inheritance of ableist ideology. This brings me to the second and more complex "fold" of Faulds' invocation.

Ableism is intergenerational; it is a way of thinking that gets passed along in local and global ways.[30] Butler describes it as a frame that is being broken and reframed as it engages new contexts:

> The frame that seeks to contain, convey, and determine what is seen (and sometimes for a stretch, succeeds in doing precisely that) depends upon the conditions of reproducibility in order to succeed. And yet, this very reproducibility entails a constant breaking from context, a constant delimitation of new context, which means that the "frame" does not quite contain what it conveys, but breaks apart every time it seeks to give definitive organization to its content. In other words, the frame does not hold anything together in one place, but itself becomes a kind of perpetual breakage, subject to a temporal logic by which it moves from place to place.
>
> What is taken for granted in one instance becomes thematized critically or even incredulously in another. (2010, 10).

As it has already been argued here and elsewhere, the location of disability is *historiographical* and the kinds of ways disabilities are defined, perceived, and sustained are inscribed by both history and geography.[31]

One important account of this intergenerational transfer of ableism is by Andreas Hechler and what he was discovered about his great-grandmother, Emilie Rau, who was institutionalized in 1936 and by 1941, murdered at the Hadamar Euthanasia Center. He argues: "Ableism has meant, among other things, that many families in the Federal Republic with similar family histories have decided to remain silent about their murdered relatives" and that "Ableism affects all human beings, even those who measure up to societal norms, while the consequences for those deemed deficient are distinctly more unpleasant and ostracizing" (2017, ¶¶2, 6). Having been deemed "unfit for living" (¶31), Hechler describes the context for Rau's extermination: "Even when one was evoking 'merciful death' and 'deliverance,' the 'burden' for society was being calculated and presented in unvarnished propaganda campaigns." The ableist framework around burdensomeness tends to not be fully discharged except through eugenic ideations[32] and is agitated by the "tension between neoliberal economic policy and the human rights approach" as it manifests in the demand to participate in the labor force and market economy.[33] Exemplified by the case of Rau, Hechler discloses the sinister connotation of this kind of ableist inheritance: "Unable and unwilling to work, incurable, rebellious—a clear case for the gas chamber" (¶36).

So, while there may be available a calculable, traceable, historical record of ableist attitudes, institutions, and ideologies, by either being testified to or in the witnessing of unnecessary conditions of harm, we cannot miss the fact that these can only be accessed through narratives in the *past tense* reconstructed for *present interests*.[34] That is not to say that ableism should not be investigated for its history. Instead, I would say that we cannot more thoroughly challenge ableism in its depth of inheritance by way of historical narratives or analyses alone and therefore, it may be insufficient even when treated concomitantly. In my context, under the heading of a "philosophical address," work coming from historical accounts of disability still need to be politicized and in dialogue with the present tense interests relative to the imagination invested in a future possible. This is a mode of thinking that is active and political in the Arendtian sense—I ask about possibilities rendered presently impossible, unthinkable, unimaginable.

This means that the content of what has been passed down and handed over is less my concern as is the fact that there are essentialisms in the content that needs to be sussed out, having naturalized certain kinds of precarity for some over others, ideologically and, for the most part, arbitrarily. This is the *sticky* character of inherited ableism; it continues to have its most sticky features attached and transferable without contest. And although we need to know where ableism has "stuck itself" at the same time we also need to imagine ways of unsticking it—perhaps, only as it is appropriate to any one particular site of lodging. I should add that even when we might free up and "unstick" one area of ableist inheritance, that this does not necessarily apply equally to other aspects of ableism's "stickiness."

One interesting aspect of this strange stickiness—one that is characteristic of much of what I have found in operational ableism currently—is described by Sunaura Taylor in "Interdependent Animals: A Feminist Disability Ethic-of-Care," in which "Dependency is a reasoning that has been used to justify slavery, patriarchy, colonization and disability oppression" (2014, 114). She reads a suspicious and ableist "logic" in the argument for sustained dependency—the idea that those living beings dependent on others for survival get negative characterizations like being a "burden," "stupid" or, as she states it, "chillingly" comparable to "domesticated animals" (115). The danger of this thinking is that it is not possible to "liberate" these communities from exploitation because—as the rationale goes—they are defined in and by the assumed right only to resources via independency, otherwise, be dependent on moral empathies of independent and ablebodied persons. To this she states:

> The ways in which romantic and conservative notions of self-sufficiency, productivity and independence are entangled in contemporary discussions of animal welfare and sustainability is troubling. . . . The idea that some dependent individuals are less valuable and more justifiably exploitable because they are understood as burdens who offer nothing of value back to their communities . . . has had a long and troubling history for disabled humans as well (117–118).

These notions—*self-sufficiency, productivity and independence*[35]—I treat here as a point of linkage with a neoliberal ideology that negotiates precarity in relation to arbitrary privilege, diminishing precarity for some while amplifying it for others. This can make it permissible to aggressively defend and posture ablebodiness, in the name of "right to life" and with assumingly unambiguous claims to those ablebodied privileges. But this posture rests on significant ideological and philosophical ambiguities. The ways in which the system of economic and political neoliberalism has come to "despise dependency as weakness" and as "intrinsically undignified" must be addressed in its multiplication and "stickiness." It has been a position deeply engrained in American exceptionalism and current national debates on the use and distribution of resources, particularly economic and environmental ones.[36] Taylor cites Donaldson and Kymlicka on this point—a particularly "sticky" ideological an affective inheritance of ableism—"Dependency doesn't intrinsically involve a loss of dignity, but the way in which *we respond* to *dependency* certainly does."[37]

One additional premise that I return to is that the globalization of neoliberal and postcolonial markets has made space and time in the ordinary sense *uninhabitable*. There are very specific, if not also accelerationist[38] tendencies in the framing of spatial relations and temporal intuitions such that some bodies are already vulnerable in ways that are politically, socially and economically conditioned, then furthered in their vulnerability by environmental and ableist normativities. Here, I follow David Mitchell: "disability serves as the 'hard kernel' or recalcitrant corporeal matter that cannot be deconstructed away by the textual operations of the most canny narratives or philosophical idealisms" (2000, 49), and too, James Charlton, when he states, "everyone is different [and these] . . . differences are real; the categories and preconceptions are false" (2000, 167). When it comes to the rigorous expectations of subsistence in a globalizing economy, there are harmful and violent demands that renders *most bodies* as *non-ablebodied*; it is a political and economic climate of building power through control of profit and production, determined at an inhuman, world-constituting pace.[39]

The manifestation of disablist attitudes and the corresponding narratives of experienced ableism are analogous to the war frames that Butler describes—in that war *enframes* life and death, value and vulnerability, violently shaping the present tense in relation to future desires. Here, I hope that I've demonstrated that neither speculating about the future of disability nor tracing the past of disability gets at ableism in the fullest way—in its *stickiness*. So again, while the condition of precariousness may be unrecognized and unrecognizable in everyday experience, there is a certain amount of readable precarity that may be admitted as in urgent need of address. Levinas might have similarly described the relation between existential precariousness and the constructed and inherited precarity as "a first injustice before all justice."[40]

WHY CAN'T WE FIX DISABILITIES?

Hope is (and perhaps pride,[41] as well) an important feeling, not just personally, but also politically and is part of the catalog of transmissible affects. Although I am highly critical of the ableist connotations, I hear a call for hope in the desire to prevent or "fix" disabilities, or in the moral impulse to want to "help" others by "fixing the situation" for people who have been identified or who identify as disabled.[42] Hopefulness becomes an important concept philosophically because it becomes contented by perceptions and imaginings for the sake of the "future tense." The precariousness of the human condition is a void that becomes contented with questions of hope and intentional desires: *What will be? How will it be?* This, despite the fact that most often the content of these futural hopes may be unredeemingly paradoxical—as in, wanting the impossible to be possible. Returning to Butler:

> For Levinas . . . the human is not *represented by* the face. Rather, the human is indirectly affirmed in that very disjunction that makes representation impossible, and this disjunction is conveyed in the impossible representation. For representation to convey the human, then, representation must not only fail, but it must *show* its failure. . . . [The] paradox must be retained in the representation we give (2004, 144).

In the Levinasian account, the desire to "fix" when faced with the vulnerable other is really more about hope against the *fixity of death*—the death mask of the other that can *no longer respond*, no longer able to voice the situation in their otherness to me. The question of "fixing" is a concern about finitude and vulnerability to the failure(s) of existence as well as the failures for any corresponding representation.

In more ordinary language, there are two ways to read the question of *fixity*:

1. *What to do* (about disabilities, deformities, disorders): that we could fix what we find "deficient" or "disordered" or "deformed"—under the heading of "diagnosing" the disability—by having the category. The naming is the "fix" that satisfies ideological ambiguities.
2. *Who to do it to*: what I had described as the "riveting" of diagnoses to bodies and persons. That the diagnostic determination of a disability "fixes" one's identity, their social and political possibilities, and too often, their personhood.

The latter of these should excite horror in regard to the outcome of this most ideological ableist formulation: "it is better to be dead than disabled."[43] In this way, to be disabled destabilizes the future tense for some more than others, rendering some lives more precarious than others, stealing the hope that comes from having been a "person in the world" to the status of non-person, closer to pethood[44] in that someone has to "claim" you, "own" you, or "represent" your interests. That is how we have been culturally and politically putting some people and their families, if I am permitted, "in a real fix," predisposing them to failure.

When we follow these metaphorics surrounding fixity, there continues to be an ableist underwriting of desire in play. As Mitchell describes in the "Materiality of Metaphor," fixity has connotations along with disability in justifying narrative expectations, "disability as a metaphor allows writers to access concerns on a metaphysical scale" (2000, 25).

This desire to fix also has masculine, paternalistic connotations, as a preference for stasis and security, an intolerance for counterevidence and cannot aesthetically perceive open-endedness as productive. This is how Butler is able to demand demonstration of *failure*—in representation and, in that sense, in expectation. There are latent necrophilic[45] and somatophobic[46] tendencies in the way the body continually gets framed and reframed as "better" or "better off" when it is distinguished then divorced from the mind as "intelligible"[47] (and we know Descartes thought this to be the composition of the material world:[48] *dead weight*); that the corpse, the inhuman loss of corporeal animation is the dominant *preference* of emotional and ideological ableism,[49] always over the interruption, the "event" of intrusion in our everyday plans, the unexpected spontaneity of the organic future.

I return to Garland-Thomson on this point; she calls it the problem of the "future perfect":[50]

> The popular utopian belief that all forms of disability can be eliminated through prophylactic manipulation of genetics will only serve to intensify prejudice against those who inevitably will acquire disabilities through aging and encounters with the environment (2011, 29).

Which leads me to the next question.

HOW IS DISABILITY ECOLOGICALLY CONSTRUCTED?

I want to argue that there is a methodological importance to the preconditionality of disability and its corresponding precarities, defined here as an *ontological precariousness*. In other words, I think it is of great importance to address ableism and, in mapping out its scope and scale, to think through

the preconditions that construct disability in all of its "afflictions" and "negative connotations," riveted to those lives rendered less grievable, less valuable. The "preconditions" are indicative of the limits previously described in
critical theories of embodiment and social construction models of disability.

I'm approaching this while following some of the thinking in *Eco-Phenomenology* (Brown & Toadvine, eds., 2003), including approaching the ideas of
the "environmental" and the "ecological" with some of the naturalism and
scientism bracketed (as per the phenomenological method) in this usage. More
specifically, Lester Embree's adaptation of Husserlian phenomenology—a
kind of ecology that provides a novel approach to nature:[51]

> the nature that phenomenologists increasingly call "lifeworldly nature" and that is
> encountered in sensuous perception and hence prior to all construction in thinking,
> . . . [o]nce abstracted from the remainder of the concrete cultural world, . . . [is]
> perceived nature . . . premathematically spatial, temporal, and causal and includes
> physical things, vital or organic things, and among the latter, things that also have
> mental lives—that is, humans as well as nonhuman animals (2003, 39).

I take this approach because I want to avoid the risk of making a simplistic,
(and ultimately questionable) analogical comparisons between animals and
disabled persons, (avoiding all together, a pseudo-discussion about who or
which has more moral value).[52]

What makes any address of ableism "ecological" is how shared themes are
brought in for analysis. What I think can be particularly helpful are questions
like: what is the role of the *object* and how does this contribute to ableist
attitudes and perspectives?[53] How do paradoxical concepts like "sustainable development"[54] and "economic growth" contribute to ongoing ableist
practices and assumptions? What would or could non-ableist conceptions of
sustainability and *habitability* mean?

I'm thinking here specifically of Vandana Shiva's injunction(s) against
the Westernization of the global economy, its policies, practices, goals, and
fundamental assumptions as unsustainable as well as uninhabitable (more so
for some than others):

> An obsession with growth has eclipsed our concern for sustainability, justice
> and human dignity. But people are not disposable—the value of life lies outside
> economic development.
>
> In effect, "growth" measures the conversion of nature into cash, and com-
> mons into commodities.
>
> Thus nature's amazing cycles of renewal of water and nutrients are defined
> into nonproduction [in this context]. . . . A living forest does not contribute
> to growth, but when trees are cut down and sold as timber, we have growth.
> Healthy societies and communities do not contribute to growth, but disease cre-
> ates growth through, for example, the sale of patented medicine.[55]

And it is Shiva's call for healthy societies, (even if it carries some uncritical ableist connotations) that I find is a considerably *preferable* call to the one of "health" in the context of a "productive" global growth-economy. This globalizing economy has at the same time ideologically justified pathologizing, cataloging living bodies, and communities into a fixed state of dependency.[56]

Thinking through the Greek meaning of ecology as *oikos* [home] and *logos* [rational structure[57]], we need to ask how it has become possible that ecological future possibles have become subordinated and even competitive with the economic future perfect, as if a satisfactory expression of *oikos* and *nomos* [habits or customs]? With "home" at stake, and, loosely what connotes the "affairs of the home," then any conception of "health" as it is related to "home" is made vulnerable to cultural and socioeconomic forces of *profit-making* and *profit-protectionism*, independent of any other available and possible rational accounts. With this line of questioning, ableist affections come into frame.

Perhaps, in responding to this conflict between the ecological and economical life-worlds, we need to first better translate "health" as closer to what the Greeks referenced as *harmonia*, in order to determine the preconditions for non-ableist (or, at least, *less* ableist) precarity. The theoretical models that emerge from a cultivating situation other than ones that partake in a kind of "harmony" and that are also life-bearing even as they "earth-bound." With this, I am not romantic about "an ecological wholeness";[58] rather, I'm hoping to frame the conditions for a kind of *musicality* to being—an organic "orchestration" that is interdependent, fluid, and inherently spontaneous.[59] This could also provide resource for important critical work like Shiva's to also be less ableist, perhaps also redeeming the idea of "health" by extending it to nonhuman nature (a "healthy environment"), ecological systems ("healthy biodiversity") and models of agrarian subsistence ("healthy crops," including non-genetically modified food sources that "favor the farmer").[60]

Concepts like *sustainability* and *habitability* have been uncritically attached to the demands for *privatization* and *profit*, especially in the context of a necrophilic[61] growth-economy, and therefore, is what is urgently at stake in the sussing out of ableism as it extends to health and home. I'm also thinking here of the highly refined choreography that goes into the labors and space of caretaking when a loved one becomes sick or disabled, even when they were not so before, and including when a child or elder needs twenty-four-hour care.[62] According to the Family Caregiver Alliance:

> Researchers found that more than one-third of caregivers provide intense and continuing care to others while suffering from poor health themselves. Additionally, a 1999 study indicated that as compared to noncaregivers, women caregivers were twice as likely not to fill a prescription because of the cost (26 percent vs. 13 percent). Elderly women caring for a loved one who has dementia may be

particularly susceptible to the negative health effects of caregiving because they receive significantly less help from family members for their own disabilities. To highlight this, a 2003 study found that over one in four (26 percent) of female care-givers reported fair to poor health compared to 12 percent of women generally.[63]

This work of homecare is impactful and gendered—a site of both institution-alized and inherited precarities.

Health and home are philosophical concepts that are sites of precariousness as it becomes precarity; I am going to claim them here in order to reinvigorate less ableist meanings for them while suspending any ideological investment in naturalism and scientism that has prescribed thinking about these concepts up to this point. Injunctions about "homeplace," specifically, the way it is described by bell hooks, I think, gives me some permission to follow this line of thought. It is

> the one site where one could freely confront the issue of humanization, where one could resist . . . and by doing so heal many of the wounds inflicted by racist [and sexist] domination.
>
> [H]omeplace . . . [the] small bit of earth where one rests, is always subject to violation and destruction (1990, 42, 47).

To continue to complement hooks's idealism with realism, it is worth refer-encing Cheryl Marie Wade:

> To put it bluntly . . . we must have our asses cleaned after we shit and pee. Or we have other's fingers inserted into our rectums to assist shitting. Or we have tubes of plastic inserted inside us to [assist] peeing . . . . These blunt, crude reali-ties. Our daily lives . . . usually disguised in generic language and gimp humor. Because let's face it: we have great shame about this need ... that only babies and the 'broken' have . . . . If we are ever to be really at home in the world and in ourselves, then we must say these things out loud. And we must say them with real language (1994, 88–89).[64]

And while the privacy of the home is where one can shit and pee, or take care of babies who shit and pee, (to "put it bluntly"), it is accurately a question of a more fundamental precariousness when one cannot be at home, or one is at a home without friends or family, or must share their home with service provid-ers, (and, more specifically, strangers paid by external, "third party" organiza-tions, in their house but not even their *employee*), or, is rendered homeless.

The generalized and public resource of institutionalized housing and hos-pice (as social "welfare") can inflict further wounds in that one is reduced to bodily functions and routines, in other words, just a *"body."*[65] There is no sociopolitical personhood in these kinds of "homes" and the "sign" of disability is already "on the door," prohibiting homeplace, instead rendering it as an always precarious kind of institutional homelessness, just a *"bed"* if you will. This is ecologically-conditioned ableist pollution: again, the renewal of selfhood through homeplace is found nowhere.[66] For some, there is no escaping the precarities inflicted by an ableist society with ableist affections—especially if the generalized externality of ableist anxieties is made intimate and internalized and "brought home."[67]

There is existential precariousness that Joel Michael Reynolds reveals, in a TEDxEmory talk, "Transability: or your body is not what you think," with the narrative of his brother, Jason.[68] Reynolds redresses the attempted slur made out of earshot by a schoolmate when they were young. This peer addresses Reynolds and his family as his visibly disabled brother exits the school bus via wheelchair lift: *you drool like your brother drools*. Reynolds rereads this encounter that was first intended to harm and shame with a response that reveals the ontological fact of precariousness, to paraphrase: "it is not just my brother who drools; *we all drool* ('just like Jason')."[69]

Here, Reynolds, not as brother but as philosopher, utilizes the suspension of the personal and emotive content of these words, inverting their potency in an existential explication, stating that this is one of many bodily possibilities. Precarity manifests in the ways in which *some of us* are able (and have *learned*) to "control" our drool, especially out in public, but more poignantly, how, for others, this is less so. Ableism adheres in the assumptions that follow: that to drool is to be less than human, that the one "who drools" needs to be segregated from public view, that it signals only a body in need and burdensome to the rest of "us." Infants and dogs are the only bodies who are exempt from these ableist concerns.

In terms of precariousness, it is of the human condition and the body organic that we are fluid,[70] and exist as perishable beings among the less and more easily perishable beings of the world in an *interrelation*. To not "drool," to not show or seemingly not to have drool, is to also deny life and submit to the preference for death—what I have already characterized as the necrophilic tendencies of ableist affections. I say that because, as Reynolds testifies, *having his brother alive and drooling is infinitely more meaningful than having to grieve his passing*. It begs the question: why should Jason need a defense as a grievable life?

In this way, when we socially and politically undervalue persons in an assumption of disability and impairment, we further the conditions of disablement beyond whatever good or benign intention may be built into the system *because it is a fully ableist system*. This is what is argued by Michael Bérubé as well: "it might be a good idea for all of us to treat other humans as if we do not know their potential, as if they just might in fact surprise us, as if they might defeat or exceed our expectations" (2006, 261).[71] Without vigilance for the "surprise" of the other, this undervaluing of the existing individual—as Foucault traces genealogically with the school, the prison, and the hospital— is *the most dangerous* characteristic of all institutionalization.[72]

As we continue to read for more of the original ethical injunction by citing precariousness as it preconditions precarity, I think it can be found in the need to escape the value and determinations of any and all institutionality. I'm reading this as a need to address the *excedence:*[73] that one cannot escape or discharge a condition for which there is no escape, no discharge. *Excedence* is fundamentally a site for the *exciting*, rather than the *excising* of ableism. From Levinas, *On Escape*:

> The urge is creative and irresistible. . . . escape is the need to get out of oneself, that is, *to break that most radical and unalterably binding of the chains, the fact that the I [moi] is oneself [soi-même].*
> The I that wants to get out of itself [*soi-même*] does not flee itself as a limited being. . . . Escape . . . puts in question precisely this alleged peace-with-self, . . . [therefore], the need to escape . . . leads us into the heart of philosophy (2003/1982, 54–56).

The desire to "escape the self" is not resolved by death, nor is it related to our "need for 'innumerable lives'" (55), but is, as I would like to attach it here, a defining aspect of existential precariousness. This is how not only can home be "an escape"—a retreat—de-amplifiying everyday precarity in ways that can also secure ableist attitudes and affections, but also reveals an ontological *intrigue*[74] by the way we *fix* some bodies in their precarity into the institutional "home"—*securing* the sick, insane, and enfeebled. In a Levinasian framework, because we cannot escape the intrigue with the vulnerable Other, and we cannot just kill the Other, we escape obligation to the vulnerable Other ("the widow, the orphan, the stranger")[75] in the establishment of institutionalized, sanitized homes of extended care: *I only have to visit, but they, who remain there, they cannot escape.*[76]

As narrated in the documentary, *Her Name is Sabine* (2007), in France, in childhood and adolescence, in the comforts of her home and surrounded by her mother and sisters, Sabine and her family were able to hold sway from the ridicule and rejection by those in her community and at school. Her sister, Sandrine, who directs the documentary, shows footage of when Sabine was young and energetic enough to be able to travel to New York when she was eighteen, dancing and singing in her home, and living well and seemingly carefree and autistic, although there was no such diagnosis available to them then. These images—of a young and vibrant Sabine—are juxtaposed with Sabine in her current state: physically and visibly unwell, exhausted, often incoherent and prone to violent outbursts.

Her sister suggests the causes for this change in Sabine over the years: when her sisters moved away from home, began their own families, and her brother died, Sabine's mother could no longer care for her at home and had her institutionalized. Sandrine, in making the film about her sister, then narrates a horrifyingly familiar story about the harmful outcomes of institutionalization. In this case, they utilized electroshock treatments and left Sabine with significant permanent nerve damage, physical and socio-emotional impairment, and a diagnosis of "adult infantilism." In the film, when Sandrine shows Sabine the video of her when she was young in their travels to New York, Sabine cries out. Assuming that seeing herself caused her pain, Sandrine asks Sabine if she should stop playing the footage from their trip. But it was not as Sandrine thought: Sabine responded that she should not stop the film and, in fact, she wanted to see it again, because she so missed her time in New York.[77]

When we personally and emotionally underestimate persons in an assumption of disability and impairment, we miss the "surprise in being"—the spontaneity by which *this one* who exists *is other than all others*: she/he/zee is like no other. This could also be understood through an ethics of alterity, what Derrida called Levinas' "hospitality ethics," (1999) in which every *other* is an asymmetrical relation to the "self-same." In Levinasian ethics, the other who comes upon me and interrupts my "home," my place in the world of egoic enjoyment—my *jouissance*—carries also an ethical demand. This is not the perceived "burden" that might be argued from a neoliberal perspective; rather, there is horizontal expectation in that every face-to-face encounter is an original moment of which I am intimately engaged. The ethical demand—the only "burden"—is that there is a *suspension* of ordinary expectation. As they say, ineffectually, "once you've met someone with Autism, you've met someone with Autism,"[78] but my suspicion is that the disablement comes with the degree of attitudinal posture of *disaffection*, an indifference[79] to this other—original and "on the scene"—to which there is not genuine responsiveness, but only "business-as-usual."

This affective indifference further disconnects any ethical and affective connections between less and more grievable lives—now moving toward the distinction of those who may drown and those who are "saved." In some contexts, "business-as-usual" is as ruthless as an execution with the rationale of "economic efficiency" or as an austerity-based decision. According to Mike Brown writing for *The Guardian* (Jan 25, 2017), in a report titled, "Disabled people are to be 'warehoused.' We should be livid":

Disabled people have long fought against the phenomenon of "warehousing"— storing people with care needs under one roof as a way to reduce the costs of providing them with the support they require. The word warehousing captures the full horror people feel about being forced into institutional care, losing privacy and autonomy (¶7).

And this "force" is often a question of paperwork-based policy such that "going home" is not an option:

Anita Bellows, a member of campaigning group Disabled People Against the Cuts is emphatic about what this means: "Institutionalisation is the logical conclusion of cutting the funds for maintaining people at home" (¶4).

As highlighted in the case cited in Brown's report, if we can read it as a distribution of precarity, the "saving" of some is arbitrary; the "drowning" of others into institutionalization horrifyingly more systematic:

One person told me that when discharged from hospital recently, they narrowly avoided being moved to a care home only because their sibling stepped in to organise an appropriate care package (¶6).

A more studied account comes by way of Harold Braswell's work on hospice care narratives (2014):

Through this research, I found that, when insufficient familial support is present, hospice patients frequently fail to receive appropriate care. Such patients are either left abandoned in home environments that are inappropriate for their needs or they are sent to nursing homes that are not designed for patients at the end-of-life. Consequently, the US hospice system can be disastrous for dying patients when sufficient familial support is lacking.

These observations and the conclusion that these insufficient systems of care are disastrous I take to be serious and urgent. To restate the question raised by Brown's injunction cited above, *why aren't we livid?*

Braswell's ethnographic study is an outline in how the "surprise in being" can be recognized and a form of recognition, even if only affectively. This kind of humanizing intervention could be argued as an alternative to the either/or problem of independent care or else institutionalization. He tells of how Silvia's father, Ramon, in hospice with Parkinson's and dementia, was humanized by having her there daily, and with an intimate knowledge of him, not only was able to provide selective attentiveness to his care, but also expanded the way in which Ramon was valued—a grievable life.[80] Braswell argue that this "kinship makes a difference."

For Silvia, Ramon's dementia was neither a negation of, nor in tension with his personhood. It was a manifestation of his personhood, one that linked him just as much to the father she had known growing up as the old radio songs he would occasionally like to sing. Because of her kinship relationship with him, she succeeded in redefining the very meaning of dementia; in the process, she also redefined—and challenged—some of the dominant understandings of dementia in US medical discourse.

Institutional, bureaucratized settings continue to frame precarity in such a way that barely maintain these necessary, intimate interrelations of care; if these care relations exist, they are sustained incidentally and accidentally rather than essentially.

We do not address the *interdependency* of the interrelation of labors and bodies in a temporal and spatial choreography of caretaking *against all precariousness*. In focusing on the disabled "dependent"—the unproductive "burden" that global production keeps trying to shame, domesticate, and extinguish—we easily lose track of the *other* "dependent" in the caretaker relation; the caretaker is not a more "independent individual" than a care-taker's *charge*, as much as just seemingly more "ablebodied" in this context, in this situation. Iris Marion Young roots this in the paradoxicality of per-ceived independence in an interdependent system that produces for the sake of capital:

> Thus, the mystery of capitalism arises[: if] . . . everyone is formally free, how can there be class domination? The theory of exploitation answers this question. Profit, the basis of capitalist power and wealth, is a mystery if we assume that in the market goods exchange at their values. . . . [But] Profit is possible only because *the owner of capital appropriates any realized surplus value* (13, [my emphasis]).

The exploitive potential that owners of capital have over the labor that mate-rially conditions that relation could also explain how it is that this kind of institutionalization furthers the devaluation of those diagnosed as "disabled" and "disordered." There is no accountability for noneconomic surplus, par-ticularly the kinds of value generated through intimate caretaker and caretak-ing interrelations.

In the context of institutionalized disablism, in which some are "fixed as dependents" on others, ablebodiness is internalized as privileged by a system and that will permit them to take care of themselves, privately, individually, and profiting from position in advantage. It is also externalized in modes of condescension, in attitudes of disaffection and indifference; there is no recognition that the interrelation is always existential and individuating, not interchangeable—and it is this particular person (not just any-*body*) who I have *in my charge* and to which I am responsible.

It is the following mode of thought that leads us to reread the interrelation: "I am able to take care of myself *by* being paid to take care of you" and this interpretation, therefore, should be reread more accurately as: "I am *only* able to take care of myself *because* I am being paid to take care of you." There is an assumption of a kind of "redemption" in service work—a redeeming of ablebodied value; the caretaker is, in effect, maintaining the differential of precarity toward the one "cared-for" against their own precarities. The patient, the client, the charge or ward appears as if they were the only "real" dependency in the relation.

This caretaking also transmits ableist affect in the context of an institutionality when it is an environment for which employees are not "paid enough to care."[81] We need to keep asking about which forms of permissible narcissism[82] make some lives more precarious than others. To follow Butler again: how might we better understand the obligations of those privileged from sustained precarity to affectively care for and about those lives rendered more precarious and fully precarious—"to consider the ways in which our lives are profoundly implicated in the lives of others" (2004, 6–7). Yet, also, how to consider this in ways that do not further promote ableism or excite ableist anxieties?

When we institutionalize and bureaucratize certain kinds of dependencies, we also systematize this disaffection, creating ableist climates. Similar to how segregation can encourage racist and sexist culture, even bureaucratic segregation of persons—some must fill out explicit and detailed forms in order to get basic and necessary supports while privileged others do not,[83] one must provide identification and be "tested" while privileged others do not in order to enjoy the same benefit—such that ableist disaffection can carry a sort of "logicality" in these operations of privilege to enculturate and concretize disability.

WHAT ARE THE LIMITS OF EMBODIMENT THEORIES?

Rosemarie Garland-Thomson provides some insight into one of these limits, engaging the debate as it regards the ethics of care. While Anita Silvers argues against being an object of care, and that it undermines access to equality and civil rights, Eva Kittay defends the "the fact of human dependency . . . and the asymmetries of care relations" (Garland-Thomson 2011, 29).[84] I favor the latter approach, in part, as it resonates with Levinas' and Butler's theories cited here so far. I also favor Kittay's approach because it challenges neoliberal models of embodiment, especially as it manifests latent assumptions about mobility, capacity, and function. *Sui generis*—that each "I" is self-sufficient, in the image of God, comes out from nothing—along with ideologies in defense of rational self-interest, are functioning uncritically as major fictions in global capitalism. We must recognize this in that, politically and culturally, we would rather displace or dispose of the bodies than of these ableist fictions.

A politically-challenging concept of precarity must be framed as a non-neoliberalism, a challenge to neoliberalism outright. My particular case in point is what I call the threat of "being lazy." The lazy body, the lazy attitude, these are ethical judgments made out of more implicit biases that involve ableist expectations about work and its relationship to the self-determining potential upheld by one's "own" life. That is to say that *social and political contribution still counts*; it is the assumptions about "laziness"—of the unemployable, the nonworker, the uselessness of an "impotent" (or even infertile) body—that "sticks" itself into general cultural attitudes. This excites an intolerance about the need for *rest, recovery*, and even *reproduction*; the revival of bodily systems and that needed time to *reorient* and engage with at a different tempo than the pace of capital accumulation and industry.[85] It is not just a problem in a general sense—that ablebodied fear of being judged lazy, or, the *slur* of laziness—but that it is a particularly targeted racialized and classed idea as well.[86]

But we must acknowledge the virtual reality of our present economy when it comes to the question of ableism. All bodies that have needs and dependencies are rendered absent to a system of money and banking that *requires nobody*. Automaticism in the generation of wealth, obscene wealth hidden in nonmaterial ways (in hedge funds, in bitcoin, in political influence, and global policy shaping),[87] is also inherently ableist, not without saying misogynist and totalitarian in the genuine senses of the terms.[88] I say this with a maximum ethical injunction to challenge the many ways there emerges the bias of "compulsory ablebodiedness"[89] in the movement and direction of global capital.

Following this, Siebers in *Disability Theory* (2008) treats the "preference for ablebodiness" as primarily ideological. As Siebers describes it in his introduction, the ideology of ability stems from two contradictions: one with the Cartesian dualism of the body, the other is related to time (7–8). As he states it, "The level of literacy about disability is so low as to be non-existent, and the ideology of ability is so much a part of every action, thought, judgement, and intention that it its hold on us is difficult to root out" (9). Yet, as ideological, even this "preference for ablebodiness" may wear away in time without challenging the underlying ableism that makes it such a powerful marker of social and cultural privilege: a grievable life is an ablebodied one, no matter the reference to a named or visible disability.[90]

I root this particular stickiness in a kind of accelerationism[91] that has developed in Western ideological thinking. Where the mind/body dualism has been the source of much philosophical debate, and theories of embodiment continue to provide provocative and radical critiques of this dualism, the temporality and *temporalization of spaces and bodies* that emerges through the ideological demands of ablebodiness. I find this desire for speed and efficiency more interesting to contemplate and question.

To follow from Teresa Brennan's *Globalization and Its Terrors: Daily Life in the West* (2003): "a war between space and time will do as shorthand for tracing out the struggles that ensue not only between labor and capital, but between environmental survival and the depletion of the conditions for life." When we have created a situation in which there is little or no time to rest, repair, reorient, learn, grow, and think; wealth is maintained in a virtual reality in a context by which we not only reject those body-minds that cannot keep up with the tempo of—as in keeping time with—daily life and its private and public demands, but also exhausting ourselves and the world in a "depletion of energy," we have what Brennan calls a Pyrrhic victory of "human speed over natural time" (143).[92]

HOW IS OUR TREATMENT OF THE NATURAL WORLD CONNECTED TO ABLEISM?

As I've cited elsewhere,[93] Rashida Bee, in the wake of a major industrial accident that released dangerous chemicals into the city and citizens of Bhopal, declared that she refused to be sacrificed at the "alter of [corporate] profit and power" arguing that there are slow and silent "Bhopals" all over the world, and because "mothers everywhere carry chemical poisons in their breasts," that she accuses Dow and other chemical-producing industries as peddlers of poison, as practicing a "cruelty . . . against humanity."[94]

And the case of Bhopal is a known case, still without real remediation, with the toxicity and the effects of the pollution being passed down the generations. From *Spiegel Online International*:[95]

> Thirty years after the worst chemical accident in history, the disaster is hitting a new generation. The victims have received little help, professional clean-up has not happened and there are no signs the ongoing environmental catastrophe will end.

Considering industrial pollution is now as complex as the chemicals and pharmaceuticals that are being produced, what remains is of significant environmental impact—of which would require its own calculus—as it is also a fabricated system of precarity. What I think needs further examination, one that cannot quite be taken up here, is an investigation into *the disabling effects of industrial pollution*—one that I am taking up in the near future.[96]

It is not just the chemicals and toxicity of industrial and technological production that accelerate *precariousness generally* and *precarity particularly* for those more vulnerable by other economic and cultural oppressions and marginalization,[97] it is also the conditions of global and wage-slave labor that render bodies disabled under these same ideological models of "economic productivity."

In the case of Rosa Morena, pictured here (Figure 4.2), she describes the effects of no longer being able to work because of the harms of the work she had been doing: "Injured workers like me don't ask for much of the billions these companies make off of our work. We just want enough to take care of our families" in an article for *The Guardian* titled, "When I lost my hands making flatscreens I can't afford, nobody would help me."[98]

In Morena's case,[99] the precariousness of an accident renders an already vulnerable worker and parent into a situation of full *emergency*—a call for help has now been issued in a way that signifies her dependence on anonymous strangers. Her dependence is also our dependence—anyone's dependence—but now *she* takes on the situation of urgent need. As much as we might argue the existential interrelation, as I have done here, there is an announcement of another aspect of precarious dependency that needs

Figure 4.2 Photograph of Rosa Moreno, Former Employee of HD Electronics in Mexico, Originally in *The Guardian* (June 11, 2015). *Source:* Copyright © 2013 Alan Pogue/Texas Center for Documentary Photography.

address: this address, if it is ethical, also needs to be without the paternalistic attitudes of *pity* and *charity*. Already economically and politically vulnerable as a woman of color who is also a wage-earning mother, producing products that she cannot afford to consume, in now a greater need of assistance, is rendered expendable, dispossessed of employment and income, and harmed without redress. This disablement will be handed down as a *dismemberment* to her children in a form of generated and generational precarity.

These are physical and environmental conditions that predispose some to greater vulnerability and dependencies than others. These others embody the privileged ignorance that erases interdependencies, replacing it with cultural and social biases of advantage-as-birthright. *I am and can do in ways that you cannot*; yet, ontologically, this is *because you are:* an existential truth that can be ignored. Unlimited access to resources combined with a created desire for personal consumption, and also passing within the context of the cultural biases within frames of the normate body and with domesticated behavior, means that only I can breathe the air of this refined state; yet, this state is at war rendering the oxygen of a greater environment inaccessible to most bodies and beings; a war in which lives are lost while rendered less grievable through a techno-bureaucratic filter of ableist battle-gear.

If Butler and Brennan's accounts hold here, then I read this refined state as an ideological and cultural war against disability, against the bodies and minds of those lives rendered most vulnerable and who cannot pass with privileges. Disarmament in this "war" so-called would then mean a recall of all (white, Western, hetero, and cis) privilege, especially as it has been ultimately "able" to avoid addressing precariousness in its intergenerational interrelation and in its disaffected institutions. The global economy sustains unjustified inheritances of greater precarity for many while defending the protection from precarity for the few through the pooling of resources, seemingly accepting of a dangerously fictive and fallacious thinking: that the most profitable and productive individuals are also the most valuable and deserving.

Chapter 5

Prosthesis

Prostheses are *ambiguous*: . . . they fluctuate between fields of action
and passion; they fluctuate between memorializing and experimenting.

—Sara Brill (2011, 248)

HOW WOULD ONE PHILOSOPHICALLY
"MEDITATE" ON THE IDEA OF PROSTHESIS?

Audre Lorde models what I take to be a key meditation on the question of
whether to adopt or not adopt a prosthetic in *The Cancer Journals: Special
Edition* (1997). Rejecting the breast prosthetic, she articulates what is at stake
in taking on what "feels like a lie more than merely a costume" because, in
its "empty comfort," the breast prosthetic would not allow her to feel solidarity and recognition with other postmastectomy women. This possibility
is an alternative to the artificiality of a prosthetic breast, "For silence and
invisibility go hand in hand with powerlessness. By accepting the mask of
prosthesis, one-breasted women proclaim ourselves insufficients dependent
upon pretense" (62).[1]

It is not only her careful reexamination of her own fears but also recognizing the possibility of internalizing the [woman-] phobia in the drive to adapt
this particular kind of normative sexualization of her breast, challenging commonplace and normative thinking. The resistance to the comfort of this kind
of prosthetic, differentiating it from prosthetics that, as she states, "perform
specific tasks" (65), and in favoring a kind of "truth-telling" in her meditative prose, she critically takes on the attitudes latent in the illusory comfort
of a "falsie." Without some kind of functional necessity, without calling out

121

ableism directly, Lorde still methodologically describes the operation of ableism as it can correspond with misogyny:

> The insistence upon breast prostheses as "decent" rather than functional is an additional example of that wipe-out of self in which women are constantly encouraged to take part. I am personally affronted by the message that I am only acceptable if I look "right" or "normal," where those norms have nothing to do with my own perceptions of who I am. Where "normal" means the "right" color, shape, size, or number of breasts, a woman's perception of her own body and the strengths that come from that perception are discouraged, trivialized, and ignored.
>
> In order to keep me available to myself, and able to concentrate my energies upon the challenges of those worlds through which I move, I must consider what my body means to me (66).

If we follow this meditative and methodological account, with the argument that, as Iris Marion Young states it, "Women in a sexist society are physically handicapped . . . we are physically inhibited, confined, positioned, and objectified" (2005, 42),[2] then we might also recognize how Lorde hearkens to the desires of her own body stilled by the demands of "decency." In this way, the body is commanded with moral connotations in ways that both compete and overlap. The demands of a sexist and ableist society are indifferent to the uniqueness of her situational identity. She rejects outright the possibility that she herself, with her recovering body, as also still a woman's body, (and with that a black woman's body), could be "indecent."

Lennard Davis argues that:

> . . . before the nineteenth century in Western culture, the concept of the "ideal" was the regnant paradigm in relation to all bodies, so *all bodies were less than ideal*. The introduction of the concept of normality, however, created an imperative to be normal, as the eugenics movement proved by enshrining the bell curve (also known as the "normal curve") as the umbrella under whose demanding peak we should all stand. With the introduction of the bell curve came the notion of "abnormal" bodies. And the rest is history.[3]

So, this interrogation into prosthetics is to counter the emergence of the normal body as Davis describes it here—in which, for my purposes, *normality* as it is generally privileged and *less precarious* can then entail Elizabeth Grosz's more open-ended application of prosthesis. She asks:

> Must we restrict prosthetic extension to inorganic or inert matter? Can other living beings, cultural institutions, social practices also be construed as prosthetic? . . . Is language a human prosthesis? . . . These questions make it clear

that the division between an inside and an outside, an object and a prosthesis, a natural organ and an artificial organ, a body and what augments it is not as clear-cut as it may seem and the boundaries more porous and productive than the mere addition or supplementation of an external object implies (2005, 151–152).

Yet, without becoming purely speculative and contemplative in this meditation, we remain attached to a politicized idea of prosthetic: asking more about the *fabrication of devices* and to challenge the depoliticization of generic and socially accepted prosthetics. This is important to the possibility of non-ableist thinking because it has important explanatory power in the context of our original ethical injunction about the precarity of life.[4]

Thinking through the ways in which we could devise new and more non-ableist frameworks is a kind of approach a philosopher could fashion if needed, when called upon as *necessary*. Take for example, Christine Miserandino's "theory of spoons." According to this, Miserandino devises this theory as an explanatory tool for ablebodied people to better understand the experience of disability, developed when she was out at the diner and was asked by her friend, "what is it like to have Lupus?":

> I explained that the difference in being sick and being healthy is having to make choices or to consciously think about things when the rest of the world doesn't have to. The healthy have the luxury of a life without [these] choices, a gift most people take for granted.
>
> . . . So for my explanation, I used spoons to convey this point. I wanted something for her to actually hold, for me to then take away, . . . [and] I asked her to count her spoons. She asked why, and I explained that when you are healthy you expect to have a never-ending supply of "spoons." But when you have to now plan your day, you need to know exactly how many "spoons" you are starting with. . . . She counted out 12 spoons. . . . [I] told her to be conscious of how many she had, and not to drop them because she can never forget she has Lupus.
>
> I asked her to list off the tasks of her day, including the most simple. As she rattled off daily chores, . . . I explained how each one would cost her a spoon. . . . Showering cost her a spoon, just for washing her hair, . . . [reaching] high or low in the morning could actually cost more than one spoon, [getting] dressed cost . . . another spoon . . . I think she was starting to understand when she theoretically didn't even get to work, and she was left with 6 spoons. I then explained to her that she needed to choose the rest of her day wisely, since when your "spoons" are gone, they are gone. Sometimes you can borrow against tomorrow's "spoons," but just think how hard tomorrow will be with less "spoons."[5]

This is an important theoretical tool—a kind of nonmaterial *prosthetic*, if you will—for *identifying ablebodied privilege*. The change in thinking required to go from the "unlimited possibilities" to a budget of bodily options, has also been useful as a theoretical tool for self-advocacy against an ideology of personal, economic and physical, neoliberal "independence," that is, *freedom as the ableist world would identify it*. As Sunaura Taylor states it, "In American rhetoric there is a strong emphasis on independence and self-sufficiency. . . . [But the] point is not that ablebodied people and disabled people are equally dependent, but rather that the dichotomy between independence and dependence is a false one" (2014, 112–113). As a prosthetic, spoon theory operates in a variety of culturally and politically site-specific ways.[6]

It would be remiss for me to discuss prosthesis philosophically and not mention Jay Dolmage's arguments in *Disability Rhetoric* (2014) on "Prosthesis."[7] He outlines three arguments regarding the rhetorical potency of the body: 1) the body is "invested rhetorically"; 2) the body *is* rhetorical, "it communicates"; and 3) embodied differences—disability in particular—shapes possibility and meaningfulness (289). What I find powerful about these premises is the linchpin to the emotive content of ableist ideology: "*we have always worried about bodies*" [emphasis added]. And yes, the "we" that Dolmage is invoking here is the Western preoccupation with disabled bodies—the plurality who seek out uniformity of bodily possibility; otherwise, we worry. As he states it, at the heart of truly ableist preoccupations, is "an obsession about who cannot learn, a cataloguing of deficiencies" (*ibid*).

HOW WOULD A PHILOSOPHER DEFINE PROSTHESIS?

It might be difficult for a philosopher to find good reason to define "prosthesis" as also part of the larger catalog of philosophical thought, in part because of a long intellectual history of neglect for particular areas of concern deemed "not philosophical," or that this reflective and speculative mode of thinking was not done by someone considered a [canonical or living] "philosopher." Yet, as Karen Warren, editor of *An Unconventional History of Western Philosophy* (2009), might say, any history of Western Philosophy needs to be both critical and corrective, so too is the way we have come to think and judge the meaning of the "able-body" and how it is in good need of critique and correction.[8]

It is Emily Cohen's description of why one might investigate the idea of prosthesis that gives the philosopher a place to begin meditation:

> Prostheses provide a window into understanding how cultural objects become incorporated into the body and the self and ultimately how they transform how people understand the body as a political, social, and personal entity. The way people wear prostheses leads them to diverse social roles. For this reason, it is crucial to consider how individuals incorporate cultural forms and values that

they come to call their own—how people make their bodily performances intelligible to others—to note the moments when cultural performances register a disconnect between the person and the body in ways that motivate social change or invite critical reflections on the world.[9]

Prosthetics emerge out of "a need for," which can at the same time be a perceived "absence-of" in a context that, in that absence, defines difference. In an ableist framework, it is affectively perceived as loss or deficit.

Enter the philosopher into the discussion of definition: Elizabeth Grosz's *Time Travels: Feminism, Nature, Power* (2005). As Grosz thinks about the space and time of "things and objects," she states that prosthetic objects:

> [are] parts of the material world that we are capable of accommodating into the living practices (and experiences) of the body. . . . Living bodies tend toward prostheses: they acquire and utilize supplementary objects through a kind of incorporation that enables them to function as if they were bodily organs. . . . [Prostheses] are organized by *utility, adaptation,* or *need* (145–47, emphasis added).

The materiality of prosthetics emerges out of the sociocultural resources made available—the precarity of persons also emerges in how those prosthetics function or do not function, and not only how they are organized as Grosz describes it, but also *by whom.* The existential sociality and ontological fact of precariousness means that all ought to share in the work of constructing and disposing of prosthetics—in the general *fabrication*[10] of prosthetic objects.

Sara Brill states that Grosz's "analysis of prosthetic functions is not only *dynamic,* it is also *differential,*" and is "a powerful form of critique." Brill raises more radical questions worth meditating on here: "What is the prosthetic function of this or that friendship, familial organization, form of education, social network, collective practice, conglomerate, coupling, institution, etc.?" (2011, 249). These can be analyzed in that they operate as "prosthetic complexes" in that even "*affect too can serve a prosthetic function*" (248, emphasis added).

Another way I can answer questions like this—in a meditation on how to think philosophically about prosthesis—is not simply "as a philosopher" but by providing examples. Of particular concern is the paternalistic territorialism that emerged among some philosophers when prompted by philosopher Shelley Tremain's call to attention regarding the use of ableist language. She petitioned the community to stop the use of "(double) blind-review" language in their calls for journal and conference submissions, replacing it with language referencing anonymity instead.[11] Here is one response by Neil Levy,[12] a Senior Research Fellow at Oxford Uehiro Centre for Practical Ethics, that I find curious:

Recently we have seen the stirrings in the philosophical blogosphere of a campaign, spearheaded by Shelley Tremain, to highlight and increase sensitivity to the use of "ableist" language. Ableist language stands to disability in the way that sexist language stands to gender. Just as we now avoid certain kinds of language because it suggests—and may inadvertently reinforce—the inferiority of women, so (Professor Tremain suggests) we ought to avoid certain kinds of language because it demeans the disabled.

I first came across the campaign in the context of a call to avois [*sic*] the phrase "blind review," on the ground that "it associates blindness with lack of knowledge and implies that blind people cannot be knowers." Professor Tremain suggests that we replace "blind review" with "anonymous review." I must admit my first response was to regard the whole thing as silly. But I had second thoughts. I no longer think it is silly (to be clear: I think that the campaign against "blind review" is silly, but the campaign against ableist language is not). . . . [Research] in psychology backs up the contention that the existence of—independently of belief in—stereotypes has real world effects, both on the behavior of those who are stereotyped and on others too. Those who are stereotyped may suffer *stereotype threat*, where their performance on tasks suffers because the task is stereotype atypical, while others may judge in ways consistent with the stereotype even when they don't accept it.

I remain unconvinced that the phrase "blind review" is problematic. Still, it seems easy and costless to avoid, so why not avoid it . . . ? More obviously problematic is the rich language of mental illness as insult: "crazy," "hysterical," "schizophrenic" (to mean two-faced), and so on.

What makes his response so curious is the indifference to the call as it was articulated. Although Levy seems to change his mind about the "silliness" of Tremain's campaign, he, in fact, is just appropriating it into the domain of why one might engage any other form of political correctness. I think my suspicions are fair as he strangely states, after seemingly willing to defend the campaign, that he still thinks the need to change "blind-review" to "anonymous review" is *unnecessary*. It is not clear to me what he has or has not been persuaded of because then he follows that:

The problem is once you are sensitized to possible associations and suggestions, it is difficult to stop. Double entendres are a classic example: make one inadvertently in a classroom and from then one everyone will hear one in every sentence you say. John Derbshire—not normally a fount of wisdom—notes how the "niggardly" controversy might cause further words to be become suspect: he gives the example of "snigger."

There is a cost to the raising of sensitivities. Linguistic self-censorship is time and resource consuming. It may make dead metaphors live once more, and thus lead to some of the very harms it aims to avoid. It may nevertheless be a cost worth paying—it was in the case of sexist, racist and homophobic language.

His response to Tremain's call is that it may just be a question of sensitivities.[13] Note that he initiates this point as a "problem." He ends the point with the analogy of racism and sexism[14] but not seeing that the root for the analogy is how it operates in climates of exclusion and rhetorical privilege.

What I think Tremain is *really* arguing, and what is dismissed by Levy's lackluster response, is how rhetorical tools feed the cultural imagination and become the currency of normative and normalizing power. This currency drives the symbolics of association and identity (disabled identity in particular, minoritized identity in general) and who ought to and should lay claim how these rhetorical values are generated and subsequently employed.[15] She does ask that her community have no part in driving or even contributing to ableist assumptions *at every turn*, as in to "leave no stone unturned" in the spirit of philosophical fieldwork.[16] What was described condescendingly by Levy (and his commentators do not seem to challenge) as a "stirring"—which, in fairness, is a misappropriation on his part[17]—is her point *as she makes it*. From Tremain directly:

Over the last couple of decades, disability theorists in the humanities have produced work that shows how signifiers of disability employed in literature, art, films, pop culture, the news media, and everyday discourse are paradigmatically and stereotypically oppressive to disabled people: the nasty villain with facial scars, the evil pirate with a prosthetic arm, the wicked witch with one eye, the determined cripple who overcomes all odds and is redeemed, and so on. One focus of these efforts has been the ways that "blindness" is used as a rhetorical and representational device to signify lack of knowledge, as well as epistemic ignorance or negligence and the moral downfall it implies.

I first wrote about the use of blindness as a metaphor in 1996. For the last few years, I have tried to get the APA to remove the phrase "blind review" from its publications and website. The phrase is demeaning to disabled people because it associates blindness with lack of knowledge and implies that blind people cannot be knowers. Because the phrase is standardly used in philosophy and other academic CFPs, it should become recognized as a cause for great concern. In short, use of the phrase amounts to the circulation of language that discriminates. Philosophers should want to avoid inflicting harm in this way.[18]

With Tremain, I think this is where a philosophical response to the question of prosthesis could begin *with good reason*. The philosopher needs to be receptive to harm if the work bears any challenge to biases in thinking. Levy masks his bias in that he remains "unpersuaded" to how "sensitivity" should operate in arguments about language and, from the armchair, the psychological impact of these kinds of campaigns. His response is essentially one of the indifferent attitudes in that there is no intrinsic compulsion to respond to a voiced harm (voiced here in Tremain's characterization of uncritical persistent ableist imagery in our cultural catalog), specifically how "blindness" is not a neutral "device" as a metaphor, especially in that it is now also associated with a kind of epistemological deficit.

Beyond this particular debate, is the fact that this language has greater ableist currency and impact elsewhere: "the blind leading the blind," "blind as a bat," etc., all forms of thinking and rhetorical function that has nothing to do with reality (as in the former, a cliché) or truth (in the latter, bats are not "blind"). Here, an ideological mistake is in play—as part of a usual academic game—similar to other ableist tendencies of the academy.[19] Levy is taking the campaign only on personal terms, ("*I* am not persuaded"). What Levy has missed is the professional and philosophical defense against ableism in the specificity of the demand, citing the "problem" as coming from being too sensitive and then, juvenilely in the comments, snarks and plays with puns.[20]

I want to put forth a theoretical resistance to this kind of response, exemplified by Levy's post and comments—indifferent, impersonal, disembodied, and juvenile—to the need for sensitive intelligibility and receptiveness, especially to the philosophical injunction and further, with respect for the work of the professional philosopher. There is a danger in Levy's sophistry: arguing that ableist language through the analogy with other forms of stereotype threat and political correctness, so that *he* then *misses the uniqueness of the ethical demands raised against ableist attitudes and ideologies.* Simply, Levy responds like a disablist.[21]

The resistance here is that rhetorical devices not only operate on par with other kinds of prosthesis but also maximizes a *philosophical* and *critical* effect: without which, in very specific ways, open or close off possibilities of association and inclusion. Similar to the paradoxical quality of diagnosis [chapter 2], prostheses *supplement* or *augment* interrelations and interdependence in a way that is *both essential and nonessential* to that situation. If they do not or cannot supplement or augment, then the prosthetic object becomes artifact. This making of artifact, when no longer producing a prosthetic effect, I associate with the picture of the leather-framed spectacles from the 1700s (Figure 5.1)—no longer belonging to a body or needed by a person—but the stuff of a museum.[22]

Alongside the image of these spectacles, on MuseumofVision.org, is a corresponding narrative for this kind of prosthetic need:

A simple historical timeline of eyeglasses starts with their invention, believed to be between 1268 and 1289 in Italy. The inventor is unknown. The earliest eyeglasses were worn by monks and scholars. They were held in front of the eyes or balanced on the nose. The invention of the printing press in 1452, the growing rate of literacy and the availability of books, encouraged new designs and the eventual mass production of inexpensive eyeglasses.

Figure 5.1 Image of Leather Frame Spectacles (*ca.* 1700s). *Source*: Reproduced with Permission from the American Academy of Ophthalmology Museum of Vision. All Rights Reserved.

There are many ways in which what is assumed furniture of the everyday world is *already artifact* when viewed critically for the ableist perspective. From James Cherney in "The Rhetoric of Ableism" (2011, ¶10):

> Ableism is so pervasive that it is difficult to identify until one begins to interrogate the governing assumptions of well-intentioned society. Within the space allowed by these rhetorical premises, ableism appears natural, necessary, and ultimately moral discrimination required for the normal functioning of civilization. Consider a set of stairs. An ableist culture thinks little of stairs, or even sees them as elegant architectural devices—especially those grand marble masterpieces that elevate buildings of state. But disability rights activists see stairs as a discriminatory apparatus—a "no crips allowed" sign that only those aware of ableism can read—that makes their inevitable presence around government buildings a not-so-subtle statement about who belongs in our most important public spaces.

One might imagine in the near future that buildings only accessible by way of stairs are similar to the chairs in a museum with a rope across it: in that it is archaically a "chair" of which no one forevermore can take "as a seat."[23]

In order to elaborate on this philosophical account of prosthesis I am presenting, it is worth summarizing one of the key points made in the film, *FIXED: The Science Fiction of Human Enhancement* (2013), articulated by Patty Berne, Activist:

> I really don't understand the desire for enhancement technologies. We don't have basic healthcare, not only in this country but globally. Preventable diseases

are the number one killer globally. Talk about misplaced priorities. It is . . . this huge irony that the research money . . . goes into emerging technologies as opposed to wheelchairs that are waterproof? [Scoffs]. That demonstrates the financial priorities with the healthcare system.

Wheelchairs are amazing and that's really precious. And at the same time, it's a machine. You know, I'm subject to its . . . frailties, you know, like any machine. So, it makes me feel pretty vulnerable.[24]

Non-ableist approaches and arguments, constructed in a spirit of a philosophical realism, addressing disablists that defend their ableism directly, link the personal with the political and philosophical. These defenses can also be read within a context of prostheses generally; to be clear, like prosthetic objects that no longer supplements or augments a need, or are no longer attached to particular bodies in particular situations, *rendering ableist approaches and arguments as artifact.*

There is a notable case vignette I return to when thinking about prosthetics and prognoses. It regards a story that went viral in which a young boy was given a three-dimensional (3D) printed arm prosthetic in the shape of an Iron Man arm. This story gained currency in the same way that most inspiration porn[25] does; that one (appropriately vulnerable individual) could be "saved" or "redeemed" by the generosity of strangers,[26] and that ablebodied people are always well-intended while permitting a self-reinforcing bias of ablebodied privilege through the condescending language of "helping," "saving," "fixing" and "curing."

The lesser known part of the story is of greater interest here; the boy turns down the "gift" of this prosthetic, and for good reason(s):

Although he has the best medical care and has had a prosthetic in the past that was exciting to begin with and then presented issues, Thaddeus enjoys having the authentic sense of touch that he receives from just the tip of his wrist. "I can figure out how to do stuff my own way," Thaddeus told his mom. "My brain just works different because of my hand, and I think that's a good thing." It was a revelation for Thaddeus' mother on the morning he explained to her that he was comfortable without a newfangled arm. "My friends like me just the way I am," he said. "I don't think kids would be my friend because of me. They would just want to play with my robot hand." His attitude is really a revelation for all of us, and an unexpected inspiration as well, as we see how possible it is for an eight-year-old to not only be resourceful and able to navigate around constant daily challenges, but to be completely comfortable in his own skin as well. "As a mother, I had wanted to add to him, because I wanted the best for him," said Catherine. "That morning, I finally saw that he was perfectly whole."[27]

What this "revelation" includes is that a prosthetic is sometimes for the comforts of others in their biases, not for the sake of one who wears or utilizes the prosthetic. In that way, and the insight comes from this young boy in that he makes the world sustainable for himself in his own way, he does not need a "supplement."

This is an important point about the making of the artifact versus prosthesis with the lesson of the Iron Man arm: that the "supplement" that had been fabricated for him with much fanfare is now a pure artifact in its novelty: it was made for a boy (not thinking that he will grow up or outgrow the prosthesis), a boy who must want to be a superhero (but surprisingly, even to his mother, does not), who needs a hand (misunderstanding that he was already satisfied and did not articulate a *need*). What is more powerful is that he recognized the need for *real* friends (rather than those who just liked his robotic hand) independent of any prosthetic novelty in a cultural artifact.[28]

The mother's revelation is important here too: her suggestion "that he is whole," recognizing the way that this prosthesis would have actually subtracted from the way he finds himself navigating the world (what the reporter describes condescendingly as "constant daily challenges"). How often are prosthetics really just cosmetic and for "convenience,"[29] and how often are many things ordinarily used not thought of as prosthetic? With these questions, I want to show the paradoxicality of ableist thinking: prosthetics make the world habitable, yet some prosthetics, when they are specific to a certain population or for very specific purposes can become characteristic of "disability"—as in the difference between a walking stick and a cane. The aporetic quality of this paradoxicality (for, what would be the real difference between the walking stick and cane?) is described by Grosz in the way we "carve up the world" (2005, 135–136):

> The object is that cutting of the world that enables me to see how it meets my needs and interests.
>
> This cutting of the world, this whittling down of the plethora of the world's interpenetrating qualities—[quoting Bergson[30]] those "pervading concrete extensity, *modifications, perturbations,* changes in *tension* or of *energy* and nothing else" (1988, 201)—into objects amenable to our action is fundamentally a *constructive* process: we make or fabricate the world of objects as an activity we undertake by living with and assimilating objects. We make objects in order to live in the world.

But what does this mean when this "cutting of the world" is not neutral but uncritically ableist in its "constructive process," in its "perturbations" and "tensions"? I can best describe it this way: think of all the ways in which "having a crutch" has become literally and metaphorically a slur and predetermination of one's lack of value and will. The "crutch" connects prosthesis to the other concept at play in this mapping out of ableism, precariousness:

think here the negative association with the "crutch" and all the ways it has come to symbolize the ableist desire for self-sufficiency, productivity, and independence. In our neoliberal system, no one should need a crutch but rather, "stand" on one's own "two feet." No one can afford—(or should I say) it seems as if it is unthinkable—to be so vulnerable to that kind of precarious-ness and therefore becomes a site of shame and blame, moral culpability, and bad habit. At the same time, it has become a naturalized given that those who do not need "a crutch" should get due praise and be rewarded accordingly.[31]

WHAT DOES PROSTHETICS HAVE TO DO WITH ADDRESSING ABLEISM?

More than waxing philosophical about prosthetics, if there is to be "nothing about us, without us," we should come back to those questions most relevant to addressing ableism. More than the cutting of the world, the cane and the walking stick can bring precarity to the fore quickly and expediently; this is made more clear in the ways that commercially produced prosthetics tend to be prohibitively expensive, and in the way that sometimes, objects just won't "fit," or in the way that prosthetic objects can easily fail and threaten the life they are meant to supplement or augment.

Most fabricated, material "equipment" that supplies the world with wealth and resource is for the general sustainment of normative states and skills. Jay Dolmage cites Garland-Thomson in order to outline the rhetorical appropria-tions of the body as they are mostly for the sake of the normate; so that "the constructed identity of those who, by way of the bodily configurations and cultural capital they assume, can step into a position of authority" (2014, 9).[32] Yet, even if differentiated bodily and an experiential plurality of narratives gain some cultural capital—in identification or in recognition—this enlarged capital does not necessarily challenge the more dominant and surreptitious ableist frameworks. We can understand this to be the problem when we think of how uncritically eyeglasses are thought of as non-prosthetic, while hearing aids are to be disguised and hidden as "fully prosthetic." A diversity of narra-tives will not necessarily alter these schematics of ableist affectivity.

Social and political mechanisms have become more sophisticated on this point; we overproduce personal devices that supplement and augment everyday life that is led by ableist desires and phobias, like cellphones and automobiles. They are also fabricated to be disposable, in their design, a materialization of planned obsolescence, never directed in their design toward addressing the precarity of life in humanizing and justifiable ways.[33] As Christina Cogdell states it, "Built-in product limitations, combined with manufacturer's cultivation of planned obsolescence and expendability of goods, . . . this unsustainable but profitable design strategy stems from twentieth-century machine-based methods of mass production and standardization" (2015, 59).

Add to this complexity the fact that any *denial* of basic prosthetics can be dehumanizing. We can juxtapose the Spoon Theory with the meaning of the spoon in the context of the Lager. According to Primo Levi, the spoon was "a tool for humiliation" because, even though there were plenty, those in the Lager went with one or none (1989, 114). The preconditions for disablement included the act of *stripping, shaving*, and a "public and collective nudity" (113). The precarity in any one individual body in its capacity to be "shaved and stripped" of social protective layers leads to a pooling of resources against some persons over others. This opens up a wound by which power can be further organized and consolidate the fabrication of objects in ableist ways, only augmenting or supplementing an *inaccessibility* to more needed and urgent prostheses. If one is forced to go without a spoon,[34] what then of the relation to those who have access to a surplus of spoons? Can a spoon still be viewed as simply *just another tool* or does it carry a now distorted and disproportioned meaning—especially if it indicates basic and disabling dehumanization?

Take, for another example, the demand to think through the significance and the general, but suspiciously ableist and *welcoming reception* of the development of sign-to-speech gloves that translate sign language for spoken word. According to Alex Lu:

To me, this reveals a tremendous lack of imagination from hearing people on how communication actually works. As Deaf people navigating a hearing society, we tend to pick up on all sorts of strategies to communicate with the non-signing hearing people around us. We tote around pens and notepads. We gesture. We use body language. We send emails. We ask for your texting number and instant messaging handles (I have a friend who holds mixed hearing/ Deaf parties by asking people to bring devices to join a group chat). We mouth words and lipread. We draw pictures. We work to meet you in the middle over and over again. Many of us wish you could learn sign language, but we know that's not always a realistic expectation. But that's okay—communication is about the message and the people, not the medium.

My radical suggestion to hearing people who are concerned with access issues for Deaf people is that you are casting the problem wrong. Perhaps the gap in communication does not stem from an inherent limitation in Deaf people, but from an attitude problem in hearing people. I get why this is a tough pill to swallow. For one, there are no easy technological fixes. You can't just make a bulky device that only facilitates slow and imperfect one-way communication, tell us it's our responsibility to pay for and maintain it, and wash your hands of us as we still struggle to gain an autonomous voice in a society that considers us objects of pity.[35]

The undergraduate engineers of the gloves win a student prize while the audist preference remains uncritically ableist—hearing rather than deaf; speaking instead of signing. In effect, the subtext is a self-congratulating message from and to the hearing world—*we will always accommodate ourselves*—but, if you are deaf, we are not obligated to accommodate you[36]—if not also, maybe, to learn from and communicate with you: Please, *just continue to accommodate us.* Yet, reading through these ableist entitlements and affections, it may still be considered too *ambitious* (but yet, quite *righteous*) to work toward the goals given to Universal or Inclusive Design, "to affirm human rights and dignity by designing for all *without stigma*" (Cogdell 2015, 60, emphasis added). From Aimi Hamraie in the context of discussing Universal Design:

> Rather than accounting for diverse body types, sizes, and abilities, the normate template privileges a small group of individuals in mainstream design, giving these individuals the appearance of normalcy or universality due to their fit in the environment. The resulting built environment is precisely what the social model criticizes—a world built without considering all ranges of ability.[37]

So the demand from an organic idea of prosthetics becomes not to provide a generic "refitting" of the "misfit";[38] rather, it is to initiate designs that avoid future retrofit.[39] Hamraie goes on to add:

> Understanding bodies as evidence of ableism, inaccessibility, and mis-fit, explains the underlying new materialist philosophy of UD research, which draws upon existing methods of quantifying and measuring bodies to make an intervention into the epistemic practices that materialize the built environment.

I would want to theoretically defend what might be only thought of as a common sense rule when it comes to prosthetics: one size does NOT fit all.[40]

Like the spoon and the glove, and unlike the crutch or the cane, clothing generally is not considered a prosthetic, especially as another mass-produced and disposable product fabricated by and for the normate. Sizing is stylized as generic, yet loaded with fat-shaming biases,[41] normative assumptions about gendered bodies, based on the fleeting market-worth of materials, fabrics, chemical dyes, as well as notoriously oppressive labor conditions to fabricate these objects (soon to be waste products) that are being produced invisibly and unsustainably.[42]

There are counterexamples of how tailoring clothing to the nonnormative body is how clothing could be like an "organic" prosthesis. The conditions for the social construction of organic prostheses—in which members of a local group alter the material conditions in a nonnormative way—but that allows for 1) mobility and accessibility, 2) equality of opportunity or 3) aesthetically satisfying sense of individuality (not necessarily attached to a sense of pure "independence").

An organic prosthesis does not mean just a replacement of a biological appendage, or attachment to the body out of deficit or absence of function. It is a way of extending interrelation in site-specific ways, while adapting to the sensitivities of bodies and minds that cannot fit the generic models or modes of inhabiting the world as it has been constructed.

One last example that comes to mind is of Kayden Clarke, a trans man with Asperger's,[43] who trained his service dog to recognize the signs of self-harming behaviors. The prosthetic is in the *way* he trained the dog, by his own account:

> "When I have a meltdown, I often have self-injurious behavior and I often self-harm," . . . . But [Clarke] stressed that the dog is not comforting [him], as he may appear to do.
>
> "He responds on action instead of emotion," [he] said. "That's how I trained him."
>
> And when 120-pound Samson moves to lie across [his] lap, he's providing [Clarke] with therapeutic tactile stimulation. Samson's pressure and weight helps [Clarke] check in with [himself]; without him, [he] said, [he] may not be able to consciously recognize the tantrum [he] is experiencing.
>
> "His weight has a calming effect," [he] explained. "He makes me acknowledge what's going on—he kind of snaps me out of it."[44]

His service animal was trained not only for specific responses and interventions that depended on an existential interrelation but also with a site-specific sensitivity to the situation. By sensitivity, I mean a kind of sensitivity that is intentionally *not* emotional; rather, it is self-aware and other-directed, a site-specific, responsive interrelation—Samson organically "fits" Clarke by way of therapeutic intervention.

WHAT IS POSSIBLE WITH THINKING PHILOSOPHICALLY ABOUT PROSTHETICS?

In my training as a philosopher, I studied Heidegger's phenomenology. In this approach, and what I learned from reading his *Being and Time* (1962), is the explanatory potential of an ontological and existential account of "being-in-the-world"—our "worlded" existence as we project it—distinct from our ordinary, even scientific understanding of the world and our "ontic" interpretations. Heidegger's work, particularly in this way, was influential on later philosophers, particularly, Sartre, Beauvoir, Arendt, Levinas, and, to some degree, Fanon and Foucault.

When thinking about prosthetics and, with a demand for a non-ableist account of possibility, the way in which the world is "worlded," or fashioned and fabricated, so that human existence is *survivable* in relation to the earth,[45] thinking of the world in terms of its equipmentality becomes one approach worth developing. I want to think that we might make "ready to hand" a theory about what can be "ready *at* hand." This is Heidegger's theoretical distinction: that we fabricate things in the world that are ready-to-hand and unveil the ontic, everyday meaning to those things that are "present-at-hand." Heidegger is known for the example of the hammer. There is no specific thinking about the hammer, except in relation to its function as a tool in relation to the task of making: hammering nails with the hammer makes it ready-to-hand in its proper environmental, (now invisible) functional proximity to other tools and objects. When ready-to-hand, the hammer is not only perceived as an object in itself, but also in relation to its function in the world. The furniture of the world recedes into its place, as the stuff "of a home."

Yet, when the hammer does not work, suddenly it emerges into focus as something "of ontological concern," "present-at-hand," and, for Heidegger, this concern over the broken tool is bound to an existential projection of "Care" [*Sorge*]. When a tool is present-at-hand, we become concerned about its form, its figure and function such that it is a "thing" that will need to be *fixed*. We contemplate it as an object outside of its former environmental circumscription.

Siebers describes how easily *but mistaken* the distinction can be between tools and prostheses proper:

> It is taken for granted that nondisabled people may choose when to be able-bodied. In fact, the built environment is full of technologies that make life easier for those people who possess the physical power to perform tasks without these technologies. Stairs, elevators, escalators, washing machines, leaf and snow blowers, eggbeaters, chainsaws, and other tools help to relax physical standards for performing certain tasks. . . . The moment that individuals are marked as disabled or diseased, however . . . the technologies designed to make their life easier are viewed as expensive additions, unnecessary accommodations, and a burden on society.

To this he adds, "a social construction . . . must be read" (2008, 31–32).[46]

So thinking "philosophically" about prosthetics means thinking about it not in the context of specific disabilities or to get entangled in the conflicts of interest in how prosthetic devices have served symbolically as individual identity markers,[47] instead, here I want to read not just for the social construction of disability but for the ideological connotations that reside within the dichotomy that had emerged between *prosthetics* and *tools*, and further a more non-ableist relation between them. By thinking about *inorganic* (mass produced, generic, and normalizing) prosthetics against an idea of *organic* prosthetics (as site-specific, with sensitivity, and liberatory), we might even produce a framework for fabricating world-habitability that is also, perhaps, anti-ableist.

A good starting point to challenge this dichotomy between what is ordinarily distinguished as the "tool" as opposed to the "prosthetic object" is with the experiences of those who are most subject to the differentiation. From Kathleen Downes: "Planning my daily activities—the basic things necessary to survive—is no small feat. The word spontaneous might as well belong in another language, because every aspect of living with a severe physical disability is anything but spontaneous for me."[48]

We could start with those tools most ready-to-hand in relation to the world—those that *mark time* and those that *mark space*. In fact, if the precarity of some bodies and minds manifests as a specialized vulnerability, like not having access to a spontaneity in living, we could imagine that the tools needed in these situations would be different than those for whom spontaneous and non-preplanned activities were more accessible. Here, I am really starting with the idea that every tool is a prosthetic device of some kind, inversing the ordinary assumption that prosthetics are specialized tools for those who have impairments, deficits, etc., that is, all the normative characteristics of being disabled.

When tools break as with when prosthetics no longer work, I want to argue that this is where any of us are vulnerable to the tragic. I do not find something phenomenally distinctive when a construction crane breaks[49]—in that *it is a tragic situation*—than when a motorized wheelchair fails, to when someone dies of malaria because they do not have access to mosquito nets. *What makes the construction crane related to the motorized wheelchair to the mosquito net?* It is that each shows how dependent each person can be to tools, large or small; the precariousness of our existence is in how we might not have tools that we need for survival or that tools break down, particularly and tragically render vulnerable bodies precarious in their failure, and particularly when we need them most to work.

If we follow through with this philosophical insight—that *all tools are prosthetics*—then what follows becomes more open-ended: that tools created for mass market consumption also make for *created dependencies*. Technologies available for the specialized few now become the source of market creation. The existential and political difficulty is that these created markets—with now created needs and dependencies—competes with those precarities that come with bodies and minds that cannot fold into the normative models of commodified dependency. As a good phenomenologist, allow me to experiment with the "need" to tell time.

The need for what I will call "time-telling"—to know exactly what time it is—comes into the field of concern both environmentally and physiologically. The demands of organic being require an attention to temporality—the cycles of growth and decay—in a way that we all are dependent on these rhythms for eating, expelling, housing, medicating, culturing, incubating, resting, etc. From the baking of bread and the growing of rice, to the length of a fever to throwing out garbage, the labors and conditions can be marked and compared to other like labors and conditions, giving us expectation, that power to plan, anticipate, and imagine.[50] With these expectations, we can also negotiate them against counterevidence and marked differentiation: *this time as opposed to last time.* We become dependent on past labors, labors that create new conditions, the conditions for expectation—including emotional labors like anticipation—as well as the tools needed for these labors. Keeping time needs measure; what Heidegger had described as the creation of "clock time." He also talked about the worldliness of clock time as it becomes differentiated with other temporalities: geological time, astronomical time.

Present technology has permitted an absurd amount of *exactness* in our telling of clock time in a need for synchronicity. Synchronicity in itself is not of particular virtue outside of the economic and cultural conditions that have come to demand it.[51] In fact, any *lag* against synchronicity, especially as it relates to personal and privileged forms of consumption, has become quite *intolerable* if not also carries the characteristics of "disablement." What dependency there is for so much of daily life to be "on" time! Here I take the lead from Richard Gilman-Opalsky's *Precarious Communism* (2014):

> Capitalism does not only separate the haves from the have-nots . . . our post-industrial, post-Fordist, realities have fragmented, bifurcated, and internally diversified class identifications so that class is now but one cleavage amongst others. . . . A person's level of anxiety, alienation, or precariousness does not correspond directly to their level of material security in everyday life (2014, 19–20).

In this way, the devices we now use to maintain these diversified identifications are very much tied still to the global production of capital and prioritization of profit protectionism, and these mechanisms exclude individual bodies while maintaining normative dependencies. The temporal conditionality of these dependencies are exciting anxieties over precariousness—as sites of created dependence and in need of defense—situating some as already more easily accommodated by the standards of the global economy. Yet for others, simply by their exclusion from "material security in everyday life," are in positions more dangerous and harmful, and perhaps only in how they must now sustain more emotional and invisible care labor, in the fact that this kind of situatedness is fundamentally anxiety-producing.

Gilman-Opalsky states that "it is rather easy to disclose that most everyone confesses the irrationality of certain arrangements in the relations of power, of the agenda for a 'reasonable' life of work and reward" (20) but goes on to question the "unplanned surrender of our conscious energy to work and its psychological comportment" citing Manuel Castells' *End of Millennium*:

> The information technology revolution induced the emergence of informationalism, as the material foundation of a new society. Under informationalism, the generation of wealth, the exercise of power, and the creation of cultural codes came to depend on the technological capacities of societies and individuals . . . Information technology became the indispensable tool for the effective implementation of processes of socio-economic restructuring. Particularly important was its role in allowing the developing of networking as a dynamic, self-expanding form of organization of human activity. This prevailing networking logic transforms all domains of social and economic life.[52]

Gilman-Opalsky goes on to point out how the tools and devices fabricated in service to this system, like the cellphone, and a system that contains a precognitive "irrational *cum* rational logic" are disconnecting bodies from minds, structurally shaping everyday life according to "cellular time," and with that, *free time* is "being colonized just as geographic space once was, and time is disappearing" (25–26).

What Gilman-Opalsky calls "work," ideologically manifests in the ableist meaning of "employability"—that work and reward are so intimately tied, that income-bearing productivity still weighs one's personhood as "defensible" existence. In plainer language, there is an excitableness in not being able to work, in being a "burden" to others and society if one does not "work," needing to justify one set of dependencies over another, as the most valuable "versions of the body . . . [of] morphology in general" (Butler 2010, 53). But this is not a benign framework; rather, from it emerges "scenes" of "extraordinary subjugation" (62). Butler's context:

> It follows then, that certain kinds of bodies will appear more precariously than others . . . [which] underwrite[s] the idea of . . . human life that is worth protecting, sheltering, living, mourning. These normative frameworks establish in advance what kind of life will be a life worth living, what life will be a life worth preserving, and what life will be worthy of being mourned. . . . Lives [are] divided into those representing certain kinds of states and those representing threats to state-centered liberal democracy, so that war can then be righteously waged on behalf of some lives, while the destruction of other lives can be righteously defended (53).

The aesthetic yet arbitrary framework for making war reveals how there has been an accelerated "tolerance" for indifference, an inhuman expectation of habitability according to a neoliberalized misogynist culture, and also can best reveal those ableist tendencies and dispositions, as they already do in terms of gender.

If, as Butler states it, what is at "stake are the conditions that render life sustainable," and "affects . . . [are] the very stuff of ideation and critique" (2010, 33–34), then I want to supplement this by describing the cultivation of what I call *receptive affections*, for the sake of *accepting* and *expecting* the diversified and spontaneity of being in the world as already a *failure* of preconceived, normative, and ableist expectations:

- *Patience*, as a plural and temporal openness to alterity, is a practice of resistance against the push for global markets, especially as these markets intensify the values of expediency, efficiency, synchronicity, and acceleration.
- *Generosity* is the receptive affection of extension and welcome of the other as other. This is a radical and spontaneous, existential phenomenon, as in: the moment the mother who is hungry instead gives the bread to her child.[53]

In this context, patience and generosity are a temporal and spatial redress for the general, globalizing ethos that has diminished any affection for alterity.[54]

These virtues are meant as counteractive to the insensitivity of global forces and economically-motivated indifference as some prosthetics are fabricated and made "ready *at* hand." The difficulty I am addressing here is in how inorganically—impatiently and ungenerously—tools are made for a normative world. This is to argue that *technē*—the phenomenal quality of technological innovation and production—cannot be limited to the futural imagining of transhumanist (now read: ableist) ideologies. It is important that there is a "problem-posing" of these ideological and material inheritances, especially as they divide the privileged from the marginalized, the seemingly productive and defensible from the "unproductive" and "indefensible." This also means to challenge ideas about what counts as critical need against commodified and created needs, without prioritizing or reorganizing the prioritization for the fabrication of tools for those needs that serve the normate.

As Brill reflects on Grosz's discussion of "prosthetic tendencies," she puts out a call for us to work toward "sufficient conceptual tools," especially because, "while the investigation into life's prosthetic tendency reveals many things, amongst them are new ways of conceiving of and speaking about the various forms of violence and vulnerability living beings enact" (2011, 250). In this way, these philosophical questions about prosthetics are neither apolitical nor ought they be ethically neutral. This must be a worlded, real-time exercise and not an escape[55] from the ethico-existential demands of nonviolence and vigilance for the vulnerable other. One outcome here is the concern for prosthetic conceptualization having priority for critical need: in its responsive *timeliness* and in *attentiveness* to precarity as it bears on some more than others.

Educational institutions are drivers in this system and blueprint future determinations of dependency and interdependency. Theoretical prosthetics could be modeled in such a way that there is more "room" for affective experiences, a more active address of ableism in its exercise, shaping possibilities where only impossibilities are the dominant scheme. Ableist attitudes and ideologies run unchecked in an "ignorance that poses as knowledge,"[56] especially in the ways we fill the world with "furnishings" that makes *no room* except for a fixed few.

This is my warning: if we allow a technology-driven culture, with an economy dependent on device commodification, and then leave ourselves open to the uncritical segue into an inhumanism through transhumanist ideology,[57] already literate in ableist attitudes and affections for the eradication of disability and fixing of all afflictions, then we have welcomed the fabrication of an eugenic toolkit as it uncritically and aesthetically prevails as the "free" and "best" choice for the future. The humanistic resistance to this ideological dominance of ableist affections, anxieties, and preferences would also mean demanding a more ecologically sound, sustainable *world habitation*, more pluralist and organic, sustainable and infinitely more empowering than "*each man for himself.*"

Epilogue

Parts and wholes

People with disabilities have forgotten how to suffer and be still.

Tobin Siebers, (2008, 35).[1]

IS A NON-ABLEIST FUTURE POSSIBLE?

There is a questionable *metaphysical essentialism* to ableism—pervasive in thinking and in attitudes—that, in these philosophical meditations, I have hoped to circumscribe in scale and scope. As Levinas states it: "A breakdown in essence is needed, so that it not be repelled by violence . . . [for] the little humanity that adorns the earth, a relaxation of essence to the second degree is needed . . . [this] weakness is needed. This relaxation of virility without cowardice is needed for the cruelty our hands repudiate" (1998/1981, 185). And, as Sara Brill warns: "any appeal to health understood as a return to balance or wholeness simply fails to take the full scope of prosthetic ambiguity . . . [we are required] to move beyond health . . . beyond any naïve vitalism that valorizes strength, force, the will as such, etc." (2011, 250). From Levinas to Brill, the move toward non- or even anti-ableist thinking will need to include a disposal of any eroticism toward unification and—in effect, all choreographies toward a climax in the conquering of the alien Other—presently functioning as the anthem of ableist systems.

Ableism manifests in ways that are intersectional with other biases better described, yet has its own properties of distortion and dehumanization. One important outcome of this work is the discovery of differential modes of active *dismemberment* at the heart of all ableist operations as a thematic to partially map its scope and scale. These meditations have been on those ideological and affective "hot spots"; such that I could think through those concepts dense with deeply-embedded ableist connotations. By describing some of what I found to be the more problematic cases, and by inverting affective assumptions that are sedimented into the more familiar social and cultural (and particularly neoliberal and bureaucratic) institutions, I hope to have placed a "pause"[2] where most ableist affections reside as well as opened up dialogue for what has been simply assumed in the most ableist ways, its characteristic "stickiness" that is passed along unpacked and from one generation to the next.

When teaching Critical Disability Theory, I would start the course by discussing the image by Picasso (Figure 6.1) asking for first impressions. Students, knowing the course was something about disability (and that being the only word contented and meaningful to them in the course title), stated that the image looked "broken" and "handicapped." There was an immediate surprise, sometimes audible, once I revealed Picasso's title for his image, an *acrobat*. This kind of shift in perceived expectation and normative association is intimately linked to one's vulnerability to otherness, signaled by the fact that we have yet to understand what it is that we think we know and have only assumed.

Also pictured here is Frida Kahlo painting her body cast (Figure 6.2) as an alternative to the play on the image of "bodiedness"—not clearly having

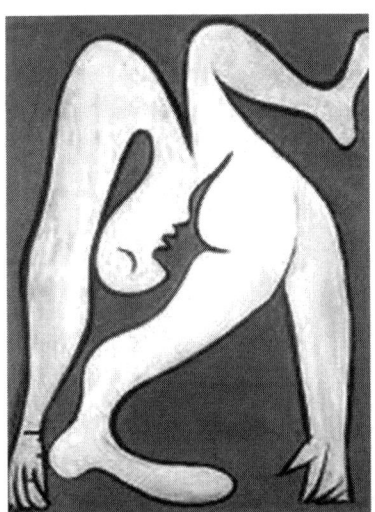

Figure 6.1 Pablo Picasso, *Acrobat* (1930). *Source*: Copyright © 2017 Estate of Pablo Picasso/Artists Rights Society (ARS), New York.

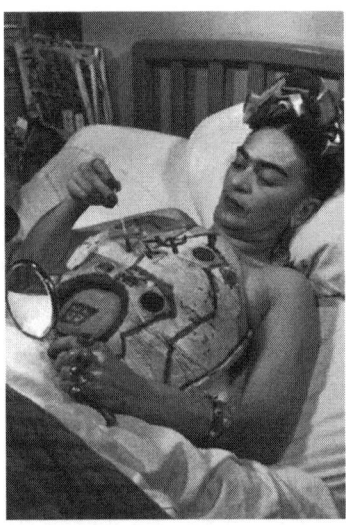

Figure 6.2 Frida Kahlo Painting her Body Cast Photographed by Juan Guzmán, (1951). Courtesy of Throckmorton Fine Art, Inc.

preference for ablebodiedness and always challenging her own sense and general imaginary of embodiment—and I tend to find her to be better reference for this challenge to the ableist imagination, particularly over Picasso's utilization and imagination of the bodily image. More specifically, I have written on Kahlo, who I argue was misread as narcissistic,[3] defending her art practice as a counterexample to the traditional idea of the "artist" (and, ironically, I had previously compared her to Picasso, who was, by my reading, narcissistic).[4]

I think Kahlo provides an exemplary case of prosthetic possibility that is both aesthetic and ethical, radically feminist, political, and personal. There is no narcissism in her returning to herself as subject matter for beautification, experimenting with abjection, as there is no narcissism in her many, diverse self-portraits.[5] I had presented an extension of this argument to a group of first-year college students, in the way that self-portraiture challenges ableist narcissism by "taking on the self" as a form of affective self-critique[6] as well as argued it to be a difficult but necessary and ethically obligating activity.[7] As an ethos, taking on a mode of affective self-critique is most challenging because it is to confront long-standing, inherited, and embedded assumptions about one's own ableist narcissism.

In this same presentation, I again compared one of Kahlo's self-portraits, (Figure 6.3) but juxtaposed with a controversial photo shoot in *Interview Magazine* of Kylie Jenner using a "golden" wheelchair as a prop;[8] the juxta-position, for me, begged the question: *what is with the insistence on ableist white-washing of women's bodies?* What is the state of the cultural imagination when the dominant and celebrated *preference* is "crip-face"[9] or finding "fun" in watching ablebodied people pretending to be disabled, or, better than that, "catching" people defrauding the "system"?[10]

As the other bookend to my Critical Disability Theory course, one of the last reflective assignments I gave to my students was to meditate on a question that I took from what is implied by Burch and Sutherland's arguments in "Who's Not Yet Here? American Disability History" (2006). I asked them: "What do you think is the future of disability?"[11] Most models, when thinking about the future, were still medicalizing disability, or instead sought some "rehabilitative" goal. From Burch and Sutherland:

> In . . . these paradigms, disabilities, and all complications related to them, reside *within* the individual. They imply or state explicitly that if an individual's disabilities could be cured, all related problems would also be cured. This has broad implications . . . [that] disabled people . . . [must] not just . . . "get better" but also to "be better" (128).

A few students caught my "test" embedded in the question: this question itself had something suspiciously ableist about it. One challenge to both of

Figure 6.3   Frida Kahlo, *Self Portrait with the Portrait of Doctor Farill,* **(1951).** *Source:* Copyright © 2017 Banco de Mexico Diego Rivera and Frida Kahlo Museums Trust, Mexico/Artists Rights Society (ARS), New York.

these limiting paradigms might need to include *asking different questions* about a non-ableist future like, "What makes for deviance? Who is deviant?" while challenging other associations with disability, like victimization or commodified performance (133). We could also ask, "What makes for consent? What are the conditions for true consent?" especially when we think of all the harm inflicted when social and emotional, political and cultural exchanges—in body, in mind, *with* bodies and minds—habitualize dependencies and codependencies into disablements. What does a social and cultural construction of rich and meaningful interdependencies look like, at least in the sense of imagining? Or rather, what would these interdependencies *feel* like—their affective and liberatory qualities if they were also to be treated as not only culturally *viable*, but also as culturally and politically *preferable*? The questions I've raised here, by not asking curiously about disability, or in order to speculate on the lives of disabled persons, or to imagine the future of disability in an unsolicitous way, are intended to instead address the ableist construction of disability in a philosophical, phenomenological way.

Burch and Sutherland find there to be a more non-ableist shift in the historiographical research and to follow the lead of Disability Studies scholars by utilizing more ethnographic than biographic narratives, "Although biographical portraits . . . are compelling, several . . . scholars have turned their attention . . . to examine Disability within the intimate history of families" (136). So, as Siebers also states it, "The autobiographical account has been the preferred method of representing disability to a wider public," while adding a caution, "the lives of people with disabilities will never be improved if we do not change the current political landscape" (2008, 47).

I take these insights to mean that the purpose of this philosophical mapping out of the scale and scope of ableism is to not neglect or to challenge the authority of these autobiographical narratives, but to politicize seemingly neutral attitudes and dispositions—what I call "affections"—in favor of self-critique: in order to "excise" ableist bias. This mode of self-critique is not just personal selfhood, (and in that way, each of us might decide to take on that task as best they can)[12]; rather, I think it includes the Western modality of "self"-hood, the egoic, "open mouth"[13] of identity in the Western world that seems to be without satiation.

In defining ableism, I wanted to examine the emotional and affective qualities of this bias. Dana Lee Baker has described the problem of *care* versus *cure* (2011, 146–150), especially as this conflict informs the mission of disability services organizations, from the nonprofit, to the governmental and for profit. As Baker states that, "An intriguing factor of the relationships between care and care-oriented agendas is the usually strong prevalence of unquestioned assumptions in the surrounding political and public discourse" (164). Yet, I take this as the problem of understanding how philosophical interventions and exorcisms[14] could also be *therapeutic*.

For example, Baker describes how educators follow current neurology that understood neurological development to take place in certain stages, but neurologists have since discovered that "[Baker quoting Lehrer] the mind is never beyond neurogenesis . . . as long as we are alive" (152). Educators, medical professionals, service providers, and family members, have all taken on ableist assumptions with less-than-critical, less-than-philosophical attitudes in the way the developmental assumptions about neurology get applied in both care and cure.

As it regards this idea of neurogenesis, if the brain is full of possibility in the way it could revise and rewire itself, haven't we closed off possibilities and maybe conditioned harm by that developmental model—in word and in deed? What I add to this question is hopefully the case as I've already made it: that these assumptions, in these everyday modes, in the corresponding media, medical, and cultural models, makes for a built environment in which ableism operates efficiently and surreptitiously—not helpful, not neutral, but are instead harmful despite all good intentions. If these kinds of overarching assumptions about the way bodies and minds work (much less what is physically, intellectually, or emotionally possible) in their assumed neutrality are instead harmful, then how removed are we from any genuinely therapeutic interventions? Simply stated: those practices based on ideas of care or cure may actually be nontherapeutic and reinforcing arbitrary distributions of precarity. The urgency in this latter assertion is really only meaningful if we also hearken to the testimonies that come from disabled experience for their truth-telling, as credible, as a command to responsibility and accountability.

How might we develop a non-ableist approach in the way we incorporate new knowledge of scientific and technological innovations? How can the political and personal content of medical diagnoses, educational pedagogical practices, and cultural understanding, (particularly popular and self-help culture) transfer less ableist thinking and affections rather than more? For instance, will the study of epigenetics[15] become another form of parent-blaming or will it distribute the investments—material and nonmaterial—for less ableist, more diverse and site-specific interventions? For whatever scientific research and cultural investments, we have funded and developed so far, too often, addressing ableism is negligible or nonexistent; instead, there is a continued and permissible sustainment of popular myths with reductive caricatures in the context of "freakshows." From Garland-Thomson's "Staring at the Other" (2005):

> We have ritualized encounters with such unexpected bodies throughout Western history by staging hyperbolic displays of what is taken to be the extraordinary. From antiquity through modernity, unusual and inexplicable bodies considered to be monsters and freaks have been displayed by the likes of medieval kings and P.T. Barnum for entertainment and profit in courts, street fairs, dime museums, and side shows. In the last two centuries, medical science has securely moved such unruly bodies into laboratories, operating rooms, and medical texts in order to establish the borders of the normal and predictable. . . . Indeed, the history of disabled people in the Western world is in part the history of being on display, of being visually conspicuous while being politically and socially erased. Like the word "fascination," a whole vocabulary of words such as "marvelous" and "wonderful" that described the common practice of staring at what I have called extraordinary bodies has faded today into vagueness now that it is considered bad taste to stare at disabled people as a middle class form of entertainment. . . . Monstrous bodies were a particular type of prodigy, which were wonderful and awful—in the sense of inspiring wonder and awe—events such as comets and earthquakes. In a pre-scientific world, unexpected and unexplainable occurrences were the maps of truth that had to be read by intense looking. The term "freak" has also been unmoored in the 20th century from its specific original meaning. "Freak" meant whimsical or capricious before today's notion of abnormal [hijacked] it.

Ralph Savarese makes what I think is a most helpful move toward a non-ableist (and maybe anti-ableist) future (if that is possible):

> If cosmopolitanism is the idea of a transnational community, the feeling of being at home everywhere in the world, then neurocosmopolitanism is the idea of a transneuro community, the feeling of being at home with all manner of neurologies.[16]

And this is where cosmopolitanism as an ethical framework is helpful—but again, not neutral when these cosmopolitan theorists remain silent on the issues of ableism and disability.[17] There is Fiona Kumari Campbell who notices the possibility of the cosmopolitan ethic:

> Cosmopolitanism is a quality of exile and strangeness to one's self through reflection. As an encounter of not knowing, cosmopolitanism is not easily cultivated. It is this regulation of the conduct of conduct in cosmopolitanism that I argue has the capacity to rethink and thus contribute to the undoing of ableist exclusions (2010, 77).

The *feeling at home* can be ableist privilege; more than this, feeling at home anywhere in the world as a cosmopolitan objective, one that must welcome the stranger, reflecting the ways in which one already feels at home in the world in how it "fits," also needs to account for those assumptions that render some more strange than fit. A future cosmopolitanism that addresses ableism must be decolonizing and challenge the ways some people never get to feel at home,[18] made to be misfits,[19] or socially, physically, economically, personally, and/or politically segregated in the way of borders and prohibitions, particularly as it may be enforced bureaucratically and institutionally.

As I finish this work,[20] the world is trying to account for Syrian refugees who flee their homes and homeland at great peril and with much violence and harm sustained; the greater media concern reinforces nationalist interests, reciting narratives of homeland security: "we cannot admit terrorists." Yet, ironically, while we give currency to and exploit the image of a refugee child washed up on a beach, there is less-to-no attention for the "hidden" victims of statelessness—the fabrication of vulnerable lives situated by fight and flight, rendered more precarious, more disposable in a new phenomenon of global homelessness, including disabled and elderly refugees.[21]

In the paradoxicality of this epilogue on "parts and wholes," it remains a state of inconclusion as a conclusion, without resolve, and necessarily so. Many questions have been raised; my responses not only have been *speculative* and *meditative*, but also, ultimately, I intend them to continue to be dialogical, rather than rhetorical. There is no holistic symbiosis or synthesis of ideas for this philosophical exorcism (so-called) of ableism. *A persistent partiality* to all that is—especially that held precariously between the world and oblivion—is the liminality that has been addressed here. By scoping out the ways in which "being in the world" is not a remembering but an ableist system of *dismembering*—a marginalization, perhaps, throughout these meditations, I provoked a serious question about the significance of an urgent ethical and political demand: that lives made precarious because of the dominance of ableist ideology and affections are now truly grievable, each one of us more morally culpable than we might have previously imagined. An alternative—a conceptual token to begin the resistance and confrontation with ableism—is that we design and defend systems of relation that *en-member* rather than merely enable (or, through deficit, disable). By *enmem-berment*, I mean imagining—truly entertaining—ways in which we ought to make space, maybe "hold space,"[22] so each member otherwise dismembered, otherwise disposed, instead can have place and context for not just being, merely existing or "surviving," but rather prosthetically sustaining a generous persistent partiality of belonging in the world.

Notes

FOREWORD

1. This volume, 144.
2. This volume, author's prologue, xxviii.

PROLOGUE

1. Thanks to Monica Vilhauer for her review of this prologue.

2. In chapter 4 on precariousness, I will expand on how this valuation of ablebod-iedness manifests in who counts and how they are counted as a "grievable life" and who does not.

3. At the outset of these meditations, I want to acknowledge that my use of the language of and identification with 'ablebodiedness' may be problematic. See Lauren Smith-Donohoe's, "It's Time to Retire 'Ablebodied'," in which she argues (2017, ¶¶4–5):

"Ablebodied" separates physical from cognitive, developmental, neurological, and psychiatric disability, it sends a message that disabled people are split between those whose "minds are fine" and are therefore deserving of respect, while implying those whose minds aren't fine are not deserving of the same respect and accommodation or inclusion. Further, it ignores that many people have physical and cognitive, developmental, neurological, or psychiatric disabilities.

Perhaps the most insidious thing that the term "ablebodied" does, is reinforce the medical model by implying that ability lies inside bodies rather than inside the social structure. It directly refutes the social model of disability, which says, in the words of the late and fabulous Stella Young, "that we are more disabled by the society that we live in than by our bodies and our diagnoses." Meaning that all the abilities in all the bodies and minds are valuable and important, but the world is structured to enable some, while disabling others. As disability activists, self-advocates, and allies seek to show the world a new lens with which to view disability, i.e. the social model, they are undermining it every time they use "ablebodied" when they are describing people who are enabled by the ableist structure of society.

Although in common use, these concerns are fair but in my context, I specifically use the distinction in order to begin the 'scoping out' of ableist bias. Ablebodiedness is a place holder and up for interrogation – and the medical model is challenged in this project specifically in my chapter on diagnosis.

4. I make this point an "arguable" one because the author of speciesism, Peter Singer, has done extensive damage in his disableism and ableist arguments about the value and status of disabled persons. See Kittay, "The Personal is Philosophical is Political: A Philosopher and Mother of a Cognitively Disabled Person Sends Notes from the Battlefield" in *Metaphilosophy*, Vol. 40, Nos. 3–4, Malden, MA: Blackwell Publishing Ltd., (July 2009) pp. 607–627.

5. I want to acknowledge Fiona Kumari Campbell's *Contours of Ableism* (2009) as well as Tobin Siebers' *Disability Theory* (2008) as foundational companion texts to my project.

6. This is in reference to one of Hannah Arendt's "favorite expressions," *Denken ohne Geländer*—thinking without banisters. Richard Bernstein describes it thusly: "If we are to engage in the activity of thinking after the break in tradition, then we can't rely on banisters or fixed points; we are compelled to forge new ways of thinking and new concepts. . . . Thinking is not to be identified or confused with calculation, means-end rationality, or even scientific knowing. . . . For Arendt, keeping thinking alive has the utmost practical significance . . . [thinking] without banisters is the alternative to both foundationalism and nihilism. And this type of thinking is urgently needed to understand violence" (2013, Preface ¶¶1–2).

7. It may be worth noting that critique is not sound critique if it is fully ableist. For example: Trump's *Crippled America*. See discussion summarized on Buzzfeed online, "Disability Activists Hijack Donald Trumps [*sic*] Book Title, Crippled America, On Twitter And Here Are The Highlights!," (Accessed Dec 1, 2015). http://www.buzzfeed.com/ninagc/disability-activists-hijack-donald-trumps-book-tit-ird7

8. See Valerie Strauss's report, (Accessed Jan 20, 2017). http://www.washingtonpost.com/news/answer-sheet/wp/2017/01/20/trump-white-house-takes-down-website-pages-about-disabilities/?utm_term=.8249d25b766f

9. Kim Sauder interviewed and quoted by Jim Brown, "Meryl Streep's speech was patronizing to people with disabilities" for *The 180*. CBC Radio, (Accessed Jan 11, 2017). http://www.cbc.ca/radio/the180/what-not-to-love-about-meryl-streep-s-speech-more-on-ptsd-and-violence-and-reform-politics-not-elections-1.3930068/meryl-streep-s-speech-was-patronizing-to-people-with-disabilities-1.3930082. More bitingly, Alistair Baldwin, self-described as "being the one designated disabled person invited to the 2017 Golden Globes after my name was pulled out of 'The Bottom Of The Gene Pool,' a rusting above-ground swimming pool filled with the names of gossip columnists who aren't legally allowed to donate their sperm," titles his response, "'Disability Impressions Offensive' Decrees Meryl Streep To Room Of

Award-Winning Disability Impressionists" with parodic interviews of Eddie Red-mayne, Emma Stone, and Tom Hanks, actors who have all been awarded and honored for "cripping-up." From SBS.com.au, (Accessed Jan 12, 2017). http://www.sbs.com.au/comedy/article/2017/01/12/disability-impressions-offensive-decrees-meryl-streep-room-award-winning. For a detailed account of the phenomenon of "cripping-up," see blogpost by crippled scholar (http://crippledscholar.com/tag/crip-face/), who states (emphasis added):

> Disability rights activists have coined terms like *cripping up*, *crip face*, *disability drag* and *cripicature* to describe the trend of nondisabled actors taking on disabled roles. There are many examples of disabled people protesting the practice and demanding better representation for disabled people on screen.
>
> In my opinion there is no actual disability representation in a film or television show unless there is an actual disabled person involved. Simply putting in a disabled character [then] casting a nondisabled actor is not representation. It is in fact the active denial of representation.

10. Established by disability activists, Dominick Evans and Lydia Brown, respectively.

11. "On Saturday, January 21, 2017, Maria Town . . . tweeted about an experience she had after the Women's March in Washington, DC and posed a question about what access truly means." Posted on storify.com by Alice Wong, http://storify.com/SFdirewolf/accessibleorganizingmeans-disabled-people-on-acces.

12. Also the title of James Charlton's book, (2000). This was a slogan he reports that he first heard used by South African disability activists.

13. See Rosemarie Garland-Thomson's "Misfits: A Feminist Materialist Disability Concept" (Summer 2011, 594):

> Misfitting serves to theorize disability as a way of being in an environment, as a material arrangement. A sustaining environment is a material context of received and built things ranging from accessibly designed built public spaces, welcoming natural surroundings, communication devices, tools, and implements, as well as other people. A fit occurs when a harmonious, proper interaction occurs between a particularly shaped and functioning body and an environment that sustains that body. A misfit occurs when the environment does not sustain the shape and function of the body that enters it. The dynamism between body and world that produces fits or misfits comes at the spatial and temporal points of encounter between dynamic but relatively stable bodies and environments.

14. From "10 Questions About Why Ableist Language Matters, Answered" posted on everydayfeminism.com, (Accessed Nov 7, 2014: http://everydayfeminism.com/2014/11/ableist-language-matters/)

15. In reference to Elizabeth Young-Bruehl's book, *Hannah Arendt: For Love of the World*, (Second Edition, New Haven, CT: Yale University Press, 2004).

16. Throughout this manuscript, I will use the term ableist for someone who expresses ableist ideas or attitudes regardless of their ablebodiedness; a disablist is

someone who defends or justifies ableist ideas or attitudes. A dominant disableist assumption is that an aversion to disabilities and people with disabilities is "natural"; the aversion itself is ableist.

17. From Arendt's essay, "Heidegger at Eighty" quoted here (*The New York Review of Books*, Oct 21, 1971, 51). Notoriously, this problem of the apolitical philosopher is embodied in her personal and professional relationship to Martin Heidegger, representing for her both a great thinker, having been both his student and lover, but also a failed thinker in his participation in Nazi Party and as rector of the University of Freiburg in 1933. Available online: http://www.nybooks.com/articles/archives/1971/ oct/21/martin-heidegger-at-eighty/?page=2). Also Arendt's "Heidegger the Fox" in *Essays in Understanding* 1930–54 (Jerome Kohn, ed., Harcourt Brace, 1994).

18. And on this point, I have good reason to hope that I am wrong. From Angela Davis' speech at the Women's March on Washington, DC, (http://www.elle.com/ culture/career-politics/a42337/angela-davis-womens-march-speech-full-transcript/ posted by Elle.com, Accessed Jan 21, 2017):

> Over the next months and years we will be called upon to intensify our demands for social justice to become more militant in our defense of vulnerable populations. Those who still defend the supremacy of white male hetero-patriarchy had better watch out.
>
> The next 1,459 days of the Trump administration will be 1,459 days of resistance: Resistance on the ground, resistance in the classrooms, resistance on the job, resistance in our art and in our music.
>
> This is just the beginning and in the words of the inimitable Ella Baker, "We who believe in freedom cannot rest until it comes."

19. By "honest," I mean something deeply Socratic: that about which we speak and think, we don't really know as much as we think we know, therefore, we must be honest and ask the honest (not merely rhetorical or speculative) questions while being open to radical reinstruction.

20. As Arendt states it: "Ideologies—isms which to the satisfaction of their adherents can explain everything and every occurrence by deducing it from a single premise—are a very recent phenomenon and, for many decades, played a negligible role in political life" (1973, 468).

21. While the "aim of a totalitarian education has never been to instill convictions but to destroy the capacity to form any," Arendt is most concerned with the iron band of terror in which: "the capacity of both and experience and thought" is lost and "the iron band of total terror leaves no space for . . . private life and that the self-coercion of totalitarian logic destroys [the] capacity for experience and thought just as certainly as [the] capacity for action." (1973; 468, 474)

22. See Julia Kristeva's *Powers of Horror: An Essay on Abjection*, (New York, NY: Columbia University Press, 1982, 9–10):

> We may call it a border; abjection is above all ambiguity. Because, while releasing a hold, it does not radically cut off the subject from what [threatens] it—on the contrary, abjection acknowledges it to be in perpetual danger. But also

because abjection itself is a composite of judgment and affect, of condemnation and yearning, of signs and drives. Abjection preserves what existed in the archaism of pre-objectal relationship, in the immemorial violence with which a body becomes separated from another body in order to be—maintaining that night in which the outline of the signified thing vanishes and where only the imponderable affect is carried out. . . . That order, that glance, that voice, that gesture, which enact the law for my frightened body, constitute and bring about an effect and not yet a sign. I speak to it in vain in order to exclude it from what will no longer be, for myself, a world that can be assimilated. Obviously, I *am* only *like* someone else: mimetic logic of the advent of the ego, objects, and signs. But when I *seek* (myself), *lose* (myself), or experience *jouissance*—then "I" is *heterogeneous*. Discomfort, unease, dizziness stemming from an ambiguity that, through the violence of a revolt *against*, demarcates a space out of which signs and objects arise. Thus braided, woven, ambivalent, a heterogeneous flux marks out a territory that I can call my own because the Other, having dwelt in me as alter ego, points it out to me through loathing.

23. Sara Brill, in discussing Plato's analogy between physical health and intellectual virtue, says that the tyrant, who is "utterly diseased and driven mad" is also "such a person [that] will have neither freedom nor friendship" (citing Plato [576a], 2005, 300).

24. For a definition of inspiration porn, see Stella Young's TEDtalk, "I'm not your inspiration, thank you very much." Posted (Accessed June 9, 2014), http://www.youtube.com/watch?v=8K9Gg164Bsw

25. This is in reference to what Arendt describes as a state of "terror" in "Ideology and Terror" in *The Origins of Totalitarianism*, p. 464.

26. See Lilit Marcus, posted by *The Wire*, (Accessed Mar 28, 2014), http://www.thewire.com/politics/2014/03/why-you-shouldnt-share-those-emotional-deaf-person-hears-for-the-first-time-videos/359850/

27. While teaching a course on Disability and Film, I cataloged films involving or featuring disability under three categories: fictional accounts like *Extremely Loud & Incredibly Close* (2011) or *Silver Linings Playbook* (2012); films "based on a true story," like *Music Within* (2007) or *The Diving Bell and the Butterfly* (2007); or, non-fiction/documentary like *The Horse Boy* (2009) or *FIXED: The Science Fiction of Human Enhancement* (2010). We would analyze the ableist connotations in the films while unpacking one's own ableist projections while watching the film.

28. In Plato's *Meno*, Socrates questions Meno's definitions of virtue in their insufficiency: from the first question to the unresolved final question, to which he says, "but we still have to define virtue." The issue that Socrates has in this dialogue is that definitions given by "one who knows" seem to have specificities and ambiguities that cannot be verified as belonging to "all cases." Meno often defined virtue (and color and bees as the dialogue goes) by giving examples but not one that is universalizable and therefore intellectually unsatisfying. The intellectual dissatisfaction with any one specific definition is part of this Socratic style, for Socrates does not provide a definition; only dialogically interrogating the status of any one working definition.

29. For example, Larry Johnson, in "Treat emergency, not disability" argues that "Assumptions [about disability] can be wrong and sometimes very dangerous." In his case, "What brought me to the emergency room was not my blindness. But, sometimes when a person has a visible disability like blindness or is a wheelchair, it's what doctors, nurses, or ER technicians will focus on first" (*Express-News*, 11 July 2014. Available online [Accessed Jul 15, 2014]: http://m.mysanantonio.com/opinion/commentary/article/In-emergency-situations-disabled-people-are-5615774.php)

30. See Kim E. Nielsen's *A Disability History of the United States* (Boston, MA: Beacon Press, 2013). This book outlines the ways in which disabled identity is historically constructed, especially as they have become associated with "monstrosities," or "aberrations" made not for public representation, but instead relegated to the margins of social life.

31. I have not yet expanded on the social construction model of disability but am, for the most part, assuming it. The different models can be reviewed here: Ian Langtree, "Definitions of the Models of Disability" (2010-09-10, Revised. 2015-10-26) posted by *Disabled World*. Available online: http://www.disabled-world.com/definitions/disability-models.php.

32. Posted as "Acceptance vs. Awareness" (Accessed Apr 4, 2012). http://autisticadvocacy.org/2012/04/acceptance-vs-awareness/

33. The "flight into the self" was a kind of disorientation that is part of modernized technology and gadgetry: we avoid the other and escape into the highly "personal" world of self-interest. The "flight from the earth" is an alienation that manifests in the way we would prefer to be: out in space rather than deal to with the world as such. Both alienations lead to a kind of "de-fanged" political activity in which one only works or labors in the world but can do nothing to reshape it in its sociopolitical constitution.

34. Thinking here of the swiftness by which the Trump administration began to repeal facets of the Affordable Healthcare Act, the impacts first affecting people with disabilities. See Michelle Chen's concerns outlined in "Trump's Obamacare Repeal Could Lead to a Mental-Health Crisis" for *The Nation* (Jan 18, 2017):

> Trump has not ignored mental-health concerns, and has in fact called for more emphasis on treating opioid addiction, and strengthening veterans' mental health–care access. However, the overarching thrust of his health care–reform agenda is to let the market do the work. An increasingly profit-driven, deregulated system would simply price out the most vulnerable (¶8).

35. My definition of "privilege" comes from Levi's preface, in which he describes the kinds of questions that need to be asked after Auschwitz, somewhat different than economic or sociological definitions of privilege: "Willed ignorance and fear . . . led many potential . . . witnesses . . . to remain silent. . . . [The] privileged par excellence, that is, those who acquired privilege for themselves by becoming subservient to the camp authority, did not bear witness at all, . . . or left incomplete or distorted or totally false testimony." (1989; 15, 18).

36. For a good example of this argument, see Joel Michael Reynolds, "Trump's Greatest Insecurity: His Body" posted in *The Huffington Post* (Accessed Jun 22, 2016.)

http://www.huffingtonpost.com/entry/trumps-greatest-insecurity-his-body_us_
57605683e4b079c7cee63caa):

> We fear a "crippled" America, as his New York Times best-seller is titled,
> because "we," the ablebodied, fear being trapped in a body, in a place and time
> and situation, that we don't want. We, and not just Trump, play chicken with
> ourselves and our bodies out of fear. But here's the catch. We aren't trapped in
> our bodies. We are our bodies, as philosophers from Frantz Fanon to Simone
> Beauvoir have argued. These changing, leaky bodies afford us opportunity and
> choice. If static or permanent, they'd be less bodies and more stones or gods. To
> be sure, bodies marked by racism, sexism, cisgenderism, classism, and ableism
> get trapped. And Trump is a great trapper.
>   But his fear of bodily change and difference is about as reasonable as a fear
> of breathing or eating: these things are the stuff of life. . . . The real question is:
> what should I do with my body? The better answers to that question are based in
> justice, not fear or pride. From those questions we, in our better moments, build
> inclusive institutions, construct just laws, and organize equitable societies (¶¶3–4).

37. Which also means that one may or may not have voluntarily identified as disabled. Sometimes society labels someone disabled, or counts differences or "disfigure-
ments" as disabilities, otherwise one may need to self-identify as disabled in order to be
recognized in the context of oppressive and marginalizing social and cultural norms.

38. This might be an argument against hypothetical and speculative case study
work that philosophers and theorists have been known to engage in and purport ableist ideas in uncritical ways. As Shelley Tremain asks (Mar 28, 2017) in reference to
the use of the case study of Phineas Gage [emphasis added]:

> That Gage's situation has been exaggerated and embellished within the con-
> texts of the literature of (inter alia) neuroscience, cognitive science, philosophy
> of mind, and medicine reminds us that science, philosophy, and medicine are
> embedded social practices rather than disinterested domains that exist apart from
> and are immune to ableist biases and other elements of the apparatus of disabil-
> ity. I suggest, therefore, that we should ask these questions (among others) about
> this line of inquiry in cognitive science, philosophy of mind, and related fields:
>   *How has this (embellished) narrative about Gage contributed to the prob-
> lematization of disability in philosophy? In what ways has this mythical narra-
> tive about Gage enabled the naturalization and materialization of impairment
> within certain subfields of the discipline and thus enabled the consolidation of
> the relation between philosophy and the apparatus of disability? In what ways
> has this mythology about certain disabled people ultimately shaped, condi-
> tioned, and determined research programs and teaching in cognitive science,
> neuroscience, and philosophy of mind?*

39. Arendt's work on ideology and terror is why I titled my epilogue "parts and
wholes."

40. She challenges conceptions of the meaningful life as also the "happy life" in her passages on "Life as the Highest Good" (1958, 313–320). I also like her more personal work and how she addresses the "problem" of Heidegger as she does in "Heidegger the Fox" addressing Heidegger's apolitical philosophical style which appeared to be benign. Only recently did Heidegger's "black books" emerge revealing the darker ideological and anti-semitic dispositions in his thinking.

41. See Patricia Bowen-Moore's *Hannah Arendt's Philosophy of Natality* (London: The Macmillan Press, 1989).

42. For a good survey of Sen's capabilities approach, see Sophie Mitra's "The Capability Approach and Disability" in the *Journal of Disability Policy Studies* (Sage Publications, 2006, 16: 236. Available online: http://dps.sagepub.com/content/16/4/236). I'm thinking here particularly of the issues with Martha Nussbaum's model. From Chad Kleist, "Global Ethics: Capabilities Approach" (*Internet Encyclopedia of Philosophy*, §6b.¶2. http://www.iep.utm.edu/ge-capab/#SH6b):

> Nussbaum addresses the question of disabilities via the capabilities approach through her list. Her early formulation of the capabilities list excluded many people from the ability to live a truly human life since she required such a life to include using all five senses, for example. She has since retracted from such bold statements. However, Nussbaum (1995) does note that it would be difficult to imagine a person living a truly human life with total lack of the senses, imagination and reasoning.

43. The idea of being "earth-bound" she describes in *The Human Condition* (1958, 7), but when tied to her concerns about the totalitarian conditions that isolate then render individuals impotent, additionally uprooting them from the world and then rendering these persons "superfluous" such that they do not "belong" in the world or to the world, she states: "For confirmation of my identity I depend entirely on other people" but in conditions of totalitarianism, "I am deserted by my own self" (1973, 474–476). These connections also indicate a greater insight into the ways in which the value of persons is in *the existential possibility* of each individual that cannot be stripped by political injunction. As Arendt states it: "Totalitarian government . . . could not exist without destroying the public realm of life, that is, without destroying, by isolating men, their political capacities. But totalitarian domination as a form of government is new in that it is not content with this isolation and destroys private life as well . . . which is among the most radical and desperate experiences of man" (475).

44. This existential belonging via natality is wholly different in analytic character than arguments from "birthright" or "right to life" discourses that are theological and political in character (not existential and pre-political as I argue here). The question of pregnancy and its entanglements with childbearing as well as my critique of the sabotages and ableist discourses of pro-life rhetoric are points I reference at length in Scuro 2017.

45. Some reference to this in *Origins of Totalitarianism*, (1973, 317–323).

46. There is overlap here between the issue of ideology that I raise using Arendt and the transhumanist movement as also an ableist ideology, despite its disabled

advocates. See Melinda Hall's *The Bioethics of Enhancement: Transhumanism, Disability, and Biopolitics* (Lexington Books, 2016).

47. Again, Arendt on this point: "To be uprooted means to have no place in the world, recognized and guaranteed by others; to be superfluous means not to belong to the world at all" (1973, 475).

48. "Run Down of #CrippingtheMighty" posted on the blog, *Cracked Mirror in Shalott* (Accessed Dec 23, 2015). http://crackedmirrorinshalott.wordpress.com/2015/12/23/run-down-of-crippingthemighty/

49. See Kittay (July 2009) on this point. Also see Nel Noddings, *Caring* (1984, 26).

50. I expand on this idea in my chapter "Theory Can Heal" in *Why Race and Gender Still Matter*, (Goswami, Yount, & O'Donovan, eds., Pickering & Chatto, 2014).

51. Chapter 5 of Butler's book, *Precarious Life* (2004), was reprinted as "Precarious Life" in *Radicalizing Levinas* (P. Atterton & M. Calarco, eds., Albany, NY: SUNY Press, 2010). I want to note this point from the reprinted reference, p. 13.

52. See Andrew Roach, *DSQ* (Vol 23, No 3/4, 2003), Dan Goodley's *Disability Studies: An Interdisciplinary Introduction*, (Sage 2011), Gladys Loewen and William Pollard, "The Social Perspective" in *Journal of Postsecondary Education and Disability, Special Issue: Disability Studies* (Volume 23, Number 1, 2010).

53. According to Charles Mills, discussing White Ignorance, discusses the "doxastic environment" as one of the ten ways White Ignorance operates, (2007, 13). This quote will be cited directly later in this volume:

Imagine an ignorance militant, aggressive, not to be intimidated, an ignorance that is active, dynamic, that refuses to go quietly—not at all confined to the illiterate and uneducated but propagated at the highest levels of the land, indeed presenting itself unblushingly as knowledge (22).

See "White Ignorance" (chapter 1 in *Philosophy and Race: Race and Epistemologies of Ignorance*, Shannon Sullivan and Nancy Tuana, eds., [Albany, NY: SUNY Press, 2007]).

54. Thank you to Devonya Havis for our discussions on this point. Further discussion of Mills on white ignorance is in chapter 3.

55. See Shelley Tremain's Dialogues on Disability, http://www.newappsblog.com/2011/07/ableist-language-and-philosophical-associations.html

56. See Rosemarie Garland-Thomson's "Disability Studies: A Field Emerged" in *American Quarterly* (Volume 65, Number 4, Dec 2013, pp. 915-926).

57. Arendt argues similarly in *Origins of Totalitarianism*, "All ideologies contain totalitarian elements" (1973, 470).

58. My emphasis. McRuer cited by Scott DeShong in "Ability, Disability, and the Question of Philosophy" (*Essays in Philosophy*. Vol. 9, Iss. 1, Article 8, Jan 2008).

59. My emphasis.

60. This was based on a paper I gave at the Society for Disability Studies, "Parenting and Allyship," June 2014.

61. This is James Stanescu's characterization of Butler's work in "Species Trouble: Judith Butler, Mourning, and the Precarious Lives of Animals" cited in the Editor's

Introduction to *Hypatia* Special Issue, *Animal Others* (Gruen and Weil, eds., vol. 27, no. 3 [Summer 2012], p. 483). Butler utilizes Emmanuel Levinas' ethical metaphysics in her work on precariousness, which will be explored in the respective chapter.

62. We might reread the idea of "temporary ablebodiedness" or TAB, less as a test for ableism, but more as a way to indicate some of this idea of existential vulnerability that Butler describes with precariousness.

63. See "The 7 Principles" from the Center for Excellence in Universal Design, developed in 1997. Posted by the National Disability Authority, 2014. http:// universaldesign.ie/What-is-Universal-Design/The-7-Principles/

64. Arendt discussed "acting in concert" (and "thinking in company") as a way that the *vita activa* could be actualized as worlded, political activity. At the heart of these considerations is the problem of bureaucratic thinking as banal thinking. See one application of Arendt's concept of plurality to administration, which could be later applied to questions of disability services and administration: Michelle Rodriguez, "The Challenges of Keeping a World: Hannah Arendt on Administration," in *Polity*, (Vol. 40, No. 4, Oct, 2008), pp. 488–508.

CHAPTER 1

1. This was subsidized with a generous NEH grant through The College of New Rochelle Faculty Development Fund and I would like to thank the Development Committee in the School of Arts and Sciences for their support.

2. Aspects of this chapter were given as talks at both St. John's University in New York, "Resisting Ableism, Renegotiating the Diagnosis" and at 2014 SDS Meeting on the "Disability and Kinship" panel, "Parenting and Allyship."

3. I want to particularly thank Harold Braswell for his paper presentation (later published in *Hypatia* as "My Two Moms: Disability, Queer Kinship, and the Maternal Subject," (Winter 2015)), for his advocacy, and his organization of the Family Members of People with Disabilities Group.

4. See "Making Space Accessible is An Act of Love for Our Communities" posted by Leah Lakshmi Piepzna-Samarasinha on the blog, Creating Collective Access (Accessed 5/9/2016). http://creatingcollectiveaccess.wordpress.com/ making-space-accessible-is-an-act-of-love-for-our-communities/:

> Embedded in this is a giant paradigm shift . . . Our crip bodies aren't seen as liabilities, something that limits us and brings pity or something to nobly transcend, cause I'm just like you. Our crip bodies are gifts, brilliant, fierce, skilled, valuable. Assets that teach us things that are relevant and vital to ourselves, our communities, our movements, the whole god damn planet.
>
> If I'm having a pain day and need you to use accessible language cause I'm having a hard time language processing and you do, that's love. And that's solidarity. If I'm not a wheelchair user and I make sure I work with the non-disabled bottomliner for the workshop to ensure that the pathways through the workshop chairs are at least three feet wide, that is love and solidarity. This is how we build past and away from bitterness and [disappointment] at movements that have not cared about or valued us.

There is so much more I can say about this, but one small thing I will add, that is one small (and huge) thing you can do to ensure access: Please be scent/fragrance free to the extent that you are able to. Folks who have chemical disabilities need to be able to participate in the AMC! So it would be great if everyone could avoid using shampoo/cologne/deodorant/detergent/fabric softener that is scented/has lots of chemicals all weekend. (This includes essential oils.)

5. "About CART: Communication Access Realtime Translation (CART), also referred to as realtime captioning or live-event captioning, is a way to transcribe the spoken word into readable English text using a stenotype machine, notebook computer, and realtime software. Through the services of CART providers using the latest realtime technology combined with a stenotype machine and notebook computer, the text appears on a computer monitor or other display and serves as an important communication tool for people who are deaf, hard of hearing, or learning a second language. CART provides a complete translation of all spoken words and environmental sounds for the benefit of an individual consumer or larger group in a variety of settings, including classrooms, courtrooms, religious services, conventions and conferences, personal appointments and events, civic events, cultural presentations, or anywhere communication access is needed." From the National Court Reporters Association (www.ncra.org).

6. And this was not really a "new normal" I was adjusting to—to borrow the cliché—because it wasn't new at all; I had just not experienced it before.

7. In their review, Lydia Brown notes my use of the term, "ablebodied(ness)":

[M]any have criticized use of that term as a stand-in for all nondisabled people because it is so physical-centric. Many neurodivergent and mad people may experience life as an ablebodied person while of course remaining disabled. Naturally, the distinction relies on a distinction between body and mind, which is itself slippery and arguably a false dichotomy—autism is often considered a mental disability (to the exclusion of physical disability unless the autistic person also has a separate physical disability), but many of us experience being autistic as a whole body experience. In any case, the term "abled" or "nondisabled" seems to better recognize the concept of someone having no disability at all—while "ablebodied" and "neurotypical" seem to be more narrowly defined, and not necessarily co-constitutive.

I think that this note is important as it stands from Brown, keeping the context of my use partial and critical. Philosophically, I respond better to the "ablebodied" identification or label with how precariousness and precarity shift the "slippery" dichotomy as needed to continue to address ableism in chapter 4. That is, as I work through the addressing of ableism, I can attend to the (appropriately suspicious) label of ablebodiedness as I better unfold how deeply embedded ableism is in our fears and projections as they emerge from a more existential and undeniable precariousness of embodied existence.

8. See Emily Ladau's account at SDS 2016 in Atlanta: "Stuck in the Dirt: Why Advocating for Justice and Access Never Stops" posted with The Center for Disability Rights, (Accessed 5/16/2016). http://cdrnys.org/blog/disability-dialogue/the-disability-dialogue-stuck-in-the-dirt/

9. Safety was one priority early on in raising my child. We quickly learned a system of "boundaries"—visible and invisible—which she could negotiate if needed. Most of this was done when she was still very young and nonverbal. My daughter would later report to us that she remembered many situations in which she challenged those boundaries, as young as two years old.

10. See Peggy McIntosh's "Unpacking the Invisible Knapsack" and her 2010 "Notes for Facilitators": "My work is not about blame, shame, guilt, or whether one is a "nice person." It's about observing, realizing, thinking systemically and personally. It is about seeing privilege, [and] is about unearned advantage, which can also be described as exemption from discrimination." http://nationalseedproject.org/white-privilege-unpacking-the-invisible-knapsack.

11. One presentation, I had made a direct demand on the parents of neurotypical children: *your kid needs to hang out with my kid.*

12. Take for example, Hara Marano, writing for *Psychology Today*, under the subtitle, a "Nation of Wimps," declares, "Helicopter Parenting—it is worse than you think" (Accessed Jan 31, 2014), posted online: http://www.psychologytoday.com/blog/nation-wimps/201401/helicopter-parenting-its-worse-you-think. Marano argues that, "There are Studies showing that some parents are especially needy emotionally, expecting their children to supply the closeness missing from . . . their marriages or their own social life. However you slice it, [helicopter] parents are putting their own emotional needs ahead of the developmental needs of their children." But this label does not always apply and is also often motivated by ableist assumptions. In addition, the accusation of helicopter parenting is usually aimed at the mothers, who were also once blamed for creating their autistic children as "refrigerator mothers." From one "Rambling Autism Mom": "When the unthinkable happens—a child with autism wanders from safety and does not survive—many people rush to judgment and blame the parents. If those people had any idea what it's like to live with the level of hypervigilance our family and many others experience 24/7, their perspective would be radically different," from "Autism, Wandering, and Helicopter Parenting" posted online (Accessed May 26, 2013): http://ramblingautismmom.wordpress.com/2013/05/26/autism-wandering-and-helicopter-parenting/

13. It is worth noting how important it is not to "overshare" as well. See Carly Findlay's "When parents overshare their children's disability" posted on dailylife.com.au (Accessed Jul 27, 2015). http://www.dailylife.com.au/news-and-views/dl-opinion/when-parents-overshare-their-childrens-disability-20150724-gijtw6.html

14. For an excellent analysis of the complexity of the role of parents (particularly mothers) in the defense of children's rights in the IEP process, see Priya Lalvani and Chris Hale, "Squeaky Wheels, Mothers from Hell, and CEOs of the IEP: Parents, Privilege, and the 'Fight' for Inclusive Education" in *Understanding and Dismantling Privilege*, 5(2), 21–41. As they argue it,

> It is worth noting that in the narratives of teachers (Lalvani 2015) and of parents, it is the parents who are positioned as "fighting"; as such, educators and institutional practices become positioned as occupying the defensive role. This is remarkable in light of the vision of IDEA for equal partnerships and raises confounding questions about why parents would need to "fight" when, in fact, education in the general education classroom for

students with disabilities is the default option as mandated by IDEA (Hale, 2013). More-over, if a "battle" is required, one can expect that it will involve a considerable amount of economic and social resources.

15. As much as this is a reference to Harry Frankfurt's *On Bullshit* (2005), I actually prefer the way Melissa Kozma and Jeanine Weekes Schroer in "Purposeful Nonsense, Intersectionality and the Mission to Save Black Babies," (2014) utilize this as an intersectional analytic tool of "calling bullshit" rather than the ordinary use as a crass term.

16. It is a motto formulated purposefully as a helpful tool for thinking through one's experiences of education: *"No student-blaming, no teacher-blaming, no parent-blaming."* As I navigate the content of my Philosophy of Education course, students easily "blame" others (and to some extent themselves) for the deficits in their own education or when we discuss very problematic cases of abuse in educational con-texts (e.g., "Student Threatens Teacher at Chicago School in Video" [abc7chicago. com, Accessed Nov 2, 2015] or "Dad wires up autistic son, 10, to expose 'bullying' by teaching staff" [usnews.nbcnews.com, Accessed Apr 25, 2012]). Once we take blame out of the reading of these cases, we could then analyze the intersectional and pedagogical difficulties of these liminal cases. In effect, from a Critical Pedagogy perspective, I ask: *What can we learn from these cases? Where could be the instruc-tion for a more democratic and pluralistic engagement?*

17. From Steve Silberman: "Obviously, even a month of acceptance will not be enough to dramatically improve the lives of people on the spectrum. What could be done to make the world a more comfortable, respectful, and nurturing place for mil-lions of autistic kids and adults—now, starting today? . . . That's the question I posed to a group of self-advocates, parents, and teachers that included Nick Walker, an autistic aikido master who founded his own dojo in Berkeley; the first openly autistic White House appointee, Ari Ne'eman; Emily Willingham, one of the sharpest science writers in the blogosphere; Lydia Brown, a prolifically articulate and thoughtful 18-year-old self-advocate at Georgetown University; Todd Drezner, director of Loving Lampposts, a groundbreaking documentary on autism and neurodiversity from a father's perspec-tive; and the editors of *Thinking Person's Guide to Autism*, which is my personal recom-mendation for parents to read after their son or daughter's diagnosis" reposted as "Why 'Autism Awareness' is Not Enough: Steve Silberman (and friends) explain 'Autism Acceptance,'" (Accessed Apr 4, 2016). http://blogs.plos.org/neurotribes/2016/04/04/autism-awareness-is-not-enough-heres-how-to-change-the-world/

18. See Catherine Lord and Rebecca Jones' account of the diagnostic changes: "Behavioral dimensions would also become the indicators of how neurobiological changes occur, how they are intermeshed and how developmental pathways might be modified or built upon (Cicchetti et al., 2011; Rutter & Sroufe, 2000). This more developmental approach would focus on change, and involve reconsidering the mean-ing of the rich, complex findings from genetics and to some degree, from neurosci-ence, based on categorical conceptions of ASD and very broad dimensions as they might be linked to more specific behavioral constructs. It would also require more attention to specificity of behaviors associated with ASD, and when non-specific dimensions are of interest, their interactions with core features." Clearly, justification

for this shift is assuming that a behavioral model rather than a therapeutic support-based model would be a better model for assessment. From "Re-thinking the classification of autism spectrum disorders" in *The Journal of Child Psychology and Psychiatry*, (May 2012, (53(5)): 490–509).

19. For one narrative, see Autistic Alex, "Why you need to stop using the puzzle piece to represent autistic people," posted (Accessed April 12, 2014). http://autisticalex.wordpress.com/2014/04/12/why-you-need-to-stop-using-the-puzzle-piece-to-represent-autistic-people/. The "People not Puzzles" countercampaign is important to note. Also see: Elizabeth Svoboda, "I am not a puzzle, I am a person" (Accessed April 27, 2009) for Salon.com. http://www.salon.com/2009/04/27/autistic_culture/

20. This fear is a dynamic and complex one, read intersectionally by Marianne Pieper and Jamal Haji Mohammadi in "Ableism and Racism—Barriers in the Labour Market" for *The Canadian Journal of Disability Studies*, Vol. 3, No. 1 (2014):

> The opportunities for participation in the general labour market, however, are extremely limited for those not deemed to reach the ideal of ableism. For one, the character of the world of work has changed dramatically in the course of the neoliberal transformation of recent years. In the transition to a service economy, there are fewer and fewer long-term, continuous employment opportunities, and more and more "precarious" jobs. Value creation in business is more and more a question of the economic exploitation of a flexible and mobile labour force, where employment is temporary so as to facilitate subsequent lay-off. At the same time, maximum performance of "human resources" has become the primary imperative.Thus, the integration service consultants we interviewed for our study, and whose task it is to aid the placement of people with disabilities in the open labour market, report an extraordinarily low willingness of companies to offer permanent employment to people with disabilities. They also testify to the scandalous "dumping" wage levels offered to disabled job-seekers. The group of people diagnosed as "mentally handicapped" have to struggle with such massive employment barriers that it is only by concealing their illness and disability status that they have any chance of employment.

21. Citing Paulo Freire, "From *Pedagogy of the Oppressed*" (2009, 59) and Henry Giroux, "Critical Theory and Educational Practice," (2009, 45) respectively, in *The Critical Pedagogy Reader* (Darder et al., eds., New York, NY: Routledge).

22. Ware (2001, 115), citing Douglas Baynton's, "Disability and the justification of inequality in American history" in *The New Disability History: American Perspectives* (P. Longmore & L. Umansky, eds., New York, NY: New York University Press, 2001).

23. In conceiving of this exercise involving a kind of "emotional inventory," I was thinking of Catriona Mackenzie's, "Imagining Oneself Otherwise" reprinted in *Self & Subjectivity* (2005), whose thesis is that "affective and cognitive effects of imaginative thinking can . . . either liberate or constrain self-conception." By training ourselves for "self-reflection" and "self-definition," (288, 290), we are closer to self-understanding as "a window into our own emotional states." She states that "For example, the process of sifting through and evaluating memories, externalizing some and appropriating others, is one way in which a person can come to terms with a traumatic event in her past and reestablish some kind of equilibrium among the different elements of herself" (287). Mackenzie goes on to state, "We can represent what we might want to

be, what we wish to be possible, or just what might be or might have been possible. This is what is liberating about imagining" (294, Kim Atkins also commenting on Mackenzie, 280–282).

24. I am purposefully striking through all of the word minus the "r" so that it is clear that, although I don't euphemize or mask the term as the "r-word," I do think this word cannot remain in the text without a clear mark of it *as a slur*. Only in the context of the clinic use and context of the term have I let the word remain as is and without strikethrough.

25. While I use the word with strikethrough, there are *many* good reasons to not use the word. See Lisa Quinones-Fontanez, "The R-Word has no Place in Literature" posted on atypicalfamilia.com (Accessed Oct 14, 2012). http://atypicalfamilia.com/the-one-word-that-can-ruin-entire-book/

26. See Lydia Brown's "Violence in Language: Circling back to Linguistic Ableism" posted on autistichoya.com (Accessed Feb 11, 2014), to which they state: "This isn't about policing language or censoring words, but about critically examining how language is part of total ableist hegemony. This is about being accountable when we learn about linguistic ableism, but it is also about being compassionate to ourselves and recognizing that to varying extents, we have all participated in ablesupremacy and ablenormativity. This is about understanding the connections between linguistic ableism and other forms of ableism, such as medical ableism, scientific ableism, legal ableism, and cultural ableism." http://www.autistichoya.com/2014/02/violence-linguistic-ableism.html

27. For example, Dan Smith's "Call a kid a zebra," his review of Donovan and Zucker's *In a Different Key* (2015) and Silberman's *NeuroTribes* (2016), quips at the end of his review that having "autism" doesn't really mean anything anymore because of the pervasiveness and range of what can be considered "under the spectrum," particularly the self-identification of those with Asperger's now that the diagnosis is no longer in the DSM. He assumes it fair to state: "Not long ago, a friend used a term I'd never heard to describe a co-worker. Her co-worker was a little brusque and unsociable and she thought he might have just a bit of an autistic impairment. The term she used was 'Splashperger's.'" I can only note how offensive it can be when ablebodied and neurotypical people get to name those who they deem not quite ablebodied or neurotypical. Clearly, one can write about autism without contributing to good scholarship. Full text posted by *London Review of Books*, (May 19, 2016, Vol. 38 No. 10) pp. 11–15. http://www.lrb.co.uk/v38/n10/daniel-smith/call-a-kid-a-zebra.

28. See Michelle Rodriguez on this point: "Under totalitarianism, as the tentativeness of the link between law and its application to particular cases is destroyed, administrative attempts to change circumstances and work specific improvements are displaced by bureaucratic planning for the benefit of 'humanity' and without intentional regard for human welfare" (Oct 2008, 493).

29. See Elisabeth Barnes, "What Philosophers Get Wrong about Disability" posted by Disablity@UVA, (Accessed Dec 8, 2015). http://disability.virginia.edu/2015/12/08/what-philosophers-get-wrong-about-disability/. See also, more generally, how PhD work is for the ablebodied: "Get Help: How the Myth of Self-Sufficiency Fails PhD

Students with Mental Illness" posted by PhDisabled, (Accessed Dec 1, 2014). http://phdisabled.wordpress.com/2014/12/01/get-help-how-the-myth-of-self-sufficiency-fails-phd-students-with-mental-illness/

30. Tremain's first comment here is in DSQ (2013): http://dsq-sds.org/article/view/3877/3402 and the follow-up response in 2014: http://www.newappsblog.com/2014/03/disabling-philosophy.html.

31. Since these posts cited here, Tremain has established "Dialogues on Disability" outlined in *The Philosopher's Magazine* (Issue 72, First Quarter, 2016) and posting regular interviews on the blog, *Discrimination and Disadvantage*. For example, with Bryce Huebner, http://philosophycommons.typepad.com/disability_and_disadvanta/2016/04/dialogues-on-disability-shelley-tremain-with-bryce-huebner.html

32. This is a concept from Emmanuel Levinas, an "ethical sensibility" (1998, 98): "The interhuman, properly speaking, lies in a non-indifference of one to another, in a responsibility of one for another. . . . The interhuman is also in the recourse that people have to one another for help, before the astonishing alterity of the other has been banalized or dimmed down to a simple exchange of courtesies that has become established as 'interpersonal commerce' of customs" (1998, 100–101).

33. From Bartky's, *Femininity and Domination: Studies in the Phenomenology of Oppression*, (New York, NY: Routledge, 1990, 27).

34. Specifically, Levinas argues, "there is a radical difference between the suffering in the other, where it is unforgivable to me, solicits me and calls me, and suffering in me. . . . It is this attention to the suffering of the other that, through the cruelties of our century . . . can be affirmed as the very nexus of human subjectivity, to the point of being raised to the level of supreme ethical principle" (1998, 94).

35. Butler cites Trinh Minh-ha when discussing the "frame": "to call the frame into question is to show that the frame never quite contained the scene it was meant to limn, that something was already outside, which made the very sense of the inside possible, recognizable. The frame never quite determined precisely what it is we see, think, recognize, and apprehend. Something exceeds the frame that troubles our sense of reality, in other words, something occurs that does not conform to our established understanding of things" (2004, 8–9).

36. Ironically, this goal of self-regulation is suspended for some based solely on their privileged and ablebodied status: "Donald Trump seems to act on pure impulse. . . . He ignores what the situation is telling him to do and obeys only his instincts. . . . Once upon a time, his supporters adored this kind of impetuous display, for it showcased Trump's authenticity, they claimed, and his willingness to 'tell it like it is.'" In asking how Trump seems to be able to defy the social and psychological demands of self-regulating behavior and emotional states, Dan P. McAdams argues ("A psychological trap: making sense of Donald Trump's life and personality" for *The Guardian* [Accessed Aug 5, 2016]. http://www.theguardian.com/us-news/2016/aug/05/donald-trump-psychology-personality-republicans-election):

> I think there are three reasons behind Trump's problem in self-regulation. Each corresponds to a distinctive feature of his personality. . .
>
> First, Trump's temperament profile—high extraversion and low agreeableness—derives much of its power from an underlying impulsivity laced with anger. . .

Second, Trump's impulsive temperament style dovetails with his central life goal—the narcissistic aim of promoting Donald Trump. . .

Finally, [and most problematically] there is Donald Trump's philosophy of life, spelled out first in *The Art of the Deal*. It is a matter of principle for Donald Trump that when you are attacked, you hit back harder. If you want to win the game of life, you must be a counter-puncher.

37. According to the US Department of Labor's Advisory Council's report, titled "Managing Disability Risks in an Environment of Individual Responsibility," it states that, "A lengthy period of disability can lead to prolonged loss of income, resulting in serious financial consequences for any individual and his/her family. . . . The consequences of becoming disabled are devastating for any worker" (2012). Raising a child that might not be employable, who ends up in "the system," exposed to unnecessary suffering because one could not "manage" in an "environment of individual responsibility" is a complexity that no one family or individual should bear without requisite interventions and supports. http://www.dol.gov/ebsa/publications/2012ACreport2. html

38. According to Noddings: "Whatever I do in life, whomever I meet, I am first and always one-caring or one cared-for." This dynamic is so important to an analysis of ableism, because the ableist tendency is to devalue the role of the one cared-for. To this, Noddings adds: "The cared-for is essential to the relation. What the cared-for contributes to the relation is a responsiveness that completes the caring. This responsiveness need not take the form of gratitude or even of direct acknowledgement. Rather, . . . [the] caring is completed when the cared-for receives the caring." Excerpted from *Caring* in *Classic and Contemporary Readings in the Philosophy of Education* (2nd edition, Steven Cahn, ed., New York, NY: Oxford UP, 2012, pp. 387, 390).

39. Citing Adrienne Asch and Harilyn Rousso, "Therapists with Disabilities: Theoretical and Clinical Issues" in *Psychiatry*, 48: 1–12, 1985.

40. Sunaura Taylor calls this desire "romantic" and fundamentally *ableist* because without these qualities of independence and self-sufficiency, it could (disturbingly) be implied that those with disabilities are "better off dead." In the case of animal species, this romanticism for self-sufficiency manifests as "better off extinct" (2014, 112, 122).

41. This in not only in reference to Sartre's existential concept, but with Freire as he cites Sartre (2009, 58) as well as his Marxist critique of the "banking concept of education" as the work of bad faith. From Freire: "Those who use the banking approach, knowingly or unknowingly (for there are innumerable well intended bank-clerk teachers [and I add: therapists, service providers, etc.] who do not realize that they are serving only to dehumanize), fail to perceive that the deposits themselves contain contradictions about reality. But, sooner or later, these contradictions may lead formerly passive students to turn against their domestication and the attempt to domesticate reality" (54).

42. Tim Wise "scandal" is recounted on the blog gradientlair.com ([Accessed Sep 17, 2013] http://www.gradientlair.com/post/61521224722/i-dont-need-tim-wise-as-an-ally):

This is a person who claims expertise on that which he does not live yet rejects criticism. But rejecting criticism when you're in a place of privilege is very dangerous especially when you do justice work.

This is a part of what he recently wrote on Facebook. How someone can claim to be anti-racism yet writes this is beyond me:

> *And this is what's funny . . . every second that fools troll my site, complaining about how I take up all the antiracist space so they can't be heard, is a moment they aren't setting up their own website, blog, or writing their own book . . . but they wanna blame me for why no one knows who they are. . . it's not on me sweetheart..plenty of people of color get book deals and speaking gigs each year . . . if u didn't its not on me . . . it's cuz u havent said anything that anyone finds valuable . . . deal with that rather than wasting time trolling . . . Maybe another POC blew up your spot rather than me . . . ever think of that? No, of course not . . . cuz that would require critical thought rather than simplistic hater bs and stuff u can put on tumblr . . . seriously, it's time for people to be told to step off . . . feel free to jump off the page trolls . . . . or I can bounce you . . . and would love to . . . trust me, u will lose this beef . . . badly . . .*

. . . This comment ignores the role of White, male and class privilege and their effects on exposure, publication, platform, income . . . even being listened to as an "authority" on Black experiences.

43. For example, in one critique of allyship, the call is to encourage more fair and democratic peer-relations rather than allyship. I cannot treat my child as a peer but still can figure allyship as part and parcel to my role as parent. See Julie Greenberg, (2014), "Beyond Allyship: Multiracial Work to End Racism" for *Tikkun Magazine*. http://www.tikkun.org/nextgen/wp-content/uploads/2014/01/Greenberg.pdf

44. Judith Butler makes my point with her reading of Levinas: "For Levinas, it is the ethical itself that gets one out of the circuitry of bad conscience, the logic by which the prohibition against aggression become the internal conduit for aggression itself. Aggression is then turned back upon oneself in the form of super-egoic cruelty. If the ethical moves us beyond bad conscience, it is because bad conscience is, after all, only a negative version of narcissism, and so still a form of narcissism. The face of the Other come to me from outside and interrupts that narcissistic circuit" (2004, 137–138).

45. See Part Four titled, "Griefwork: How Do You Get Over What You Cannot Get Over?" in *The Pregnancy ≠ Childbearing Project* (Scuro 2017).

46. For a discussion of the problem of allies wanting a "cookie" see Mari Brighe, who outlines ways in which one needs to be a better trans-ally, arguing the sixth point: "Don't expect cookies. Trans people are extremely grateful for our allies. You're absolutely critical in helping us move our causes forward. That being said, don't expect a constant outpouring of thank-you's for what you're doing. Don't get huffy if you don't get hugs and cookies and rainbow glitter for every single thing you do as an ally. Don't pout if you don't get the 'props' you deserve for the work you're doing. And no, you don't get a special ally flag. Allies don't do their work because they want gratitude and recognition—they do it because they genuinely care about trans people and want to see the world improve for them. If seeing positive change isn't enough of a motivator for you, then you're failing as an ally." From "There Are No Cookies: Ten Ways to Take Action as a Trans Ally (Even If

You're Also Trans)" posted on autostraddle.com, (Accessed Jan 13, 2015). http://www.autostraddle.com/there-are-no-cookies-ten-ways-to-take-action-as-a-trans-ally-even-if-youre-also-trans-268945/

47. See Dan Ariely, "Our Buggy Moral Code" TEDtalk (Accessed Feb 2009). Transcript posted online: http://www.ted.com/talks/dan_ariely_on_our_buggy_moral_code/transcript?language=en, (3:15 / ¶11).

48. More exactly, Ariely states, "We have very strong intuitions about all kinds of things—our own ability, how the economy works, how we should pay school teachers. But unless we start testing those intuitions, we're not going to do better. And just think about how better my life would have been if these nurses would have been willing to check their intuition, and how everything would have been better if we just start doing more systematic experimentation of our intuitions" (15: 30).

49. See a critique of the recent "helping" videos by David M. Perry, "Inspiration Porn Further Disables the Disabled: Objectifying people with disabilities creates the wrong kind of hero" posted *Al Jazeera America*, (Accessed Jun 2, 2015). http://america.aljazeera.com/opinions/2015/6/inspiration-porn-further-disables-the-disabled.html

50. Rachel Cohen-Rottenberg, "The Complexities of Giving: People with Disabilities as Help Objects" posted on Disability Blog, the official blog of Disability.gov, (Accessed Aug 19, 2013). http://usodep.blogs.govdelivery.com/2013/08/19/the-complexities-of-giving-people-with-disabilities-as-help-objects/

51. This is an injunction that comes from intersectional approaches to allyship (specifically meaning "shut the fuck up"). See "Sometimes, Intersectionality Means You STFU" posted by April Hathcock on her blog, *At The Intersection*, (Accessed Mar 15, 2016): "The fact is that if we're going to be good allies to each other, we have to be good allies to each other. We have to wear our many intersectional hats. . . . And as an ally, it's my job to put on my ally hat and shut my beautiful intersectional mouth. I listen, I learn, and I only speak up to signal boost. I don't bring up my issues because that conversation isn't about or for me. My intersectionality tells me to STFU. . . . Does that mean I never get to speak? No. I get my space. And if one of my identities gets mentioned in this other space in a way that seems less than aware, I can certainly offer correction. But I do that later. I do that in a separate conversation. Because I recognize the importance of respecting the focus of the discussion, the purpose of the space at that moment. I realize that space isn't about or for me, and I respect the space by not seeking to derail the conversation with my own concerns." http://aprilhathcock.wordpress.com/2016/03/

52. Recently, Sheryl Sandberg has apologized for her "Lean In" advocacy now that she is a single mother. See Penelope Trunk, "Too little too late: Sheryl Sandberg apologizes for Lean In" posted on her blog, (Accessed May 11, 2016). http://blog.penelopetrunk.com/2016/05/11/too-little-too-late-sheryl-sandberg-apologizes-for-lean-in/. Since the death of her husband, Sandberg has gone on to write another book, *Option B: Facing Adversity, Building Resilience, and Finding Joy*, and a companion non-profit site called *Option B*.org. It is an unreflectively ableist propaganda project for "building resilience" and overcoming tragedies or difficulties utilizing inspiration porn strategies. http://optionb.org/build-resilience/lessons/the-importance-of-resilience

53. To further this experiment in an intersectional way, how often are women of color outright and uncritically assumed to be "the help"?

54. See, for example, Harold Braswell's, "My Two Moms: Disability, Queer Kinship, and the Maternal Subject" in *Hypatia* (Winter 2015), Vol. 30 Issue 1, pp. 234–250.

55. See Stella Young's argument against "compassionate homicide" and "mercy killing" in "Disability is no justification for murder" (Accessed Sep 2, 2013), posted by *The Drum*. http://www.abc.net.au/news/2013-09-03/young-kyla-puhle-death/4930742

56. This is the extension of my argument in *The Pregnancy ≠ Childbearing Project* (2017), in which I graphically and phenomenologically "disentangle" pregnancy from its childbearing expectations. As a "phenomenology of miscarriage," I found that because not all pregnancies lead to the birth of a child, that it is philosophically and politically significant to future solidarity among women to challenge the entailment of childbearing simply because "she is pregnant."

57. From Emmanuel Levinas' *God, Death, and Time*. (Bettina Bergo, trans. Stanford, CA: Stanford UP, 2000). Parts of this argument was delivered in my presentation, "Receptive Affections: Toward an Eco/Alter Ethic" for *Power, Time and Agency* Conference, University of Manchester, January 2013.

58. Discussed at length in my chapter on Griefwork (Scuro 2017).

59. There has been recent use of the term "snowflake" to indicate someone who is too sensitive, "in need of trigger warnings," not "strong" enough to handle or navigate political discussions. It is code also for liberal, progressive ideology by the conservative and alt-right extremists. From Dana Schwartz in GQ.com (Feb 1, 2017): "Snowflake is an ad hominem attack, a taunt of a schoolyard bully by way of Ayn Rand. You're a wuss, and so your argument is invalid" (http://www.gq.com/story/why-trump-supporters-love-calling-people-snowflakes). This operates as an ableist slur because it assumes that the kind of ethical sensitivity I am defending in this chapter is "weak," supplemented with a kind of effeminacy ("wuss"/"pussy") riveting disabled characteristics in the ad hominem ("snowflakes can't . . . " and "snowflakes aren't able to . . . ").

60. As discussed in the Prologue.

61. Referencing McMahan's position as described in Kittay (2005, 102).

62. From Rudy Simone, *Aspergirls: Empowering Females with Asperger Syndrome*, (Philadelphia, PA: Jessica Kingsley Publishers, 2010).

63. A study by Wallace, Case, et al., http://www.ncbi.nlm.nih.gov/pmc/articles/PMC3448486/. There are good critiques of the psychological standards set for the reception and understanding of emotional states by people on the spectrum, including outright challenges to Sasha Baron-Cohen's "Theory of Mind" hypothesis. Some of these critiques are important because, in practice, these theories suggest that more eye-contact is better than less, despite the discomforts and even harms it causes non-neurotypical people. See Rachel Cohen-Rottenberg (no relation), "A Critique of the Empathizing-Systemizing (E-S) Theory of Autism" posted on her *Autism and Empathy* blog (2009). http://autismandempathyblog.wordpress.com/a-critique-of-the-empathizing-systemizing-e-s-theory-of-autism/. For a discussion on the problem of forced eye contact, see "Autism Discussion: Eye Contact, IEPs and Compliance"

posted by M. Kelter on the blog *Invisible Strings*, (Accessed Apr 22, 2015). http://theinvisiblestrings.com/autism-discussion-eye-contact-ieps-and-compliance/

64. For a discussion of this term, see Rosemarie Garland-Thomson's work, *Freakery: Cultural Spectacles of the Extraordinary Body* (New York, NY: New York University Press, 1996).

65. Butler, responding to the question of her commitment to non-violence, especially when "the subject is formed out of violence," states that non-violence is already a conflicted position coming from an "injured, rageful subject." She clarifies this: "It is crucial to distinguish between (a) that injured and rageful subject who gives moral legitimacy to rageful and injurious conduct, thus transmuting aggression into virtue, and (b) that injured and rageful subject who nevertheless seeks to limit the injury that she or he causes, and can do so only through an active struggle with and against aggression" (2010, 171–172).

CHAPTER 2

1. This chapter was a presentation originally given at the 2015 SDS in Atlanta called, "Ableist Implications of Diagnostics and Diagnoses" on the panel, "Philosophy of Disability: Ethics, Ableism, & Affect" with Joel Michael Reynolds and Lauren Guilmette. It was revised and presented again at the American Philosophical Association Eastern Meeting, 2015. I am grateful for their direct feedback.

2. From *The Oxford Classical Dictionary*, (Third Edition, London: Oxford University Press, 1999). Thanks so much to Kathy Mannino for assisting me with access to these reference materials.

3. Butler discusses this under the umbrella concern, "Survivability, Vulnerability, Affect" in *Frames of War* (2010): "To perceive a life is not quite the same as encountering a life as precarious. . . . An ethical attitude does not spontaneously arrive as soon as the usual interpretive frameworks are destroyed, and no pure moral conscience emerges once the shackles of everyday interpretation have been thrown off. . . . The tacit interpretive scheme that divides the worthy from unworthy lives works fundamentally through the senses, differentiating the cries we can hear from those we cannot" (51).

4. Butler argues that we do "not want to celebrate a full deregulation of affect" (2010, 52).

5. Defined by Rosemarie Garland-Thomson as: "the corporeal incarnation of cultures collective, unmarked, normative characteristics" (2011, 23).

6. Appropriately, when I read these narratives at 2015 SDS, one commentator suggested I include and compare these narratives of neurotypical parents of non-neurotypical children with the narratives of non-neurotypical parents to non-neurotypical children, commenting that "this experience would not be the same."

7. Lisa Quinones-Fontanez blogs on AutismWonderland.com, and this blog post was reposted on Parents.com, (Accessed May 15, 2013). http://www.parents.com/blogs/to-the-max/2013/05/15/autism/five-years-after-an-autism-diagnosis-part-1/

8. Jim Sinclair's "Don't Mourn for Us" (1993) is important to note here in order to temper the parent narratives of "grief" as it regards the handing over of the autism diagnosis:

> *Autism is a way of being. It is pervasive; it colors every experience, every sensation, perception, thought, emotion, and encounter, every aspect of existence. It is not possible to separate the autism from the person—and if it were possible, the person you'd have left would not be the same person you started with. . . . This is important, so take a moment to consider it: Autism is a way of being. It is not possible to separate the person from the autism.*
>
>   *Therefore, when parents say,*
>   *I wish my child did not have autism,*
>   *what they're really saying is,*
>   *I wish the autistic child I have did not exist, and I had a different (non-autistic) child instead.*
>
> *Read that again. This is what we hear when you mourn over our existence. This is what we hear when you pray for a cure. This is what we know, when you tell us of your fondest hopes and dreams for us: that your greatest wish is that one day we will cease to be, and strangers you can love will move in behind our faces.*

Reposted on the Autism Network International newsletter, Our Voice, Volume 1, Number 3. http://www.autreat.com/dont_mourn.html.

9. See Solomon's and Movius' video interviews on *Katie!* (The Katie Couric Show) posted on andrewsolomon.com (Jan 8, 2013). http://andrewsolomon.com/coverage/video-katie/

10. There is something about the openness of these narrated experiences I do not want to critique here. The difficulty with these parent narratives is twofold (and could apply to me as well): 1) that they share in the stories of their children and not necessarily with their children's full consent and 2) that the narrative tone is a loss of ableist privilege, as "something about us without us" contrary to the demand of disability advocacy about *who* gets to speak and about *what* experiences.

11. Kittay's "The Personal is Philosophical is Political: A Philosopher and Mother of a Cognitively Disabled Person Sends Notes from the Battlefield" in *Metaphilosophy*, (Jul 2009), Vol. 40, Nos. 3–4, Malden, MA: Blackwell Publishing Ltd., pp. 607–627.

12. DisCrit is defined as such because, "Given the small but growing interest in ways that race and dis/ability are co-constructed, we argue that the time is right to propose Dis/ability Critical Race Studies . . . [exploring] ways in which both race and ability are socially constructed and interdependent" (Annamma et al., p. 5).

13. From "How The Flint Water Crisis Could Send An Entire Generation To Prison" reported by Carimah Townes, posted by ThinkProgress.org, (Accessed Jan 22, 2016). http://thinkprogress.org/justice/2016/01/22/3741585/flint-juvenile-justice-catastrophe/

14. In "Environmental Racism: Beyond the Distributive Paradigm" (2013), Sheila Foster and Luke Cole argue that there was statistical significance in the correlation between the percentage of people of color in a community with the increase in commercial "hazardous waste management." To their point: "race was the most significant

variable in determining the location of commercial hazardous waste facilities" (122–123). While the "market" and "lifestyle" were assumed sufficient for causal explanations, the authors argue that structural racism of residential segregation did not emerge naturally or by choice: "discriminatory real estate practices, exclusionary and expulsive zoning, redlining . . . [that] would also result in closed social networks" (129).

15. Even the calls to repair infrastructure fell upon the private sector. From Jared Bernstein (Jan 25, 2016) for *The Washington Post* (http://www.washingtonpost.com/posteverything/wp/2016/01/25/the-water-crisis-in-flint-and-the-strategy-of-government-failure/?utm_term=.7d748ffe2e65 [emphasis added]):

> [One] Flint pediatrician compared kids' lead levels in their blood before and after the switch, and found that they'd doubled and tripled. State officials dodged once again, accusing the doctor of causing unnecessary hysteria. Finally, outside pressure forced the Michigan government to acknowledge the accuracy of the pediatrician's data and reverse course.
>
> That is decidedly not a happy ending. *Brain damage from lead poisoning is irreversible.*
>
> But those of us who advocate for [government] interventions cannot assume away government failure, any more than free-market conservatives can assume away market failures. Progressives can and should make the point that public goods, such as safe water, must be provided by governments as private firms will not adequately provide such goods to everyone. . . . [We] must recognize that government failure is not an accident. It is a strategy of those who benefit from less government.

16. Elizabeth Barnes, *The Minority Body: A Theory of Disability*. (London: Oxford University Press, 2016)

17. In this essay, Silvers seems to argue in defense of Barnes's work as it is more from the position of how disability is represented than philosophical approach per se; after narrating Barnes' responses to typical philosophical position-taking, like narrating Barnes' arguments for the social construction of disability—which for Disability Studies (DS) communities is fairly established while in (predominantly analytic) philosophy communities it is not—and narrating the typical kinds of response philosophers tend to give, (who "parade medical conditions" as evidence for example), she states (859–860),

> If, as Barnes's ontological theory maintains (rightly, in my opinion), disability is not a natural kind . . . referring instead to social facts, what social construction of disability should philosophers choose? What should philosophy do?
>
> I have argued here that a conceptualization like Barnes's idea of disability as mere difference, or mine of devising a normatively neutral understanding, avoids both moral and epistemic wrongs to which versions that connote negativity fall prey. An important purpose for philosophers (and other people as well) is to facilitate aspirational efforts to improve disabled people's access to opportunities nondisabled people commonly enjoy. Such fairness aims for what ought to be.

As I have argued in this text, this, as a whole—Barnes's defense of a positive or value neutral meaning for disability as well as Silvers' defense of her work—still rivet the problem of disability to the disabled person. Argued in chapter 1, by addressing ableism rather than the meaning and corresponding value for the status of disability, my hope is to liberate philosophers and nonphilosophers from a harmful bias rather than primarily debate the moral, political or social identification of disability.

18. Kittay references Evelyn Fox's Keller's and Barbara McClinock's work on how it is possible to not know the capacity and emotional states of others with an "everyday eye" (619).

19. From the *Oxford Classical Dictionary* (1999).

20. *Stanford Encyclopedia of Philosophy*, "Ancient Conceptions of Analysis." http://plato.stanford.edu/entries/analysis/s2.html

21. Although this may be debatable. Commentators conflict as to whether the later dialogues that show Socrates engaged in more the elenctic style is a move toward generating nominal or real definitions related to working hypotheses (*ibid*). From the entry: "there has been more controversy over precisely what the presuppositions of the elenctic method are, and how to respond, in particular, to the charge that Socrates commits the so-called Socratic fallacy. Socrates appears to be committed to the principle that if one does not know what the *F* is, then one cannot know if *F* is truly predicable of anything whatever, in which case it seems pointless to try to discover what the *F* is by investigating examples of it via the elenctic method."

22. In Paul Shorey's translation of the Divided Line in Book VI of Plato's *Republic* notes the "division" of the Line that is least "clear and precise," the thinking related to objects least related to "truth and reality," is "picture-thinking or conjecture [εἰκασία']" (Plato 511e; *Republic*, 116–117).

23. This point can be illustrated by the debate about whether subjects who are blind or blindfolded make the same errors as those sighted when it comes to optical illusions like the Poggendorff effect and the Müller-Lyer illusion. There is some evidence that these "optical" illusions, when provided to blind subjects, seem to display the same set of miscalculations tactually as do sighted subjects looking visually. This might support my suggestion that there is diagnostic thinking at work (and to some degree that also fails) when encountering these "illusions" of parts in relation to wholes. See, for example, S. Millar and Z. Al-Attar, "The Müller-Lyer illusion in touch and vision: Implications for multisensory processes" (*Perception & Psychophysics*, Apr 2002, Volume 64, Issue 3, pp. 353–365) and P. Wenderoth and D. Alais, "Lack of evidence for a tactual Poggendorff illusion" (*Perception & Psychophysics*, 1990, 48 (3), 234–242).

24. See Stanley Rosen's *The Quarrel between Philosophy and Poetry: Studies in Ancient Thought* (New York, NY: Routledge, 2014), pp. 62–66.

25. My emphasis.

26. Sara Brill aligns this with the work of an excellent doctor, and that it is "necessary to cultivate the capacity for self-diagnosis" (2005, 309).

27. This is in direct reference to my graphic novel account in *The Pregnancy ≠ Childbearing Project* (Scuro 2017, 29–33).

28. Estrich, George (Apr 2016). "Open Letter to Medical Students." *AMA Journal of Ethics*, Volume 18, Number 4: 438–441. Available online: http://journalofethics. ama-assn.org/2016/04/mnar1-1604.html

29. Ashley Taylor citing Thomas Hehir, "Eliminating Ableism in Education," *Harvard Educational Review* 72, No. 1 (2002).

30. Paraphrasing Hehir.

31. Arendt more precisely argues it: "Men now live in an earth wide continuous whole where even the notion of distance, still inherent in the most perfectly unbroken contiguity of parts, has yielded before the onslaught of speed. Speed has conquered space . . ." (1958, 250).

32. An updated medical coding system, ICD-10, began transition in October 2015. Medical practices have been mandated to convert to the newer system, train and hire staff to manage the coding systems. See AHIMA.org:

> WHO owns and publishes the international version of the ICD classification system, and ICD has become an international diagnostic classification system used for all general epidemiological and healthcare purposes. In 1992 WHO published the tenth revision of the ICD system (ICD-10), which represents the broadest scope of any ICD revision to date.
>
> The goal of the tenth revision was to expand the content, purpose, and scope of the system. It was designed to include ambulatory care services, increase clinical detail, capture risk factors in primary care, identify emergent diseases, and develop group diagnoses for epidemiological purposes. ICD-10 provides more categories for disease and health-related conditions than previous revisions through its alphanumeric coding system. Currently the ICD-10 classification system is used by many countries to record both mortality and morbidity data. Although the U.S. won't fully implement its ICD-10 based classification systems until October 1, 2014, the U.S. has used the WHO ICD-10 classification to report mortality data since 1999.

From the "ICD-10-CM/PCS Implementation Toolkit" (2012) posted online by the American Health Information Management Association [AHIMA]: http://bok.ahima. org/Doc/7/2/F/107049#.V0xktpErKhd

33. It is important to note the unreflective use of ableist language in the narrative. Nika C. Beamon is a journalist in New York City. She is the author of the memoir *Misdiagnosed: The Search for Dr. House*. http://www.huffingtonpost.com/nika-c-beamon/medical-misdiagnosis-nearly-killed-me_b_8441082.html

34. Posted in the *Express-News*, (Jul 11, 2014). Available online (Accessed Jul 15, 2014): http://m.mysanantonio.com/opinion/commentary/article/In-emergency-situations-disabled-people-are-5615774.php

35. Thank you so much to the Neonatalogist at Emory University Hospital for her wonderful feedback on many of these points. Our discussion provided me a working counter-narrative to this account, hopefully not as exceptional as she seemed in her practice to be.

36. Available in full text online: http://dsq-sds.org/article/view/341/429

37. See Lei Wiley-Mydske's Review of the documentary, "Sounding the Alarm: Battling the Autism Epidemic" posted on Autism Women's Network blog (Jul 19, 2014). As Wiley-Mydske states it: "Throughout the film, the 'cost' of Autism is brought up several times. From Bob Wright [co-founder of Autism Speaks] lamenting that 'you don't die of autism,' to doctors talking about the millions of dollars we cost, to parents distraught about paying out of pocket for therapies that are not covered by insurance. There is not one point in this film that talks about the fact that not only do many Autistics find [Applied Behavior Analysis] (the therapy they bring up the most) to be

dehumanizing and abusive, but also that childhood should not be spent in 8 hours a day of therapy. Autistic children are children first. They are not your science project. . . . By far, the most disturbing part of the film for me was the filming of Autistic children and young adults in crisis. Shown at their most vulnerable and since all of the parents claimed they were unable to communicate, certainly without their permission." Available online: http://autismwomensnetwork.org/film-review-of-documentary-sounding-the-alarm-battling-the-autism-epidemic/

38. Jenell Johnson (2013) citing Roy Richard Grinker's *Unstrange Minds: Remapping the World of Autism* (New York, NY: Basic Books, 2008).

39. See Tobin Siebers' evaluation of "narcissism" in *Disability Theory* (University of Michigan Press, 2008). He argues that there is a countertransference that leads to therapeutic failures when, "analysts cannot bear to work with patients with disabilities." It is not the people with disabilities that are narcissistic, it is the rules of psychoanalysis (or even the ordinary rules) that do not fit," pp. 41–42.

40. See Philip Ferguson and Emily Nusbaum, "Disability Studies: What Is It and What Difference Does It Make?" from *Research and Practice for Persons with Severe Disabilities*, (Vol 37, No 2, 2012).

41. I presented this twice as workshops titled "Diagnosis Stories" in 2016.

42. Reprinted here with permission from author. From the blogsite: http://wearelikeyourchild.blogspot.com/2015/07/reclaiming-dignity-lost-in-diagnosis.html (Accessed Jul 23, 2015). Thank you to the SDS attendee of our 2015 panel who made the comment about including autistic parent narratives alongside the recitation of the non-autistic parent narratives.

CHAPTER 3

1. From Wong's Facebook post dated Jun 9, 2015 regarding the difficulties for Desi and Asian Americans with Disabilities to find meaningful employment, http://www.news-indiatimes.com/desi-leaders-urge-improved-employment-for-the-disabled/15837

2. The reference to intersectionality and the post of Wong's meeting President Obama were from different posts, same page. See Disability Visibility project (http://disabilityvisibilityproject.com/).

3. Shildrick includes an analogy that I utilize as well. For addressing ableism, this needs to not be seen as the "disable person's problem" in the same way that a critique of racism needs to address the problem of whiteness (2009, 15).

4. Lending itself is required.

5. See ref. from Young about aversion.

6. From bell hooks (1994, 143–44):

There is a critique of progressive pedagogical practices that comes at us not just from the inside but from the outside as well. . . . Its frightening to me that the mass media has not only offered the public a sense that there really has been some kind of revolution in education where conservative white men are just completely discredited when we know that very little has changed . . . almost no paradigm shifts, and where knowledge and information continue to be presented in the conventionally accepted manner.

Of course, . . . students who have had a more conventional education would be threatened by and even resist teaching practices which insist that students participate in their education.

7. Abjection is discussed in chapters 1 and 4. See Kristeva (1982).

8. For a good narrative of how this kind of psychological terrorizing operates, see Brown's account, "Why They Hate Us" (Aug 19, 2013; http://www.autistichoya. com/2013/08/how-they-hate-us.html).

9. For instance, "Make America Great Again" operates as conservative and nationalist code and carries this kind of terroristic effect. From Rebekah Frumkin (Nov 14, 2016 for Medium.com):

Swastikas and the words "make America white again" spray painted across a baseball dugout. The repeated verbal and harassment of Muslims. A wall tagged with "Black lives don't matter" and rainbow flags set afire. As a queer woman, I fear for my own safety and the safety of my friends who are Black, Latinx, refugees, Muslim, trans, immigrants, disabled, or otherwise marginalized by cishet white moneyed patriarchy. I fear, as many do, the roiling aggression of Trump supporters, the righteous pale hand reaching across our country's political divide to strangle us cold. The hateful words of Trump supporters are intended to terrorize and dehumanize all those who don't match their demographic profile. Even the sentence "make America great again" is easily recognizable as a speech-act of white nationalist intimidation.

10. Only with a twitter search of the #disabilitytoowhite discussion on social media will demonstrated the truth of this terrorization. "Vilissa Thompson, the founder of disability equality organization, Ramp Your Voice, started the hashtag after stumbling upon an xoJane article that only presented white women in a story about disability and beauty . . . " (From Laura Donovan, "New Hashtag is calling out the Media . . ." [posted by attn.com on May 20, 2016].)

11. I'm indirectly referencing Levinas' idea of the *il y a* as a characteristic of non-human and even dehumanizing experience ("without a face"). For more on this, see Michael Marder, "Terror of the Ethical: On Levinas's *Il y a*" in *Postmodern Culture* (Jan 2008, Vol. 18, No. 2).

12. As it regards the link between racism and Post-Traumatic Stress Disorder (PTSD), see *Psychology Today*, (Sept 6, 2015; http://www.psychologytoday.com/ blog/culturally-speaking/201509/the-link-between-racism-and-ptsd).

13. See Kessler et al., "Associations of Housing Mobility Interventions for Children in High-Poverty Neighborhoods with Subsequent Mental Disorders During Adolescence" in *JAMA* (2014; 311(9), pp. 937–947).

14. Subini Ancy Annamma, David Connor and Beth Ferri (2013), "Dis/ability critical race Studies (DisCrit): Theorizing at the intersections of race and dis/ability" in *Race, Ethnicity and Education* citing T. Parrish (2002), "Racial Disparities in the identification, funding, and provision of special education' in *Racial Inequality in Special Education* (Losen & Orfield, eds. Harvard UP).

15. Aug 28, 2015. http://politicalphilosopher.net/2015/08/28/featured-philosopher-devonya-n-havis/

16. This is lowercased purposefully.

17. She made it clear that the precondition for my daughter's future participation is that I watch over her at every meeting—as if to babysit her, stating,

"they cannot get through a song because she is distracting the group." Ironically, Juliette Gordon Low, the foundress of the Girl Scouts was also a disability activist and intended the Girl Scouts to be fully inclusive. See Mac Pogue's "Adventures in Feministory: Juliette Gordon Low, Founder of Girl Scouts, Disabled Activist," posted by BitchMedia.org, (Jan 30, 2012). http://bitchmedia.org/post/adventures-in-feministory-juliette-gordon-low-girl-scouts-disability

18. See Kittay's, "The Personal Is Philosophical Is Political: A Philosopher and Mother of a Cognitively Disabled Person Sends Notes from the Battlefield" in *Metaphilosophy*, (Jul 2009) Vol. 40, Nos. 3–4, Malden, MA: Blackwell Publishing Ltd., pp. 607–627.

19. LB Note: I wrote two articles that I was responding to: 1) http://lisybabe. blogspot.com/2008/05/disablism-vs-ableism.html and 2) http://lisybabe.blogspot. co.uk/2013/07/ableism-stop-insulting-me.html. [A sample of the position from lisybabe:]

> Historically it's been the case that the single word to describe disability-based discrimination in British English has been "disablism." North Americans have always preferred "ableism," but you didn't see it used by Brits that often. Sadly the word "ableism" is creeping further and further into British English usage. I've seen it used repeatedly by journalists and popular bloggers which validates its use; and every time I see it I feel hurt.
>
> Let's crack on to why I find the word "ableism" insulting. As you will have read, there are . . . two ways of considering disability. There's the medical/individual model in which a person with an impairment is seen as lacking in ability, and there's the social model in which a person with an impairment is considered disabled by social barriers.
>
> The problem with the word "ableism" is that it's predicated on the medical model. The "blame it on their brain/body" individualised perspective of disability should be consigned to the history books and instead we need to focus on dealing with disabling barriers—from architectural to financial—that make life difficult/impossible for disabled people.

> I posted this as a status (and comments) on Facebook originally, in June 2014, and Lisa Egan participated in the ensuing discussion, all of which is public: https://www. facebook.com/lmxzb/posts/10152196981853157. I also read this article by A.J. Withers, who identifies as a disabled, queer, trans, and anti-poverty activist: http://stillmyrevolution. org/2013/01/01/disablism-or-ableism/. [JS addition to LB's note: Withers argues, "We all have able bodies. If we don't have able bodies we are dead—otherwise our bodies are working, they are able. The opposite of disabled is not able-bodied, it is non-disabled."]

20. Sami Schalk also discusses the important transitivity of Larsen's main character in the novel *Passing*, Clare, as having a "both/and" desire, that is not limited to the politics and identities of "passing" but as "transing" (2015, 155):

> Here, it becomes necessary to emphasize the *desire* of both/and desire. Though Clare does not explicitly cross the binary by having sex with a woman, she does dance on the boundary in her public actions and attitudes. This appearance of transing hetero- and homosexuality is just as important for Clare's characterization as her more direct transing of race and class because it raises the other characters' suspicions and prevents them from reading her body and actions in the same way she seems to be able to read theirs.

21. Jenny Saul discusses the implicit bias when it comes to intellectual ability in the academy—particularly in academic philosophy—and how this bias manifests as a stereotype threat. She does not name this as ableist but is a good example of ableist operations and exclusionary practices by way of stereotype threat (2013, 53–54):

> If intellectual ability [should be] viewed as a more complicated set of abilities and skills, . . . [and] I think this is an especially important point for philosophers to reflect on, because it seems to me that philosophers are very prone to claims regarding "who's smart" and "who's stupid." . . . It could only be a good thing for the profession if philosophers stopped talking this way. (And this is so for reasons other than stereotype threat as well. Fear of being labeled "stupid" undoubtedly makes everyone more hesitant to try out a really new and different idea, or to discuss one's work at an early stage, when it's still a bit inchoate but would really benefit from discussion) . . .
>
> In addition, it is very likely that judgments of "who's smart" are affected by implicit bias. We've already seen plenty of reason to think that evaluative judgments are in general, but it seems likely to think that "smartness" judgments are especially susceptible to this. After all, they're judgments of what someone's capable of rather than their actual output: E.g. "He's really smart, but it just doesn't come through in his work" is a perfectly normal sort of thing to say. The same is true of the negative judgments: E.g. "She writes good papers, but that's just because she works so hard. I don't think she's really smart." The lack of sensitivity to actual results means that these judgments can be influenced *even more* by implicit biases.

22. Doxxing is the practice of making a person's personal/private information public. I personally know of a couple of cases in which academics were doxxed but because they debate they were engaged in made it to general or non-academic (and politically conservative) websites. For more information, http://theconversation.com/doxxing-swatting-and-the-new-trends-in-online-harassment-40234

23. A description of the American Philosophical Association's (APA) need to craft a public statement against bullying based on the case of George Yancy: http://www.insidehighered.com/news/2016/02/15/philosophy-association-issues-statement-against-bullying. Here, as a critique of "call out culture," is an example of how these situations may be read differently from a disability lens: http://feministphilosophers.wordpress.com/2015/03/04/call-out-culture-the-case-of-ableist-language/

24. From DH: For example, I am thinking about a cordial but critical exchange at a recent Eastern APA meeting where I inquired about the title of a new text on disability. Elizabeth Barnes' book, *The Minority Body* (2016) raised concerns for me as a Black woman about the positioning of one as "minority" as well as what it means for a "minority" to be a minority body. Racialized bodies are structurally always already constructed as "other" so how does the addition of disability, marking an already "defective" body yet again as "minority" further disempower rather than empower.

25. Part of this right included in the act is that a student be in "the least restrictive environment." Children should be integrated as much as possible with the general; not segregated in special education classes. From the IDEA (2004) legislation:

> Disability is a natural part of the human experience and in no way diminishes the right of individuals to participate in or contribute to society. Improving educational results for children with disabilities is an essential element of our national policy of ensuring equality

of opportunity, full participation, independent living, and economic self-sufficiency for individuals with disabilities.

. . . Before the date of enactment of the Education for All Handicapped Children Act of 1975 (Public Law 94–142), the educational needs of millions of children with disabilities were not being fully met because—

(A) the children did not receive appropriate educational services;
(B) the children were excluded entirely from the public school system and from being educated with their peers;
(C) undiagnosed disabilities prevented the children from having a successful educational experience; or
(D) a lack of adequate resources within the public school system forced families to find services outside the public school system.

26. Emily Willingham, for Forbes.com, reports on the perceptions of Autistic women in "Autistic Girls Are Undiagnosed, Underserved and Misunderstood" (Sept 4, 2015).

Mildred: Neurotypicals go to great lengths to avoid situations that make them anxious. It seems to only be a disorder when we do it as well. And the first person I ever had to block on fb was actually an autistic male who was angry that no one would be his girlfriend. Who wrote this thing? I am beginning to wish no one be allowed to talk about autistic people but other autistic people.

Emily B.: Yeah–non-autistic people can't see the things that make us anxious.

27. From Rachel Cohen-Rottenberg, "It's an oft-repeated and erroneous stereotype that autistic people lack empathy . . . Ironically, in the face of the myth of nonexistent autistic empathy. I have an intensely empathetic response. I intuitively recognized the potential for harm and suffering to millions of people, I feel grief, anger, and a powerful need to speak to the issue." She goes on to add, "unfortunately, too many lay people look to credentials as opposed to experience when it comes to understanding non-normative conditions." *On Autism and Empathy: Dispelling Myths and Breaking Stereotypes* edited blog, (2011). http://autismandempathyblog.wordpress.com/on-the-matter-of-empathy/

28. Ableism contributes to the traumatization: "It is tragic that the very methods a traumatized Autistic person may use to calm themselves from the trauma they've experienced, are often the very things those who are not Autistic pinpoint as "behaviors" or actions that must be stopped. Not only is the person trying as best they can to deal with the initial traumatic event(s), but they are often being punished and told to stop using the only ways they know of that actually help them cope, thus creating further trauma." From *Emma's Hope Book: Living Being Autistic* blog post, (Jun 25, 2013). http://emmashopebook.com/2013/06/25/trauma-autism/

29. Beauvoir's *Ethics of Ambiguity* (1949, Citadel Press), posted online through marxists.org, http://www.marxists.org/reference/subject/ethics/de-beauvoir/ambiguity/

30. JS and DH had a secondary conversation whether it was possible to use "crazy" in non-ableist ways. For reference to this question, see "Replace 'Crazy' with the Adjective You Actually Mean" by Katie Klabusich for The Establishment.

co (May 25, 2016) and the hashtag #replacecrazywith. http://www.theestablishment. co/2016/05/25/replace-crazy-with-the-adjective-you-actually-mean/

31. As discussed in the Prologue.

32. See *Fat Studies: An Interdisciplinary Journal of Body Weight and Society* (Taylor & Francis Online).

33. See LB's post, "Ableism/Language" on autistichoya.com (updated Dec 7, 2016). http://www.autistichoya.com/p/ableist-words-and-terms-to-avoid.html

34. See Amy Sequenzia, "Privacy Versus Popularity": "Your child's disability is not about you. Your child's disability is not your story to tell. If you do it in public at your child's expense, you are not doing your job, which is parenting. . . . Let me repeat that: Parents are posting private information about their children, they are posting difficult moments of their disabled children for praise from other parents." Posted on ollibean.com (Accessed Dec 2016).

35. Note Ferguson and Nusbaum, "DS: What is it and What difference does it make?"

36. See my chapter. 4, ref. to Siebers 2008, pp. 126–127.

37. DH Note: Thinking here of Kristie Dotson's work on testimonial smothering and silencing. See "Feminists We Love" posted online: http://www.thefeministwire. com/2015/01/kristie-dotson/

38. I had a colleague discuss my daughter's teacher within earshot and how upset her daughter was because my daughter's class was disruptive to her daughter's class. My colleague actively named my daughter's teacher with intention to antagonize me. My daughter was subsequently removed from that class *and that school* before the end of the school year.

39. See Crenshaw's more recent work as cofounder and executive director of the African American Policy Forum (AAPF), including initiatives like #SayHerName (http://www.aapf.org/sayhername/):

> Although black women are routinely killed, raped, and beaten by the police, their experiences are rarely foregrounded in popular understandings of police brutality. Yet, inclusion of black women's experiences in social movements, media narratives, and policy demands around policing and police brutality is critical to effectively combating racialized state violence for black communities and other communities of color.

40. See Crenshaw's seminal text, "Mapping the Margins: Intersectionality, Identity Politics, and Violence against Women of Color" in the *Stanford Law Review*, Vol. 43, No. 6 (Jul, 1991), pp. 1241–1299.

41. As quoted in an article by Bim Adewunmi, "Kimberlé Crenshaw on intersectionality: 'I wanted to come up with an everyday metaphor that anyone could use.'" Posted in *The New Statesman*, (Apr 2, 2014). Available online: http://www.newstatesman.com/lifestyle/2014/04/kimberl-crenshaw-intersectionality-i-wanted-come-everyday-metaphor-anyone-could

42. bell hooks interprets this idea from Freire effectively when thinking of how this critical consciousness or conscientization is linked to a process of decolonization: "Because the colonizing forces are so powerful in this white supremacist capitalist patriarchy, it seems that black people are always having to renew a commitment to a

decolonizing political process that should be fundamental to our lives and is not. And so Freire's work in its global understanding of liberation struggles, ... Again and again Freire has had to remind readers that he never spoke of conscientization as an end itself, but always as it is joined by meaningful praxis" (1994, 47).

43. See my discussion in chapter 2 of Kittay (2009, 612)

44. For example, see Geoff Livingston, "No Thank You, Trump America: I will not give him an open mind" (Nov 13, 2016) for *The Huffington Post*, (http://www.huffing-tonpost.com/entry/no-thank-you-trump-america_us_58285b7de4b02b1f5257a42c):

> Trump and that small group of supporters who are using this election as an endorsement of xenophobia, bigotry and misogyny cannot be given mulligan after mulligan. We will lose everything that makes America free and inclusive if we allow that to happen.
>
> A word of caution to those who disagree with Trump: We cannot fight hate with hate. Violence destroys the message. Protestors have invoked the swastika as a method of pro-testing against Trump. I have been the subject of persecution in my past. My relatives in Europe flee-ed the Nazi threat. This is not a casual reference. In fact, it is a hurtful one, one that inspires as much fear and hate in protest as it seeks to combat. The more mindful we can be about our use of symbolism, the more impactful our message will be.

45. It is worth a reference to but not an extensive discussion of *Hypatia*'s publica-tion of Rebecca Tuvel's essay on the possibility of transracial identity, utilizing the case of Dolezal. I cite Kristie Dotson's conclusion on this particular matter (cited with permission, [Facebook post; May 7, 2017]):

> [As] I grow wearier with the *Hypatia* debacle and increasing number of "considered" and "balanced" pieces on the article and its responses (which were predictable . . . this is what makes the provocateur approach so successful . . . people are forced to respond to pieces that never should have made it through peer-review . . . and this demand is exacerbated by controversy, not lessened), this article is the best reflection on the kind of epistemic environment and discriminatory peer-review processes that spark these debacles and the tangible harms that result.
>
> I work on teasing out epistemological engines to structural and systemic states of affairs. As a result, this debacle has been of great concern to me. And I have learned a great deal about a great many. I have seen much of my own work confirmed throughout the course of these discussions: from the brute deniers of epistemic violence; to the people who fail to realize harms can be facilitated and hidden as harms due to epistemological failings; to the people who at once assume some conception of epistemic violence only to then deny its existence in their various statements; to people who apply it to every-thing without an analysis of what the structures and systems look like that generate the epistemology-related issues; and so much more.
>
> In the end, and I am coming to an end on this particular issue, this piece reflects each and every concern and disappointment I have with *Hypatia*, its review process to date, and the Tuvel article.

46. Or rather, the more appropriate use of the term. From Zack Ford's "The Real Meaning of 'Transracial.'" (Jun 17, 2015) for ThinkProgress.org. http://thinkprogress.org/the-real-meaning-of-transracial-ebfb6e18544a

> Kimberly McKee, an assistant professor at Grand Valley State University and assistant director of the Korean-American Adoptee Adoptive Family Network (KAAN) . . . told

ThinkProgress, "I hope that we recognize that the term transracial describes a specific type of adoption experience. At the same time, I encourage us to use this as an opportunity to ask ourselves why are we not hearing more about the experiences of black women in the US and #SayHerName." If the term is co-opted to describe Dolezal, "it erases the lived experiences and realities of transracially adopted individuals."

I am one of the signatories on the controversial open letter to *Hypatia*'s editors regarding the publication of an article by Rebecca Tuvel that hypothesizes the idea of a "transracial identity" via Dolezal as also permissible. A copy of the open letter is still available online: http://gendertrender.wordpress.com/alexis-shotwell-open-letter-to-hypatia/

47. There have been recent examples of people who "see color for the first time" videos, showing the subjects putting on glasses and looking at a set of colorful balloons. This is similar to the cochlear implant videos in which the subject "hears for the first time" a loved one's voice.

48. See Ann Jurecic's discussion in "Neurodiversity" (2007, 427).

49. See Doston's and Sheth's contributions to the Special Issue of *Hypatia* on interstitiality (Feb. 2014).

50. See Scuro (2017).

51. See commentary from National Women's Law Center, posted by Lauren Khouri, "Pregnancy's Not a Disability, But the ADA Helps Pregnant Workers" (Dec 18, 2013). http://www.nwlc.org/our-blog/pregnancy%E2%80%99s-not-disability-ada-helps-pregnant-workers

52. As in the case of Rachel Dolezal. As described by Brubaker (2015, ¶¶60–61), which may be parallel to the discussion in chapter 1 about "my interloper problem":

Passing, on the objectivist view, intrinsically involves deception (Kennedy 2003)—justifiable deception, perhaps, for the many light-skinned blacks who have successfully passed as white, but deception nonetheless. Passing is always trespassing (Harris 1993).

The deception involved in performing an identity on which one has no legitimate claim underwrites the charges of appropriation and cultural theft. [Noting: "The notions of appropriation and cultural theft presuppose an understanding of identity, culture, and history as forms of property. The notion of race as property has been articulated by legal scholars, beginning with Harris's (1993) influential analysis of 'whiteness as property.'"] In a context in which who is what can determine not only who (legitimately) gets what but also who (legitimately) gets to do what, Dolezal was accused of selectively indulging in "blackness as a commodity," of "donning blackness" in order to "negotiate black spaces," while retaining the privilege of removing her "costume" at will (Blay 2015). While gender transitions are understood to be undertaken at great personal cost, and to bring no extrinsic benefits, Dolezal was asserted to have "capitalized on her fake blackness" (Modkins 2015), "building a career and persona off it" (Noman 2015): she selectively "appropriated aspects of blackness" for her "personal benefit" (Fang 2015) and "occupied and dominated spaces ostensibly reserved for people who had life-long experiences of racial marginalization and disenfranchisement" (White 2015).

53. For a good account of how anti-black racism works, see George Yancy's "Walking While Black in the 'White Gaze'" (Sept 1, 2013) for *The New York Times*. http://opinionator.blogs.nytimes.com/2013/09/01/walking-while-black-in-the-white-gaze/?mcubz=0&_r=0

54. See Emily Tess Katz report, "Transitioning To Female Taught Rebecca Juro A Valuable Lesson About Male Privilege" including a live interview of Juro on

The Huffington Post (May 19, 2014). http://www.huffingtonpost.com/2014/05/19/
rebecca-juro_n_5353520.html. Also reported by Lane Florsheim for *Marie Claire*,
"A Study in Sexism: What Happens When Trans Women Lose Their Male
Privilege," (Aug 14, 2015). http://www.marieclaire.com/culture/news/a15510/
male-privilege-transgender-people/

55. From Anthony J. Williams, "Why Black Queer Men Must Fight Misogynoir" for WearYourVoiceMag.com (http://wearyourvoicemag.com/identities/race/
black-women-everything-youd-never-know):

> Misogynoir is a term created by Black feminist scholar Dr. Moya Bailey to discuss anti-
> Black misogyny. Misogynoir teaches us that the material reality of living as a Black
> woman is often dire.
>
> A society that approves of only the lightest Black people and minimizes women at
> every opportunity will inevitably produce men who hate women. This planet is full of men
> who enjoy sex with women and love women's body parts, but whose actions reflect a deep
> disrespect for women as fellow humans. I have seen Black men disparage dark-skinned
> people as "ugly," despite their beautiful dark-skinned mothers who protected them from
> the world that seeks to destroy us. Regrettably, I have kept quiet more than once in that
> swiveling chair as the barbers and customers talked about women as if they were pieces of
> meat. My silence was complicity in an anti-Black patriarchal society that lives on because
> we reproduce it daily.

56. See Rachel McKinnon's video presentation on "calling in" instead of "calling out,": "Allies, Active Bystanders, and Gaslighting" presented at Rice University,
posted Sep 3, 2015. http://www.youtube.com/watch?v=T4cGNF2y40c

57. I am ethnically Italian American and so this complicates whether I am "white
enough," complicated again by class and gender differences by not being "white
enough."

58. See Fanon's *The Fact of Blackness* (1952). http://www.nathanielturner.com/
factofblackness.htm

59. Particularly the case of David Washington in Fredericksburg, Virginia,
as reported by Jason Molinet for the New York *Daily News* (updated May
23, 2015). http://www.nydailynews.com/news/crime/va-resigns-taser-peppe-spray-
stroke-victim-article-1.2232948

60. PoC: People of Color. Thinking here specifically of the "attitude test" and how,
as in the case of Sandra Bland, since she failed that test, was detained and eventually
died in police custody. This problem, and the corresponding real danger of "having an
attitude" when one (marginalized) is expected to defer judgment, the authority, even
genuflect and be grateful for the interaction, can be paralleled with the ways in which
caretakers, beyond their caretaking roles, also expect similar deference and will issue
similar "attitude checks" without which there may be penalties, withholding of care,
exploitation and abuse.

61. Note from LB: See: http://autisticadvocacy.org/2015/07/asan-calls-for-justice-
in-troy-canales-police-brutality-case/. I drafted that statement for ASAN and was
deliberate about connecting the case it was about to broader patterns of racism and
ableism.

62. See *LA Times* (Mar 5, 2011), "Police Commission overrules chief, says LAPD shooting was wrong. The commission rejects the chief's finding that officers made mistakes but were ultimately justified in killing an unarmed autistic man" reported by Joel Rubin. http://articles.latimes.com/2011/mar/05/local/la-me-shooting-20110305

63. See *LA Times* (Jan 24, 2011), "Ex-LAPD officer found to have used excessive force in slaying. Federal jury rejects former officer Joseph Cruz's account of the March 2008 shooting that killed Mohammad Usman Chaudhry, a 21-year-old autistic man" reported by Joel Rubin. http://articles.latimes.com/2011/jan/24/local/la-me-lapd-verdict-20110124

64. See the *Chicago Reader* (Dec 17, 2015): "Black, autistic, and killed by police. Stephon Watts was diagnosed with Asperger's at age nine—and shot dead by Calumet City cops at age 15. Now his family is working to keep other kids with autism out of the line of fire" reported by Adrienne Hurst. http://www.chicagoreader.com/chicago/stephon-watts-police-shooting-autism-death/Content?oid=20512018

65. For example, see the case of a North Miami Beach Police Department using mug shots of black men for target practice, as reported by BBC.com: "Florida police shot images of black men in training" (Jan 17, 2015). http://www.bbc.com/news/world-us-canada-30860057

66. Like NIMBY (Not In My Backyard), recently there was a letter from a neighbor that asked to remove a boy from the neighborhood because he behaved and interacted in nonnormative, non-neurotypical ways. See the case from Newcastle Canada, reported by Channel 7 Eyewitness News, (Aug 20, 2013): "Autistic Boy Hate Letter: Neighbor Suggests Euthanizing Child." http://abc7chicago.com/archive/9213250/. Ableist expectations of what makes a "neighborhood" is not the actual "neighbors" who live there, but an assumption of regulated and enforced normalcy. There are ableist preoccupations in the Stand Your Ground laws, clearly illustrated by the murder of Trayvon Martin.

67. Sami Schalk cites her intersectional approach based in Corrinne Blackmer's assertion, quoting her in this way: "exclusive focus on one category of difference tends to inhibit analysis of how overlapping differences operate in syncopation ([Blackmer 1993] 232)," (2015, 149).

68. According to Schalk on *both/and* desire, exemplified by Claire's "refusal to stay on one side of any binary and her attempt instead to exist on both sides at once." This renders Claire "and Claire's challenging of their implicit binaries . . . as 'peculiar,' 'unfathomable,' 'queer,' 'undecided and uncertain,'" (154, 155–56).

69. See Diane Duane's *The Young Wizards* series, http://www.youngwizards.com/category/young-wizards-series/

70. From Davidson's *Black Girl Dangerous* blogpost, "Angry about the White Lesbians Suing for Having a Black Child? You're Missing Something" (Oct 6, 2014). http://www.blackgirldangerous.org/2014/10/angry-white-lesbians-suing-black-child-youre-missing-something/

71. From the blog, prettyqueer.com, "On Ableism within Queer Spaces, or, Queering the 'Normal'" (Dec 7, 2012). http://prettyqueer.com/2012/12/07/on-ableism-within-queer-spaces-or-queering-the-normal/

72. From a Facebook post [with permission], http://www.facebook.com/kay.ulandaybarrett/posts/10152776478728356

73. From "Poetry is not a Luxury" in *Sister Outsider* (1984).

74. See autistichoya.com on this point.

75. Note from LB: This is important, because it was the murder of a white, class-privileged autistic living in an affluent area that started the vigils happening.

76. The National Day of Mourning is March 1. http://www.disabilityleadership.org/index.php?option=com_content&view=article&id=25:day-of-mourning&catid=1:about-us

77. It is worth noting Brown's latter publication: "Our movement first rose with Jim Sinclair's speech 'Don't Mourn For Us' at the 1993 International Conference on Autism in Toronto. Sinclair founded Autism Network International (ANI), the first autism organization ever led by autistic people, around the same time. The impetus for ANI developed from the frustrations of autistic people struggling to organize under existing parent-run autism organizations that stymied their efforts and co-opted their self-advocacy."

78. See Lydia Brown here: http://www.autistichoya.com/2013/11/an-unholy-alliance-autism-speaks-and.html and here: http://www.autistichoya.com/2012/07/georgetown-say-no-to-autism-speaks.html. For more on the critique of Autism Speaks, see one video critique of "Autism $peaks": http://www.youtube.com/watch?v=wUKIatCarMA

79. There was a *New York Times* (NYT) exposé alleging that The Wounded Warrior Project engaged in inappropriate expenditures ("lavish") and expensive promotion without the aid going to wounded veterans (Dave Phillips reporting for NYT, [Jan 27, 2016]). As discussed in a review article posted on Alternet.org:

> "Veterans need organizations that provide real assistance and address the underlying issues affecting us, from war to healthcare to poverty, not another business profiting from our trauma and sacrifices," Kelly Dougherty, cofounder of Iraq Veterans Against the War, told AlterNet.

From Sarah Lazare's "Famous Charity for Veterans Accused of Inappropriate and Lavish Expenditures" (Jan 27, 2016). http://www.alternet.org/famous-charity-veterans-accused-inappropriate-and-lavish-expenditures

80. Elder Robinson stepped down from his voluntary position at Autism Speaks in 2013. See Online: http://www.autismdailynewscast.com/john-elder-robison-leaves-autism-speaks-amid-controversy/4773/laurel-joss/

81. See the ASAN "Position Statements" http://autisticadvocacy.org/policy-advocacy/position-statements/

82. After these interviews, Morénike Giwa Onaiwu was appointed to the ASAN board. Accessed May 21, 2016; http://autisticadvocacy.org/home/about-asan/leadership/

83. The "anti-vaccination" campaigns were led by affluent suburban parents who exemplified the bias that children are "better off with measles [or dead] than with autism," similar to the traditional articulation of ableist thinking; "it is better to be dead than disabled." See here for the "anti-vaccination" body count, http://www.latimes.com/local/california/la-me-measles-oc-20150126-story.html

84. See Scuro (2014), p. 185.

85. Specifically, in utilizing Karen Warren's metaphor of Western philosophy's "canonical house," I argue that "theory-building needs revision so that it isn't just an exercise in exclusivity, arrogance, and general "House-maintenance." . . . Theory-building must become more like bridge-building than house-building if it is at all to engage intersectionality" (Scuro 2014, 183).

86. On autistichoya.com, http://www.autistichoya.com/2014/09/the-empty-room.html

87. On autistichoya.com, http://www.autistichoya.com/2015/07/how-not-to-plan-disability-conferences.html

88. See Kozma and Schroer (2014), in discussing anti-abortion billboard campaigns, they discuss this point: "Bullshit, like lying, is a mode of misrepresentation; . . . [an] assertion fails the bullshit test for multiple reasons: different version of [a] claim each have different specious explanatory theories; . . . some evidence supports the opposite claim; [etc.] . . . In our view, this is not a sufficient critique; it fails to hold the speaker accountable for the potential harm done by the inflammatory nature of the rhetoric" (105).

89. There is an affinity of Brown's approach with another narrative position: see Siebers' discussion of "philosophical realism" (2008, 126–127) and his citation of Cheryl Marie Wade, (184), discussed in chapters 1 and 4.

90. By "shit-show" I am also referencing the original IEP meeting discussed in chapter 1. But here, it could be extended to the SDS "shit-show" when there was a parade to celebrate and many people in wheelchairs were stuck in the mud and sun while others just went into the stands and the shade. See Emily Ladau's, "Stuck in the Dirt: Why Advocating for Justice and Access Never Stops" posted with The Center for Disability Rights, (Accessed May 16, 2016). http://cdrnys.org/blog/disability-dialogue/the-disability-dialogue-stuck-in-the-dirt/ cited in chapter 1.

91. See, for example, the warnings issue to women about the Zika Virus, as reported in *The Independent* (Jan 25, 2016) by Steve Connor, "Zika Virus: Pregnant Women Advised to Stay Away From Rio 2016 Olympics" especially women who are even "planning to be pregnant." http://www.independent.co.uk/life-style/health-and-families/health-news/zika-virus-pregnant-women-warned-to-stay-away-from-rio-2016-olympics-a6833311.html

92. Siebers (2008) cites Adrienne Asch on this point.

93. See Hamraie on this point: "Universal Design Research as a New Materialist Practice" in DSQ, Vol. 32, No. 4. (2012). http://dsqsds.org/article/view/3246/3185

94. Butler quoting E. Levinas and R. Kearney, "Dialogue with Emmanuel Levinas" in *Face to Face with Levinas*, (New York, NY: SUNY Press, 1986). In *Precarious Life* (2004), pp. 131–132.

CHAPTER 4

1. (2010; 1, 2, [emphasis added]). The debate over the use of Butler in Disability Studies is well laid out by Ellen Samuels in "Critical Divides: Judith Butler's Body Theory and the Question of Disability" in *Feminist Disability Studies* (Kim Q. Hall, ed. Indiana University Press, 2011). Butler's newer scholarship openly draws upon

Levinasian ethics in a way that *Bodies That Matter*, the material referenced in recent DS scholarship, still uses Foucauldian theory.

2. There has been recent scholarship and use of the term precarity in a variety of contexts, including through a capabilities approach. I am limiting my usage to Judith Butler's usage of the terms. Thanks to Joel Michael Reynolds for this point.

3. Here it is important to note that Butler in an interview with George Yancy (for *The New York Times*, Jan 12, 2015) takes the position that #blacklivesmatter does have a greater and justified demand than #alllivesmatter. http://opinionator.blogs.nytimes.com/2015/01/12/whats-wrong-with-all-lives-matter/?_r=0

4. An excerpt from Brian Miller and Mike Lapham's *The Self-Made Myth: The Truth About How Government Helps Individuals and Businesses Succeed* (Berrett-Koehler Publishers, 2012), "Despite what [Donald] Trump may espouse, his success would in no way possible without his father, the general public, and the US government. Unfortunately, Trump decided to forget or selectively ignore these truths while forming his political philosophy, a sentiment made particularly clear during his brief bid for the 2012 Republican presidential nomination." Reposted on Alternet.org (Jul 29, 2012, accessed May 28, 2016). http://www.alternet.org/story/156234/exposing_how_donald_trump_really_made_his_fortune%3A_inheritance_from_dad_and_the_government's_protection_mostly_did_the_trick

5. "The more or less existential conception of 'precariousness' is . . . linked with a more political notion of 'precarity'" (2010, 3).

6. She cites Levinas' theory with authority early on in the text: " . . . as Levinas has said, . . . the obligations 'we' have are precisely those that disrupt any established notion of 'we'" (2010, 14).

7. Citing Weil's "Human Personality" in *Simone Weil: An Anthology*, (S. Mills, ed., New York, NY: Weidenfeld & Nicolson, 1986, pp. 50–78), p. 70.

8. See my discussion of the "fugue state" and "ontological shock" of being "handed over a diagnosis" in chapter 2.

9. See Melinda Hall's *The Bioethics of Enhancement: Transhumanism, Disability, and Biopolitics* (Rowman & Littlefield 2016). I had the privilege of attending the symposium on the book organized by Shelley Tremain in April 2017. The papers presented in these symposia are available on the Discrimination and Disadvantage blog online: http://philosophycommons.typepad.com/disability_and_disadvanta/2017/06/symposium-on-melinda-halls-the-bioethics-of-enhancement-hall.html

10. I find some of this intellectual nihilism in Elizabeth Barnes' *The Minority Body* when she discusses possible worlds in which disability exists within and not in an ableist context or even a world in which there is neither ableism nor disability. She also hypothesizes a "Disability Fairy" in which the fairy grants "the prevention of all future disabilities." Even with this, Barnes questions how this fairy might also have to alter the *causes* of disability in order to prevent future disability and that it may be a "deal worth taking." To her credit, she also states, "while the Disability Fairy case is interesting, . . . I don't think it actually gets a grip on the issue. The question of whether we should prevent disability can come apart from the question of whether disability is, by itself, bad for you" (2016, 68–69). This intention (to pull the

questions apart) seems to indicate identifying disabilities as relative to certain kinds of objectives and natural facts—which is exactly the concern I raise here. She asserts as much in arguing disability as a "neutral feature" out of the mere-difference view of disability (78–79).

11. Cora Diamond discusses how even philosophers engage in deflection, in which "the philosopher's understanding is deflected; the issue becomes deflected, as the philosopher thinks it or rethinks it in the language of philosophical skepticism. . . . [which can] further deflect from the truth . . . I want the notion of deflection, for describing what happens when we are moved from the appreciation, or the attempt at appreciation, of a difficulty of reality to a philosophical or moral problem apparently in the vicinity." From "The Difficulty of Reality and the Difficulty of Philosophy," (reprinted *in Philosophy & Animal Life*, New York, NY: Columbia University Press, 2008), p. 57.

12. Barnes argues against this negative construction in her chapter "Disability Pride," stating the error thus (2016, 168–169):

> The dominant conception of disability in contemporary society is an explicitly normative one. Disability is a tragedy. Disability is a loss. Disability is a misfortune. Within this normative conception of disability, there is little room for understanding the experience of the thriving disabled person. And so we develop narratives of disability to accommodate the fact that many disabled people seem to thrive. . . . We tell the story of the inspirational disabled person . . . thriving *in spite of* disability. . . . [Instead] Pride, I argue, is a crucial part of undermining the idea that disability is somehow essentially or inherently tragic.

13. The "ability" to identify as "employable" has much currency in our society—often a *costuming* of potential contribution. I would argue, much like there is embedded racism and sexism in how one can "get a job," there too rests latent, unpacked ableist assumptions. I would add to "employability" the idea of "fuckability." The overlapping of the "sexy" and "able" body as important currency for generating capital and status is a site of ableist assumption, framing some lives as more precarious and disposable than others.

14. An interesting point of discussion in my Philosophy of Education class was the pervasive standardized testing strategy: "when you do not know the answer, just choose c." My students were quite familiar with it and we asked about it in the context of Critical Pedagogy. Here, a parody video becomes a "lesson plan" defending the Common Core curriculum—again out of ableist anxieties for job-holding, intellectual understanding, social comportment, etc., the complexity of "I choose C" through a philosophical, pedagogical, and ableist analysis yields a number of thought problems. See TEDed's posting of M. Thomas' Lesson Plan: *Why We Need Common Core: "I choose C."* Video originally posted on YouTube by rngutierrez1. (Accessed May 29, 2016) http://ed.ted.com/on/agod4tzg

15. Counter examples are worth nothing here: "Happy Being Himself, This Little Boy Turns Down a 3-D Printed Prosthetic Hand" by B. B. Millsaps (3DPrint.com, Accessed May 22, 2015), as well as Audre Lorde's meditation over whether to utilize a prosthetic breast, a "falsie." Discussed further in chapter 5. http://3dprint.com/66657/boy-happy-without-prosthetic/

16. Barnes gives an account of McBryde Johnson as she argued against Peter Singer's assumptions about disabled people being worse-off. Despite her testimony,

in which, "I've had enough. I suggest to Singer that we have exhausted our topic" as it regarded the negative correlation between disability and happiness, Singer still was chosen to write McBryde Johnson's obituary in *The New York Times*. To this, Barnes states, "They titled it 'Happy Nevertheless.' McBryde went to great lengths – including her famous essay in the same paper that published the obituary – during her life to explain that she was not happy *nevertheless*. She was just happy, like so many of other flourishing disabled people" (2016, 137–138). Barnes notes Kristie Dotson's concept of "testimonial smothering" as a form of testimonial injustice as well.

17. This is in specific reference to Stella Young's argument: disability should not be made exceptional.

18. I argue earlier in chapter 1: calling someone "special" or "special needs" can easily translate into an ableist slur.

19. See Quentin Davies' narrative of the Judge Rotenberg Center, which used electroshock therapy as "behavior aversion techniques," an institution still in operation:

> In the very recent history of the JRC, a study by Mental Disability Rights International caused the United Nations Special Rapporteur on Torture to investigate the Judge Rotenberg Center, declaring the treatment of disabled people by the JRC to be torture. The previous Rapporteur on Torture, Manfred Nowak, urged the investigation, and said, "This is torture. Of course here they might say, but this is for a good purpose because it is for medical treatment. But even for a good purpose – because the same is to get from a terrorist information about a future attack, is a good purpose. To get from a criminal a confession is a good purpose. [. . .] You cannot balance this. The prohibition of torture is absolute" (Hinman and Brown). After the investigation, the Judge Rotenberg Center was mentioned in the Report of the Special Rapporteur on torture and other cruel, inhuman, or degrading treatment or punishment, written by current Special Rapporteur Juan E. Méndez. The report states that "the rights of the students of the JRC subjected to Level III Aversive Interventions by means of electric shock and physical means of restraints have been violated under the UN Convention against Torture and other international standards" (85). In 2011, Matthew Israel resigned his position as part of the probation agreement after Israel was indicted on counts of misleading a witness and destroying evidence that contained footage related to the investigation, involving the treatment of the two students after the prank phone call (Jrolf). Glenda Crookes took over Matthew Israel's position after his resignation. Also in 2011, the Massachusetts Department of Developmental Services (DDS) ruled that electric shock and other physical aversives cannot be used on new admissions to JRC (Markham). This was very important in that students who are admitted to JRC after this date can no longer be subjected to physical aversives, but the JRC still has many students who can be and are abused in this way.

From "Prisoners of the Apparatus: The Judge Rotenberg Center" posted by The Autistic Self-Advocacy Network [ASAN], (Accessed Aug 9, 2014). http://autisticadvocacy.org/2014/08/prisoners-of-the-apparatus-the-judge-rotenberg-center/

20. See, for example, *Rosemary: The Hidden Kennedy Daughter* by Kate Clifford Lawson, (New York, NY: Houghton Mifflin Harcourt, 2015).

21. From Anne Shlay in "Low Income Homeownership: American dream or delusion?":

> Given . . . the precarious financial situation of many low-income households and the significance of financial loss for them, the opportunity costs of their capital should be

scrutinised like those of households with more economic resources. Examined along these lines, the conclusions reached by economists Goetzman and Spiegel in their analysis of housing's economic performance are severe.Overinvestment in housing by families with modest savings means underinvestment in financial assets that will grow and provide income for retirement. In fact, *encouraging homeownership among low-income families will only increase the wealth gap in the United States* (Goetzman and Spiegel, 2002, p. 272; emphasis added).The continued high level of racial segregation in most US cities also means that returns to investments may be affected by what has long been regarded as a dual housing market (Denton, 2001). Neighbourhoods of Black homeowners, on average, have been found to be better than those housing Black renters. But the differences between neighbourhoods of White owners and White renters were much larger. Therefore, benefits accrued to White low-income homebuyers may be greater than those accrued to Black low-income homebuyers. Both place, race and neighbourhood are vital parts of the equation when assessing economic benefits to low-income homeownership. Is homeownership a quality economic investment for low-income families? The answer is complex (Mar 2006, 520).

22. There is a brief but excellent account of the historical practice of government-sponsored redlining by A. C. Jemison for Urban Intellectuals, "Did You Know Black Ghettos Were Deliberately Created By Gov't Sponsored Redlining?" (Accessed Feb 8, 2017). http://urbanintellectuals.com/2017/02/08/know-black-ghettos-deliberately-created-govt-sponsored-redlining/. This practice continues as Lisa Guenther describes in a post, "Phenomenology as a Practice of Liberation" discusses a sketch by planners for a new construction in Nashville, titled "SoBro" (Jun 19, 2013):

It's a developer's vision of how Nashville could look someday, if we just built enough live/work environments and planted a few trees. The sketch invites you to insert yourself into this scene, to "catch" the vision, to *want* what you see depicted here.This invitation is very different from the task of phenomenological epoche and reduction. It does not ask you to *suspend* the natural attitude, but rather to embrace a certain version of it. It asks you to suspend your capacity for critical reflection and become absorbed in the sketch, in a way that both gives you a ready-made fantasy of (sub)urban life, and also constitutes you as a particular kind of subject: a consumer, an investor, a city-dweller, even a citizen.What's wrong with this picture? This is where the social dimensions of phenomenology need to be expanded beyond the practice of classical phenomenology, narrowly-conceived. It's where phenomenology must become *critical*, not only of the naïve positivism of the natural attitude but also of the ideological horizons that frame our perception of the world from different perspectives. (Guenther goes on to assess it this way:) What will happen to these people if the developers have their way? Some will be arrested for sleeping in parks or under bridges; they will be punished for being homeless, and jail will become their most viable "housing option." Some will die of exposure and/or untreated medical conditions. Some will be lucky enough to crash with family or friends, or to find their own form of housing. Many will be displaced to other homeless shelters, many of which already function as de facto carceral spaces. The Nashville Rescue Mission is equipped with metal detectors and security cameras. One inhabitant says: "It's like a prison in there. . . . Too many beds crammed into one spot" (5). The mission provides a bed for 400–500 men a night and serves between 1800–2000 meals a day.Any way you cut it, the SoBro is a scene of mass incarceration, displacement, and death—from the perspective of those who are *already there*, but who are not represented in the developer's vision except as a threat to be managed, a blight to be removed, and a problem to be solved.

23. For instance, see Lydia Brown's full critique of disability simulations in "A Critique of Disability/Impairment Simulations" (posted on autistichoya.com, Accessed Feb 24, 2013), citing Valerie Brew-Parrish here:

> Disabled activist Valerie Brew-Parrish further identifies three particular problematic ideas that may emerge from participation in disability simulations: the belief that life is a tragedy for disabled people, the belief that they (as non-disabled participants) are lucky not to be disabled, and the belief that disabled people are especially inspiring or courageous for living their ordinary lives. She notes further that these simulations are usually organized and implemented by nondisabled professionals without the input of actually disabled people, which begs the question of whether or not it is ethical to engage in such activities.

24. Siebers goes on to state that "It demonstrates both the social construction of experience and the political promise arising from the knowledge that experience is constructed . . . [a] valuable weapon against the oppression of minority people" (2008, 127).

25. See chapter 1, my discussion of the interloper problem.

26. See Siebers, "Ablebodiedness is a temporary identity at best, while being human guarantees that all other identities will eventually come into contact with some form of disability identity" (2008, 5).

27. I follow Greta Gaard's interest in an ecofeminist examination of the "boundary conditions" that have become "anti-ecological," especially as they inform gender and heteronormativity. Citing Karen Warren's work, in which Warren outlines eight boundary conditions of at length, Gaard offers a useful groundwork for defining how "eco-masculinity" would work and, for my purposes, offers me a possible continued intersectional analysis with ableism. Borrowing Gaard's citation (2014, 231) of Warren:

> (1) not promoting any of the "isms" of social domination; (2) locating ethics contextually; (3) centralizing the diversity of women's choices; (4) reconceiving ethical theory as a theory-in-process which changes over time . . . (5) responsive to the experiences and perspectives of oppressed persons . . . ; (6) it would not attempt to provide an objective viewpoint . . . As with feminist ethics, an eco-masculinity would (7) provide a central place for values typically misrepresented in traditional ethics (care, love, friendship, appropriate trust), and most significantly, (8) reconceive what it means to be human "since it rejects as either meaningless or currently untenable any gender-free or gender-neutral description of humans, ethics, and ethical decision-making" (Warren 1990, 141).

28. From Faulds', "Reclaiming the Dignity Lost in a Diagnosis" posted on blogsite, *We Are Like Your Child.* (Accessed Jul 23, 2015). http://wearelikeyourchild.blogspot.com/2015/07/reclaiming-dignity-lost-in-diagnosis.html

29. I discuss this in chapter 1.

30. Sheth's approach through interstitial analysis can include the difference between generations and social and political identity formation better than traditional intersectional theory and even Critical Race Theory, there is a "dynamic is . . . generationally specific." Her example includes South Asian identity, in which the "history of second- and third- generation South Asians is not the same as the histories of first-generation Indian-, Pakistani-, Bangladeshi- and Sri Lankan migrants;

the former straddle the tensions between the country of their parents' origin and the regions in which they were raised in ways that are fundamentally different from their parents' struggles to straddle similar tensions" (2014, 86).

31. Discussed in chapter 1. Also see Paul K. Longmore, Lauri Umansky, eds. *The New Disability History: American Perspectives.* (New York, NY: New York University Press, 2001) and Kim Nielsen's, *A Disability History of the United States.* (Boston, MA: Beacon Press, 2012).

32. Joel Michael Reynolds in "The Silence of the Abled: Kristeva, Levinas, and the Sagamihara 19" (unpublished paper delivered at philoSOPHIA 2017) discusses the ideological implications of "getting rid of the disabled from the world," and how "It is better disabled people disappear," or "It is wasteful to have the disabled continue living": statements from Satoshi Uematsu who was responsible for the worst mass murder in Japan in which he targeted and stabbed to death nineteen people in an assistance facility. Reynolds notes the absence of interest in global and national media suggesting that this indifference is ableist.

33. Specifically, "Proponents of disability rights and national governments both view increasing labor market participation of people with disabilities as a central goal, albeit for different reasons. From the disability perspective, employment is about rights and participation in society; while for national governments, especially OECD countries, employment is about reducing welfare expenditures and activating beneficiaries. The low labor market participation of people with disabilities is a significant problem in the UK, as is the high level of people receiving disability benefits rather [than] participating in the workforce" (Owen & Harris 2012, ¶¶3–4). Authors go on to cite the ways the burdensomeness related to employability:

> The economic and social incentives to work were recognized by policymakers and people with disabilities alike, and there were discussions of how work increases social interaction and helps people feel a part of society. However, one of the concerns when discussing the rights and responsibilities of work was the lack of choice that people face. Many people with disabilities felt that they had very limited choice in the types of work available and who would hire them. This concern raised broader policy questions about the expectations of moving from welfare to a job, rather than being encouraged and supported to move from welfare into a career. People with disabilities felt that the workfare programs were pushing them into "any work" rather than a career of their choosing. As one participant put it: "I don't think we have the same choice as an able bodied person. . . . Other people can go out to work and enjoy what they do, because it's their choice to go into that profession" (Fran, female, age 38, physical disability). (¶22).

34. Reference to my chapter on voiced harm, *Why Race and Gender Still Matter* (Scuro 2014).

35. An example of this distinction between a sense of individuality but not necessarily pure "independence" is in the discussion about going for a walk between Sunaura Taylor and Judith Butler. Both get to enjoy each other's company (at one point helping each other shop for clothes) and neither is alone in the walk. The individuality of both comes by way of the dialogue they share when they walk; there is a humanizing interdependence in walking together rather than walking alone, "having to go it alone." Taylor gives an example in the dialogue about how she retrieves her cup at

the coffee shop when she is on her own and how, since it is disorienting to the people around her (she uses her mouth), it also becomes a political act. See the documentary *Examined Life*, (Astra Taylor, dir., 2008).

36. In the wake of a Trump presidency, this position—as a fully ableist and disablist position—has been further entrenched as he delivers a series of executive orders in his first week of office. See Lisa Desjardins' report for PBS Newshour, "The 12 Executive Actions Trump has signed (so far)." (Accessed Jan 24, 2017). http://www.pbs.org/newshour/rundown/10-executive-actions-trump-signed-far/

37. Emphasis added. Taylor, p. 123 citing Sue Donaldson and Will Kymlicka, *Zoopolis* (New York, NY: Oxford University Press, 2011).

38. James Stanescu gives a good sum of accelerationism with references on his blog, *Critical Animal.* (Accessed Dec 15, 2013). http://criticalanimal.blogspot.com/2013/12/accelerationism-animal-ethics-and.html

39. See "Too Fast to Fail: How High-Speed Trading Fuels Wall Street Disasters" by Nick Baumann for MotherJones.com, (Accessed Jan/Feb 2013 Issue). http://www.motherjones.com/politics/2013/02/high-frequency-trading-danger-risk-wall-street

40. From Levinas' *Entre Nous: Thinking-of-the-Other.* (New York, NY: Continuum, 1998), pp. 24–25.

41. Along with hope, perhaps "pride" too can be important in this same way but does not necessarily challenge or address ableism as it is both "sticky" and inherited. I'm thinking specifically of Barnes' final chapter, "Disability Pride" in *The Minority Body* (2016) in which she seeks to resolve the tension set up by the premise of the book: that disability needs not have a negative connotation but rather one that can be connected to a value-neutral model that participates in the construction of well-being.

42. The critiques of these desires were discussed in chapter 1.

43. There is a disability rights grassroots movement called, Not Dead Yet, worth citing here. See notdeadyet.org.

44. Sunaura Taylor discusses the overlap between the perception of domesticated animals and people with disabilities, suggesting instead that "Disability asks us to question our assumptions about who counts as a "productive member of society" and what sort of activities are seen as productive. It asks us to question the things we take for granted—our rationality, the way we move, the way we perceive the world. Animals ethics also requires critical engagement with our assumptions about who is valuable and who is exploitable and a reimagining of what it means to contribute to the world" (2014, 120).

45. To use Erich Fromm's term, see Freire discuss "necrophily," (2009, 55)

46. Susan Wendell more specifically discusses disability-phobia (1996, 32).

47. I use the concept of "intelligibility" out of the Levinasian model of ethical theory. The first intelligibility is in *meta*-phor in which what is other cannot quite be represented. "The act of signifying would be more indigent than the act of perceiving. Rightfully, reality would have an immediate signification. Reality and intelligibility would coincide." This is not the same as intellectualism (2003, 7).

48. See Louise Derksen's summary, "Anne Conway's Critique of Cartesian Dualism." Published online in *ΠΑΙΔΕΙΑ*, (Accessed Sept 2015): http://www.bu.edu/wcp/Papers/Onto/OntoDerk.htm

49. I often ask students why it is that in learning Anatomy and Physiology (as future doctors and nurses especially), why are they learning the corpse first? How do they feel about opening up and examining the dead body? How come they not study the "body" more ecologically in that all living things are bodies in relation to other non-like bodies, engaged in their living through a *habitat*.

50. Citing Priscilla Wald "Future Perfect: Grammar, Genes, and Geography." (*New Literary History* 31(4), 2000, pp. 681–708).

51. The specific way Embree adapts Edmund Husserl's phenomenology is from his work in Husserl's later work, *Ideen II*, as "Constitutive phenomenology" in which nature as a concept is already "correlative to the naturalistic attitude" and "part of the cultural world." Embree goes on to state, "Pretheoretically, this world is where humans fundamentally live their lives. It is called the 'lifeworld' by Husserl and subsequent phenomenologists. Even though the emphasis in his work is on lifeworldly nature, which could be further specified as the lifeworldly environment, the lifeworld is concretely cultural for Husserl. The adoption of the naturalistic attitude requires abstraction from the values and uses of cultural objects and yields naturalistic objects" (2003, excerpted from pp. 37–40).

52. As discussed in chapter 1. See Eva Kittay (Jul 2009) as she argues against Singer and McMahon.

53. See Elizabeth Grosz's *Time Travels: Feminism, Nature, Power*, (Durham, NC: Duke University Press, 2005), on prosthetic objects, to be discussed in chapter 5.

54. Vandana Shiva is one of the most prominent, ecofeminist voices on this issue. For example, see *Staying Alive*: *Women, Ecology and Development*, (NJ: Zed Books Ltd, 1989) or more recently, *Earth Democracy: Justice, Sustainability and Peace* (MA: South End Press, 2005).

55. Vandana Shiva writing for *The Guardian*, "How Economic Growth has Become Anti-Life." (Accessed Nov 1, 2013). http://www.theguardian.com/commentisfree/2013/nov/01/how-economic-growth-has-become-anti-life

56. For example, I find it interesting the way there is discussion and unquestioned use of metaphor about how first-world economies can be "crippled" by slowed growth, yet there is no connection to the way in which foreign aid dependency becomes a way to disable non-"first-world" cultural and political autonomy. The case of Haiti comes to mind. See Dupuy, "Foreign Aid Keeps the Country from Shaping its own Future" in *The Washington Post*, (Jan 9, 2011).

57. At least this is the way the word might be understood from the Ancient Greek.

58. This is Sara Brill's concern (2011, 250).

59. Defending this idea of organic spontaneity was the topic of an unpublished paper I wrote on "*Ursprung*: Reading for the Root."

60. Shiva has also been criticized for being overly essentialist and romantic about the idea of the seed (see Cecile Jackson's "Radical Environmental Myths" [*New Left Review*, I/210, March/April 1995]), yet, this is not a purely ideological ecofeminism. She has been a leader in radical and outspoken resistance to the patenting of seed by transnational corporations with the establishment of seed banks. See navdanya.org.

61. For an interesting use of Fromm's term, see P. Gounari's "Neoliberalism as Social Necrophilia: Erich Fromm and the Politics of Hopelessness in Greece" in

Reclaiming the Sane Society: Essays on Erich Fromm's Thought (S. J. Miri, R. Lake, & T. M. Cress, eds., Boston, MA: Sense Publishers, 2014), pp. 187–201.

62. This is in honor of my dear friends, sisters Bernie and Katie, and their children and families. Their lives are scheduled, movements choreographed, with "many moving parts and people" in their respective households. Sometimes it is well-timed, sometimes less so, all with a clear design—to have made and to make Emma and Finn's lives less precarious than they already were and are. This book is dedicated to Emma who passed away in 2016.

63. From "Women and Caregiving," (Accessed Dec 2003). http://www.caregiver. org/women-and-caregiving-facts-and-figures

64. Also cited in Siebers, 2008, 65.

65. Devonya Havis had described this when it came to her husband's condition; discussed in chapter 3.

66. One example of this is of Willowbrook, a school for children with developmental disabilities, documented in *Unforgotten: Twenty-five Years after Willowbrook* (Jack Fisher, dir., 1996).

67. There also is some of this precarious dislocation in the distribution of the student "body" in a school district. Our recent experience with Special Education had my daughter moved mid-year out of one classroom and school (more affluent and integrated) to another school in the "other" part of the district (and to an enclosed classroom). Considering that children spend more of their waking life in school than at "home," this kind of "homelessness," in which students are shuffled around a district in terms of which seats in which classrooms they should occupy, it is hard to not take this ableist framework "home." In fact, we were told by the principal of the former school that we need to take her home because he could not ensure her safety. We homeschooled her for two weeks in order to restore her sense of self from some of the feelings of rejection and eroded self-esteem. It is worth noting again Lalvani and Hale's "Squeaky wheels, mothers from hell and CEOs of the IEP: Parents, privilege and the 'fight' for inclusive education." *Understanding and Dismantling Privilege*, 5(2), (2015), pp. 21–41.

68. See Reynolds' TEDxEmory talk, "Transability: or your body is not what you think." (Accessed Jul 7, 2014). http://www.youtube.com/watch?v=nBk8YeJv7Dg

69. Worth noting is Leroy Moore's "Droolilicious" in *Criptiques* (C. Wood, ed., May Day Press, 2014).

70. This is also the site of Reynold's account of transability.

71. Also cited in Siebers 2008, 184.

72. Hechler cites the same in relation to the case of his great-grandmother, (2017, ¶25):There is another possible reason for Emilie's increasing destabilization. As noted in her medical records:

> "*I didn't actually want to come here. I wanted to go home. The institution is too hard on me,*" and "*I'm getting sick here and it is making me weak.*" Physicians note repeatedly that she asserts she is "*not sick*" and "insists" on "being released." Additionally, repeated notes in her records allege that she is aggressive, that she curses, and that she does not want to work. One may also infer that she was perceived to be rebellious and an "unpleasant" patient who upset the smooth running of the psychiatric ward. One may also presume that

physicians and caretakers had the upper hand and let her know that. This is admittedly speculative, but the overarching nature of psychiatry as a disciplining and normalizing institution is by now well known. Moreover psychiatric clinics in their history have again and again been sites that, instead of alleviating crises, instead intensify them or even cause them in the first place. ...

73. Levinas coins this as a play on the idea of transcendence, but instead as signifying "the need for escape" (2003/1982, 54).

74. This is a term that Levinas employs when describing the desire for the Other that is not always an openness to the other (1998/1981, 25), also "the crux of the diachronic plot" and the "knot tied in subjectivity."

75. See Bettina Bergo's entry on Emmanuel Levinas in *The Stanford Encyclopedia of Philosophy*: "Levinas speaks of the face of the other who is 'widow, orphan, or stranger.' These figures are more than allegorical. Each one lacks something essential to its existence: spouse, parents, home." http://plato.stanford.edu/entries/levinas/

It is as summons that we see expression precipitating transcendence. In other words, if I am self-sufficient in my everyday cognition and my instrumental activities, then that is because I am a being that inhabits overlapping worlds in which my sway is decisive for me. The approach of the other person halts the dynamism of my cognitive and practical sway.

76. Harold Braswell's work on hospice and end-of-life care is important to note. An insight into his broader work can be found in his entry "Euthanasia" for *Keywords in Disability Studies*, in which he states, "While the relationship between hospice and euthanasia remains contested (Putnam 2002), Disability Studies scholars can work with hospice professionals to implement end-of-life care that is astute about ableist power dynamics and responsive to the needs of the terminally ill" (2015, 81).

77. Her sister Sandrine Bonnaire, a French supermodel, established a small assisted housing facility for her sister and others like her. She is interviewed by Mick LaSalle, "Sandrine Bonnaire tells her autistic sister's tale." Posted by the SF Gate. (Accessed Mar 30, 2008). http://www.sfgate.com/entertainment/article/Sandrine-Bonnaire-tells-autistic-sister-s-tale-3220169.php

78. This is a cliché that was used to justify the mistreatment and misrepresentation of my daughter during the (other and worse) IEP meeting, 2016.

79. Instead, non-indifference is a much more dynamic invocation in Levinas, here inspired by Gabriel Marcel: "Non-indifference of the one for the other! ... What I call the non-indifference of Saying is, in its double-negation, the difference behind which no commonality arises in the guise of an entity. And thus there is both relation and rupture, and thus awakening: awakening of Me by the other, the Me by the Stranger, of Me by the Stateless person, that is, by the fellow human being who is but a fellow human being. ... Expiation, assigned to me without any possible evasion and in which my own uniqueness is exalted, irreplaceable" (1998, 63).

80. The more striking account that Braswell observes is here:

Silvia, in contrast, was able to provide her father with an extremely different experience of dementia care. First, she had a broader context in which to interpret utterances that might seem nonsensical to others. For example, one day, while I was sitting with Ramon, he began to address me as Manuel. I tried to engage him in conversation about this, asking him who Manuel was and what he did, but he ignored my questions and continued on obliquely. When Sylvia came into the room, however, she immediately was able to recognize Manuel as a friend of her father's from sixty years prior, when he was in his twenties. "Ah, Manuel," she said to him. "You liked drinking rum with Manuel." On hearing this reference to rum, Ramon noticeably perked up, and he began speaking about Manuel and rum. He was not addressing us directly, and yet, because of Silvia's knowledge of him, she was able to enter his consciousness in a way that I, a relative stranger, could not. But Sylvia was able to provide a deeper context for Ramon's utterances even when they did not contain any clear biographical referent. For example, one day she told me that Ramon had done something incredible: He had woken up and, as opposed to being sullen—which had been his state for previous days—he was elated. His eyes were wide open and he was making a chewing motion with his mouth "I'm eating peace [*Estoy comiendo paz*]," he said. This poetic statement was not one that Silvia could readily situate in Ramon's life history. Nevertheless, her response to it was contextualized in a manner that, I believe, was specific to her status as his caretaker: She interpreted it as a sign that he was happy, and that her care was being successful. She smiled at him and echoed his chewing motion, repeating back to him "I'm also eating peace." Thus, she saw his seemingly nonsensical remark as both as a vindication of her particular care for him, as well as a potential bridge to engage him more fully.

81. See Marion Young's description of "menial" service work: "Menial labor usually refers not only to service, however, but also to any servile, unskilled, low-paying work lacking in autonomy, in which a person is subject to taking orders from many people. Menial work tends to be auxiliary work, instrumental to the work of others, where those others receive primary recognition for doing the job" (2014, 17).

82. From Butler (2004): "A narrative form emerges to compensate for the enormous narcissistic wound. . . . [We] respond to the exposure of vulnerability with an assertion of US "leadership" . . . [yet] we will need to emerge from the narrative perspective of US unilateralism and, as it were, its defensive structures . . ." (6–7).

83. See Shildrick and Price on the "clinical encounter." When it comes to disability claims, "far from liberating the claimant from an authoritarian and intrusive situation . . . [the] gaze now cast over the subject body is that of the subject herself. What is demanded of her is that she should police her own body, and report in intricate detail its failure to meet standards of normalcy; that she should render herself in effect transparent" (1999, 434).

84. Garland-Thomson citing Silvers (1995) and Kittay (1999).

85. See Richard Gilman-Opalsky (2014) on this point, discussed in chapter 5.

86. See Pfeiffer, (2009, 53–54), arguing that characterizations of "incompetent and lazy" folk come from the "interests of the oppressors." From Pfeiffer, "Usually these passively accepted hypotheses about human behavior and people are called stereotypes. In Western society due to the modern ontology there are a number of stereotypes about groups of people" (2002, ¶¶72–73). Also see *Theories of Race and Racism: A Reader*, Les Back and John Solomos, eds. (New York, NY: Routledge, 2000).

87. The two hallmarks of economic neoliberalism are trade liberalization and governmental deregulation. One example of this, was in the crafting of the Trans Pacific Partnership (TPP) trade agreement designed on behalf of transnational corporate interests and investments, while protecting patent and copyright rights. For

a narrative analysis, see: "TTIP and TPP: Arc of the Neoliberal Order" posted for Katehon.com. (Accessed May 30, 2016). http://katehon.com/1234-ttip-and-tpp-arc-of-the-neoliberal-order.html

88. I use Arendt to define. This totalitarianism is not to say "monolithic" at the same time. There is a pluralism within it that does not shape it into a pure propagandism. There is no clear "us" in this virtual global economy.

89. Garland-Thomson (citing McRuer, 1999) 2011, 34.

90. One example I am thinking of is the initiation of programs by tech companies to specifically employ neurodiverse and autistic persons. It is, as a simply stated rationale, because neurodiverse colleagues *will benefit the company*. There is no clear attempt to alleviate the ableist tendency to ostracize neurodiverse persons or to distribute these benefits more evenly among autistic communities. See Bourree Lam reporting for *The Atlantic*, "Why Some Companies Are Trying to Hire More People on the Autism Spectrum." (Accessed Dec 28, 2016). http://www.theatlantic.com/business/archive/2016/12/autism-workplace/510959/

91. "Acceleration is one of the features of capitalist subjugation. The Unconscious is submitted to the ever increasing pace of the Infosphere, and this form of subsumption is painful—it generates panic before finally destroying any possible form of autonomous subjectivation." I don't completely subscribe to a psychoanalytic reading of accelerationism, but an interesting summary here: Franco Berardi Bifo, "Accelerationism questioned from the point of view of the body" posted by e-flux (2013). http://www.e-flux.com/journal/accelerationism-questioned-from-the-point-of-view-of-the-body/

92. I find that this problem is exemplified in the fact that, even with United States being one of wealthiest countries in the world, it cannot sufficiently fund and distribute health care to all people in equal and democratizing ways. See Anu Partanen's "The Fake Freedom of American Health Care" for *The New York Times*. (Accessed Mar 18, 2017). http://www.nytimes.com/2017/03/18/opinion/the-fake-freedom-of-american-health-care.html?mcubz=0

93. See Scuro (2008), "Thinking of Bhopal" (141–142).

94. See *The Bhopal Disaster: Twenty Years without Justice*, Sanford Lewis, dir., 2007. http://www.youtube.com/watch?v=0csW97x8d24

95. This quote is the subheading of "Generations of Victims: Bhopal's Unending Catastrophe" by Anne Backhaus and Simone Salden. (Accessed Dec 9, 2014). http://www.spiegel.de/international/world/disaster-persists-30-years-after-bhopal-gas-catastrophe-a-1006101.html

96. In particular, I am writing a documentary, *The Bayside Women*, questioning the impact on the health, particularly the reproductive health, of a set of friends who were in downtown New York City during September 11, 2011. I am also in the process of drafting a proposal for a project that seeks out testimonies of people who live and raise families near Superfund cleanup sites.

97. Thinking here of the young men profiled in Frontline/WORLD's *Ghana: The Digital Dumping Ground* (pbs.org, 2009). Available online: http://www.pbs.org/frontlineworld/stories/ghana804/

98. From *The Guardian*, (Accessed Jun 11, 2015). http://www.theguardian.com/commentisfree/2015/jun/11/lost-hands-making-flatscreens-no-help.

99. In my correspondence with Alan Pogue, the photographer:

[Rosa] wants and deserves modern prosthetic hands but LG won't help and neither the Mexican government nor NAFTA will help. LG is a huge South Korean electronics firm and one of the worst employers along the border. Rosa Sarmiento Moreno lives in Reynosa, Mexico and reaching her is difficult. . . . Any payment I receive would be given directly to Rosa.I am happy that the photograph was used in the Guardian but they had nothing to do with the taking of it. I am an independent photographer. Ed Krueger, 85 years old, is the force behind the Comite de Apoyo, the workers union, took me to meet Rosa shortly after her injury. Her story is on my web site. . . . I took this photograph with an 8" × 10" Deardorff view camera. I bought the big screen TV and drove it to her home as no ne of the workers could afford to have one.

See http://www.documentaryphotographs.com/rosamoreno1.html for Rosa's story and to donate.

CHAPTER 5

1. Lydia Brown in review of this book notes: "the meaning/function/appearance of breasts can be different for some trans women. Some transwomen begin growing breasts if they choose to medically transition, as a result of taking estrogen, and some also choose to undergo breast augmentation surgery as well. There is also a critique to be made of the implicit imperative for transwomen to perform gender essentialist aesthetics of femininity including by having breasts of particular size/shape, but I know that having visible breasts can be very affirming for many transwomen too."

2. Also cited in Siebers (2008, 23). Here, Lydia Brown responds to Young's conflation in my manuscript review: "In discussing Iris Marion Young's assertion that women in a sexist society are physically handicapped, I would suggest adding a bit more critical analysis—women don't become 'disabled,' but disability can be a useful framework for analogizing/understanding women's bodily subjectivity in a sexist/patriarchal/misogynistic society. At least acknowledging that disabled and woman as identities are not identical, and Young's assertion without context/analysis is reductive."

3. Davis's *Bending Over Backwards: Disability, Dismodernism, and other Difficult Positions* (New York, NY: New York University Press, 2002) as cited by Sara Hendren her article, "All technology is assistive: Six design rules on 'disability'" posted by *Backchannel Online Magazine* (medium.com, Accessed Oct 16, 2014). http://backchannel.com/all-technology-is-assistive-ac9f7183c8cd#.43hz72wji

4. Discussed in chapter 4.

5. Full text here: http://www.butyoudontlooksick.com/articles/written-by-christine/the-spoon-theory/

6. As prosthetic, spoon theory still *holds* even when it cannot be adapted for everyone in all cases. See Jenny Smales' "The Spoon Theory Gave People the Wrong Idea About My Illness" posted on *The Mighty*. (Accessed May 27, 2016). http://themighty.com/2016/05/why-the-spoon-theory-doesnt-fit-my-life/

7. Jay Timothy Dolmage, "Prosthesis" from *Disability Rhetoric* (Syracuse University Press, 2014).

8. She calls her project, the inclusion of women in a survey of canonical philosophical authors, *An Unconventional History of Western Philosophy* (New York, NY:

Rowman & Littlefield, 2009), a "recovery project" that challenges the basic assumptions about the canon, that it is "objective, impartial, and gender-neutral." To this she argues, "Canonical philosophy's long-standing comfort with such illusions comes at a high price. . . . [This project] corrects that complicity" (3).

9. "From Phantoms to Prostheses" in *DSQ*, Vol. 32, No. 3, (2012).

10. An exploration into Arendt's idea of *homo faber* with the need to fabricate prosthetics would be useful. See *The Human Condition* (1958).

11. See Tremain's "Ableist Language and Philosophical Associations" post (and comments that follow), posted with New APPS, (Accessed Jul 19, 2011). http://www.newappsblog.com/2011/07/ableist-language-and-philosophical-associations.html

12. Posted on the University of Oxford "Practical Ethics: Ethics in the News" webpage. (Accessed Aug 15, 2011). He links to Tremain's campaign, (under "stirrings") on the blog site: New APPS, Jul 11, 2011. (Accessed Aug 17, 2015). http://blog.practicalethics.ox.ac.uk/2011/08/ableist-language/

13. The issue of this patronizing dismissal of "sensitivity" or being "too sensitive" as itself ableist is discussed in chapter 4.

14. Edited from the excerpt: "Here's one reason to be suspicious of this initial reaction: when women (and a few men) began to question the unthinking use of sexist language, I think lots of well-meaning people reacted by thinking that the notion was silly. The people I had in mind may not have been sexist, in their explicit commitments. Rather, they thought that words do not harm, that we should save our energies for fighting for equal rights, that the movement brought feminism into ridicule, and so on. But gradually people became sensitized to the use of sexist language and we now avoid it."

15. The power to reclaim the slur—as a kind of rhetorical device—is unavailable if the privileged position then also dismisses (as Levy does) or bans the tool from reclamation. One narrative by Nia Ashari Harris for *affinitymagazine.us*, "How Black People Are Reclaiming The N-Word and Embracing Their Heritage" (Feb 23, 2017), highlights my point:

> Black people have managed to create our own subculture that thrives so much so that we set the trends for other ethnic and racial groups. I'm not saying that the success of black culture is attributed to the word nigga, but I am saying that the word nigga and the reclaiming of it as very exclusive has become an important part of the black subculture. Through the word "nigga" and redefining it for ourselves, I feel like we have been able to redefine what it means to be black.

16. This is from Karen Warren's "Lead Essay" when discussing philosophical methodology that includes women: "it was my deep philosophical commitment to 'the search for truths' and my emotional temperament to 'overturn every stone' until I found what survived gender (and other) criticisms of [the canon]—that is, doing philosophy in the spirit of Socrates" (2009, 10).

17. Is he accusing her of "stirring the pot" or "stirring the shit"? She raises objections and he trivializes it as "stirrings."

18. Tremain, "Ableist Language and Philosophical Associations," (Jul 11, 2011; my emphasis). Accessed Aug 2015 online: http://www.newappsblog.com/2011/07/ableist-language-and-philosophical-associations.html

19. See Anita Silvers, "Philosophy & Disability: An Overview" for *Philosophy Now*. Another interesting example: "In *On Blindness*, an exchange between philosophers Bryan Magee and Martin Milligan, disability elucidates how we know what we know. Magee initiates the conversation to explore how much someone like Milligan, blind nearly from birth and with no memory of seeing, can understand from other people's descriptions of visual experience. . . . In this discussion, rhetorical convention clearly privileges the sighted over the blind interlocutor, since Milligan is expected to bear the burden of convincing Magee that being blind is not a significant drawback in acquiring knowledge of the world. This rhetorical assumption prevails even though, as Milligan argues, blind people enjoy a more comprehensive standpoint on the subject than sighted people," (Accessed Jun/Jul 2016). http://philosophynow. org/issues/30/Philosophy_and_Disability_an_overview

20. Levy responding to another insensitive commenter, "Anthony, I agree that's the right thing to do, but alas, justice is blind," (Accessed May 30, 2015). I think it is fair to state that this is still a *completely ableist* (and unapologetically paternalistic and condescending) way to address the issue. It is a poor effort on behalf of the(se men) "philosopher(s)," but as discussed in chapter 2, sometimes those in a position of privilege and authority have opinions *that do nothing more than opine*.

21. In the same way that Kittay calls Peter Singer and Jeff McMahan "disablists" despite them not "wanting to hurt her feelings" while ideologically dehumanizing her daughter and those like her daughter.

22. Even when placed in the context of artifact—"stuff of a museum"—the context can still preserve ableist attitudes. As Amanda Cachia who identifies "as a curator and as a disabled person" describes it, if the curator can play a powerful role in the generation of knowledge in the context of the museum, citing Francesca Rosenberg of the MOMA in an interview, she then argues, "In [Rosenberg's] experience, she has found that one of the biggest incentives for curators to work on disability and engagement is because of their personal encounter with a disabled person, such as the curator whose mother has dementia, or the curator who breaks their leg and must use a temporary crutch to move through the gallery space" (2014, 56). An exhibit dealing in an artifact like the sixteenth century spectacles pictured in this chapter could easily reinforce the ableist assumptions that some objects are prosthetics (for disabled people) while other museum objects (artifacts) are tools of a natural kind—like shoes and clothes. Cachia adds, "Ultimately, discourses on education might be the new norm, but it is also the 'norm' for the educational turn to leave disability out of the conversation" (64).

23. This concern for artifact comes back to the discussion of homelessness in chapter 4, in which, in the context of institutional housing, the concern is only for "bodies" and "beds."

24. From the film: *FIXED: The Science Fiction of Human Enhancement*, Regan Brashear, dir. (2013). US: New Day Films, www.newday.com

25. Also referenced in the prologue: Stella Young's TED talk, "I'm not your inspiration, thank you very much." Posted online (Accessed Jun 9, 2014): http://www. youtube.com/watch?v=8K9Gg164Bsw

26. Nietzschean thinking is worth mentioning on this point because his suspicion of "philosophies of betterment" has become my suspicion when there is a strange satisfaction that comes from these moments when prosthetics are some kind of "gift"—not a right to resources for self-determination.

27. Reported by Bridget Butler Millsaps in "Happy Being Himself, This Little Boy Turns Down a 3D Printed Prosthetic Hand" posted by *3DPrint.com*, (Accessed May 22, 2015). http://3dprint.com/66657/boy-happy-without-prosthetic/. I challenge this problem of "desiring wholeness" in the epilogue on parts and wholes.

28. This is in concert with the questions raised by Sara Brill earlier, repeated here: "What is the prosthetic function of this or that friendship, familial organization, form of education, social network, collective practice, conglomerate, coupling, institution, etc.?" (2011, 249).

29. The problem with tools fabricated for convenience is that they are usually made in the context of consumer and commodified market systems.

30. Grosz cites Henri Bergson's *Matter and Memory*. New York, NY: Zone Books, 1988.

31. In chapter 3, Devonya Havis described this as the reward for "functioning" that was the impetus for "passing" as ablebodied.

32. See Garland-Thomson's "Integrating Disability: Transforming Feminist Theory." *NWSA Journal*, (2011).

33. Thinking here of "Google Glass." In one way, Google Glass was considered a helpful device for people with disabilities:"Google Glass has a ton of potential to transform lives for people with disabilities," says Mark Perriello, president and CEO of the American Association for People with Disabilities. "Not everyone has had the good fortune to experience Google Glass at this point. But for those who have, the technology features a number of things that make it really user-friendly for people with disabilities—voice-activated technology, the potential for speech-to-text, face recognition—all of which can help people with a variety of disabilities."(As reported by Alan Neuhauser in "Google Glass Offers Disabled People Access to a Bigger World" for *US News & World Report* [Jun 10, 2014]). Yet, within a year or so, described as a commercial failure:

> Google Glass failed to help consumers understand why they needed such a device. With a recent move to larger and larger screens for users, it might be a risky move for Apple to shift its focus to a user interface the size of a watch face. But, diehard Apple fans will cite Steve Jobs' quote, "People don't know what they want until you show it to them." Remember that the Apple Watch is an accessory for your phone, not a replacement. If you are used to wearing a watch, getting notifications without taking your phone from your purse or pocket might seem appealing.

From "Why Google Glass Failed and Why Apple Watch Could Too," reported by Ian Altman for Forbes.com (Apr 28, 2015).

34. I am connecting the symbol of the spoon as Levi uses it to describe the dehumanizing conditions of the Lager (and as I had referenced his The Drowned and The Saved [1989] in chapter 1) but intentionally to parallel with Miserandino's "spoon theory."

35. Alex Lu, "Deaf People Don't Need New Communication Tools—Everyone Else Does" posted by *The Establishment*. (Accessed May 11, 2016). http://

www.theestablishment.co/2016/05/11/deaf-people-dont-need-new-communication-tools-everyone-else-does/.

36. This is not limited to deafness. A good example of this is documented in the film, following four blind teenagers as they navigate the school system and getting sufficient accommodations: *Do You Dream in Color?* (Fuller & Ivy, dirs. 2014).

37. From Hamraie's "Universal Design Research as a New Materialist Practice" (*DSQ*, Vol 32, No. 4, 2012). http://dsqsds.org/article/view/3246/3185. Hamraie continues this argument in *DSQ* 2013:

Supposedly neutral design often privileges the most common bodies through (what I have called) the "normate template" for architectural design (Hamraie 2012). Garland-Thomson's term normate represents the unmarked privilege of majority embodiments—white, male, cisgender, heterosexual, ablebodied, and middle-class bodies—that appear neutral when their social location is in fact highly specific (Garland-Thomson 1996, 8–10).

38. Hamraie citing Garland-Thomson on this point: "Normate and the mis-fit form a conceptual scheme that takes more common binary notions, such as normal and pathological, and gives them context within the built environment. Normates are unremarkable and perhaps even impossible figures, yet their intended presence permeates the world. Mis-fit is a material construct and a nearly universal experience that demands accountability by the built environment" (2012).

39. As Hamraie describes it (2013): "Universal Design (UD) is an approach to access to the built environment that goes beyond barrier-free design (Mace 1985). UD seeks to design built environments to be as accessible as possible from the outset, to as many people as possible. That is, UD seeks to design built environments that will not require future retrofitting or alteration. Furthermore, UD goes beyond legal accessibility requirements (for example, what is required to comply with the Americans with Disabilities Act) to integrate into disability-access strategies the specific requirements that accrue when designers take into account aging, gender, size, and health (among other variables) (Steinfeld & Maisel 2012; Welch & Jones 2002)."

40. See Hamraie's "diffracted reading" of UD, in "Designing Collective Access: A Feminist Disability Theory of Universal Design" (2013): "These professional debates hinge on the very concept of a universal, one-size-fits-all approach to design (Hannson 2007, 17; Sandhu 2011; Steinfeld & Tauke 2002)."

41. Or, as Cara Leibowitz describes it when referencing not fat-shaming, but the issue of "palsy skinny." She states, "sizeism doesn't exist in a vacuum. It interacts with and impacts other forms of oppression, including ableism" (2014, 63).

42. This disposal of clothing is worth noting because "Americans now buy five times as much clothing as they did in 1980" and "send 10.5 million tons of clothing to landfills every year" equivalent to 193,000 tons annually according to Elizabeth Cline for *The Atlantic*, (Accessed Jul 18, 2014). http://www.theatlantic.com/business/archive/2014/07/where-does-discarded-clothing-go/374613/

43. On Feb 4, 2016, Clarke was shot and killed by police outside his home in Mesa, AZ, after a suicide call. The dehumanization and violence that queer, transgender, disabled people experience and suffer is narrated by Lydia Brown in chapter 3. As reported in the NY Daily News: http://www.nydailynews.com/news/national/woman-asperger-shot-dead-police-article-1.2520902

44. As reported by Kate Bratskeir for *The Huffington Post* (June 17, 2015). Kayden Clarke is deadnamed and misgendered in the original article. http://www.huffingtonpost.com/2015/06/17/aspergers-dog-video-samson-danielle_n_7594598.html.

45. On Heidegger's environmental philosophy, see Michael Zimmerman's "Heidegger's Phenomenology and Contemporary Environmentalism" in *Eco-Phenomenology: Back to the Earth Itself* (C. Brown & T. Toadvine, eds. Albany, New York, NY: SUNY Press, 2003), pp. 73–101.

46. Siebers also cites Joseph Shapiro ("Disability Policy and the Media" in the *Policy Studies Journal*, 22.1, 1994, 123–132) on the latter point.

47. See Kathleen Downes, in "When the Bus Driver Called Me 'The Wheelchair'": "My wheelchair is my constant companion, and rather than calling me 'a wheelchair' or willing the chair away to see me, I challenge you to see me and the wheelchair, and—at the same time—see someone who is moving along in the world, looking for the same opportunities so many people take for granted." Posted by *Estanara Magazine*, (Accessed May 4, 2015). http://e-newsletter.pdpi.pk/?p=662

48. Kathleen Downes, "Why I long for spontaneity as a Young Person with Cerebral Palsy" posted in TheMighty.com, (Accessed Aug 28, 2015), [no longer available online].

49. See the statistics for fatal crane accidents, posted by Arnold and Itkin, LLP, (Accessed Jun 16, 2015). http://www.arnolditkin.com/Personal-Injury-Blog/2015/June/Fatal-Crane-Accident-Statistics-in-the-United-St.aspx

50. I had discussed this in an unpublished paper, "Sexist Time Structures."

51. Levinasian ethics is the stuff of *diachrony*—the interruption or "out-of-time" event of the Other, the break from the *il y a* of existence.

52. Cited in Gilman-Opalsky, pp. 22–23, nt. 28. See Castells' *The Information Age: Economy, Society, and Culture*, Volume III. (Second Edition. Blackwell Publishers, 2000, 367–368).

53. See Rosalyn Diprose's description of Levinas' idea of generosity: "a witness to alterity . . . commands me 'to give to the other taking the bread out of my own mouth, and making a gift of my own skin.' [citing Levinas 1998/1981]" (2002, 165).

54. Part of an unpublished paper I've given elsewhere, "The Consequences of a Heliocentric Epistemology."

55. As discussed in chapter 4.

56. As discussed in chapter 3, citing Charles Mills, (2007, 13).

57. I would want to argue that transhumanism as an ideology usually operates as desirable and futural possibility as if also in an apolitical, nonviolent context. In support of my assertion here, in her discussion of the cyborg soldier, what seems like a "cause for celebration. As a post-human subject . . . a transgressive image of disabled subjectivity," Nirmala Erevelles questions this in the context of militarism in which the cyborg soldier emerges: "the social, political, and economic context of an imperialist war highlights a more sobering scenario of violence, invisibility, and dehumanization" (2011, 124–125).

EPILOGUE

1.   Important for me in addressing ableism, as Siebers indicates, is how I want to account for how some lives are precariously preconditioned upon these dismembering operations and can no longer *existentially afford* unacknowledged ableist indifference. For evidence of this "forgetting to . . . be still," see: "For Defeat of Trumpcare, Thank Disability Rights Activists, Not John McCain" by Jake Johnson for CommonDreams.org, (July 28, 2017). https://www.commondreams.org/news/2017/07/28/defeat-trumpcare-thank-disability-rights-activists-not-john-mccain.

2.   By this, I mean, that one can be given or give oneself permission to "stop and think," or take what might be referred to as "the sacred pause." See Tara Brach on this point, (from *Psychology Today*, Dec 4, 2014): http://www.psychologytoday.com/blog/finding-true-refuge/201412/the-sacred-pause

> We may take a pause from our ongoing responsibilities by sitting down to meditate. We may pause in the midst of meditation to let go of thoughts and reawaken our attention to the breath. We may pause by stepping out of daily life to go on a retreat or to spend time in nature or to take a sabbatical. We may pause in a conversation, letting go of what we're about to say, in order to genuinely listen and be with the other person. We may pause when we feel suddenly moved or delighted or saddened, allowing the feelings to play through our heart.
>
> A pause is, by nature, time limited. . . . But much of our driven pace and habitual controlling in daily life does not serve surviving, and certainly not thriving. It arises from a free-floating anxiety about something being wrong or not enough.

3.   This does run a parallel to Siebers's analysis of assumed narcissism of disabled people; in fact, by his account, the caretakers or therapists retreated into a kind of narcissism and made issues "about them" and not the patient or client. See his concluding injunction to the chapter on "Tender Organs, Narcissism, and Identity Politics" (2008, 52):

> Some of you have disabilities. Some of you do not. Most of you will someday. That is the reality of the human mind and body. Remember what you already know about people with disabilities, so the knowledge will be useful when you join us. The blind do not lead the blind. The lame do not want to walk alone. We do not love only our own kind or ourselves. You others are our caregivers—and we can be yours, if you let us. We of the tender organs are not narcissists.

4.   See Scuro (2004).

5.   This was my claim, (*ibid.*).

6.   See chapter 1.

7.   I argued that radical self-portraiture required 1) license: that you give yourself the *permission* to take on your comforting self-identity; 2) medium: one must decide *how* to portray oneself in a way that is radicalizing; and 3) means: finding the *time and space* to dedicate to the work of (and usual failures in) self-portraiture practice. Another example of radical self-portraiture was Casey Jenkins' *Casting Off My Womb* (2013), in which the artist knitted from yarn in her vagina during her menstruation, who stated in relation to the work, "The piece for me is about assessing and being intimate with my own body" (Quoted from DailyMail.com, Dec 5, 2013).

8. Photoshoot published online, *Interview Magazine* (Dec 1, 2015), http://www.interviewmagazine.com/culture/kylie-jenner. As it is noted, the magazine "never intended to cause offence" and stated: "Our intention was to create a powerful set of pictures that get people thinking about image and creative expression, including the set with the wheelchair. But our intention was certainly not to offend anyone." Despite both the photographer and Jenner arguing that the shoot was defensible, "Kylie might want to avoid the internet . . . as people have taken to twitter to accuse her of ableism." One example from Jennifer (@WordsmithJenn), "Kylie Jenner's shoot in a wheelchair is ableism at its worst. Disabled bodies in wheelchairs are not fodder for the fashion industry" (Brett 2016).

9. See Frances Ryan, "We wouldn't accept actors blacking up, so why applaud 'cripping up'?" for *The Guardian* (Accessed Jan 13, 2015). http://www.theguardian.com/commentisfree/2015/jan/13/eddie-redmayne-golden-globe-stephen-hawking-disabled-actors-characters

10. See the discussion by Ronald Berger of the "disability scam artist storyline" in films, "What's So Funny About Disability?" posted with *The Society Pages*, (Accessed Dec 26, 2012). http://thesocietypages.org/specials/whats-so-funny-about-disability/.

11. A summary of this exercise is discussed in chapter 4.

12. And arguably, from an ethical standpoint, if you can, you *ought*. See the ethical minimum argued in chapter 1.

13. See Levinas, "Secularization and Hunger," which he asks, "Have we measured the depths in which the human I (*Moi*) attends to itself and, deaf to language, ("a famished stomach has no ears"), closes itself to all serenity, . . . any equilibrium which would be merely that of totality? . . . In fact he never ceases to fly from his responsibility" (GF1998, 10–11).

14. As I have mentioned throughout, to "excise" ableist phobias and affections is to "liberate" oneself or "out" the possession of these biases.

15. According to Mark A. Rothstein, Yu Cai, and Gary E. Marchant in "The Ghost in our Genes: Legal and Ethical Implications of Epigenetics": "The refinement of philosophical analyses of transgenerational environmental epigenetics will be greatly influenced by scientific developments and the emerging understanding of biological mechanisms." See *Health Matrix*, Cleveland, OH, (2009) Winter; 19(1): 1–62.

16. Quoted from a reprint of Savarese's chapter from Academia.edu (2013, ¶6).

17. Anthony Appiah's *Cosmopolitanism* does not address this; Selya Benhabib's work is also without mention of the question of ableism. Benhabib's approach has potential to be developed into a non-ableist cosmopolitanism. In an interview, she states, "I believe that democracies require boundaries, not borders. There is a difference. Boundaries are limitations, boundaries can be porous, boundaries can be flexible: they can let people in and they have to let people out. And the reason why you need boundaries in democracy is because you need to have boundaries of representation" in "Toward a Converging Cosmopolitan Project?" with M. Croce, D. Archibugi, (Jan 28, 2010) on OpenDemocracy.net. Fiona Kumari Campbell cites Benhabib as well: "A cosmopolitan ethic acts as a reminder of belonging to humanity beyond a singularity of identity. The right of hospitality is situated at the boundaries of the polity; it delimits civic space by regulating relations among members and strangers. (Benhabib, 2004, p. 27)." (2010, 77).

18. As discussed in chapter 4.

19. Garland-Thomson defining misfit in *DSQ* (2014, ¶20) [Also see p. 165 nt. 13]:

A fit occurs when a harmonious, proper interaction occurs between a particularly shaped and functioning body and an environment that sustains that body. A misfit occurs when the environment does not sustain the shape and function of the body that enters it. The dynamism between body and world that produces fits or misfits comes at the spatial and temporal points of encounter between dynamic but relatively stable bodies and environments. The built and arranged space through which we navigate our lives tends to offer fits to majority bodies and create misfits with minority forms of embodiment, such as people with disabilities.

20. To update this as I am completing the manuscript from when I first wrote this epilogue, President (#notmypresident) Trump issued an executive order halting all settlement of Syrian (and other) refugees into the United States, "triggering fears across the globe." As reported in *The Washington Post* (Jan 26, 2017):

As news of the impending order spread, lives were quickly affected across the world, particularly among the citizens of the countries immediately targeted. For them, it is already difficult to get visas or immigrate to the United States. Vetting has been stringent since the Sept. 11, 2001, terrorist attacks, rights activists say. Even so, many potential Muslim immigrants went through long screening processes, often lasting years, to gain entry to the United States. Now, many find themselves in an emotional and bureaucratic limbo.

http://www.washingtonpost.com/world/trumps-impending-bans-on-refugees-and-immigrants-triggers-fears-globally/2017/01/26/c698e67e-e33d-11e6-a419-eefe8eff0835_story.html?utm_term=.7adea17212a8

21. From Marcus Skinner, Humanitarian Policy Manager at HelpAge International: "Half of the surveyed refugees affected by impairment, injury and non-communicable disease reported at least one frequent sign of psychological distress: changes in emotional state, behaviour, relationships or cognition. Again, the older population is disproportionately affected with more than 65 percent reporting such signs, a level three times higher than the general refugee population." Posted on Forced Migration Review, Accessed Sept 2015. See more at: http://www.fmreview.org/syria/skinner#sthash.qO0JUuhu.dpuf

22. See for example, Lynda Terry: "It is time for humanity to remember and recommit to this important practice and service that [usually] women, in particular, . . . [have been] called to offer to people and to the earth. I am holding space for that time when seeking out keepers of the heart and vessels of peace will become commonplace. I envision a day when non-profit organizations and business enterprises will have holders of space present at their board and staff meetings to support their intent to reach agreements for the highest good of all. . . . And I envision a day when holders of space will not only be routinely present at times of birth and death but in operating rooms and ERs and cancer treatment clinics and refugee camps." Posted on the Gaiafield Project (Accessed May 25, 2016). http://gaiafield.net/holding-space-as-subtle-activism/

Bibliography

Annamma, S.A., D. Connor, and B. Ferri. (2013). "Dis/ability critical race Studies (DisCrit): Theorizing at the intersections of race and dis/ability" in *Race Ethnicity and Education*, Vol. 16, No. 1, pp. 1–31.

Arendt, Hannah. (1958). *The Human Condition*. Chicago, IL: University of Chicago Press.

_____. (Oct. 21, 1971). "Heidegger at Eighty" for *The New York Review of Books*.

_____. (1973). *The Origins of Totalitarianism*. NY: Harcourt Brace and Co.

Ariely, Dan. (Feb. 2009). "Our Buggy Moral Code" VIDEO: TEDtalk. http://www.ted.com/talks/dan_ariely_on_our_buggy_moral_code.

Asch, Adrienne and Harilyn Rousso. (1985). "Therapists with Disabilities: Theoretical and Clinical Issues" in *Psychiatry*, Vol. 48, pp. 1–12.

Baker, Dana Lee. (2011). *The Politics of Neurodiversity*. Boulder, CO: Lynne Rienner Publishers.

Baldwin, Alistair. (Jan. 12, 2017). "'Disability Impressions Offensive' Decrees Meryl Streep to Room of Award-Winning Disability Impressionists" posted online by SBS.com.au.

Barnes, Elizabeth. (2016). *The Minority Body*. New York, NY: Oxford University Press.

Bartky, Sandra. (1990). *Femininity and Domination: Studies in the Phenomenology of Oppression*. NY: Routledge.

Bates, Karen Grigsby and Karen E. Hudson. (2005). *The New Basic Black: Home Training for Modern Times* (Revised Edition). NY: Random House Publishing, Inc. (Knopf Doubleday).

Beamon, Nika C. (Nov. 2, 2015). "Medical Misdiagnosis Nearly Killed Me" posted on *The Huffington Post*. http://www.huffingtonpost.com/nika-c-beamon/medical-misdiagnosis-nearly-killed-me_b_8441082.html.

Beauvoir, Simone de. (1949). *The Ethics of Ambiguity*. Citadel Press. http://www.marxists.org/reference/subject/ethics/de-beauvoir/ambiguity/.

Bergson, Henri. *Matter and Memory*. NY: Zone Books, 1988.

Bernstein, Richard J. (2013). *Violence: Thinking without Banisters.* Malden, MA: Polity Press.

Benhabib, Seyla. (2004). *The Rights of Others: Aliens, Residents, and Citizens.* UK: Cambridge University Press.

Berger, Ronald. (Dec. 26, 2012). "What's So Funny about Disability?" posted with *The Society Pages.* http://thesocietypages.org/specials/whats-so-funny-about-disability/.

Bérubé, Michael. (2006). *What's Liberal about the Liberal Arts?: Classroom Politics and "Bias" in Higher Education.* New York: W.W. Norton & Co.

Bonnaire, Sandrine, dir. (2007). Film: *Her Name is Sabine (Elle s'appelle Sabine).* Mosaique Films, prod. NY: Film Movement (US Distribution).

Brashear, Regan, dir. (2013). Film: *FIXED: The Science Fiction of Human Enhancement.* US: New Day Films, www.newday.com.

Brennan, Teresa. (2003). *Globalization and its Terrors: Daily Life in the West.* NY: Routledge.

———. (2004). *The Transmission of Affect.* Ithaca, NY: Cornell University Press.

Brett, Hattie. (2016). "Photographer Steven Klein explains that Kylie Jenner wheelchair shoot" posted online for *The Telegraph* (Jan. 5). Online report: http://www.telegraph.co.uk/fashion/news/people-are-outraged-by-kylie-jenners-wheelchair-shoot-for-interv/.

Brill, Sara. (Spring 2005). "Diagnosis and the Divided Line: Pharmacological Concerns in Plato's Republic." *Epoché,* Vol. 9, No. 2, pp. 297–315.

———. (2011). "The Prosthetic Cosmos: Elizabeth Grosz's Ecology of the Future" in *Philosophy Today,* Vol. 55, Issue Supplement, pp. 245–254.

Brown, Charles S. and Ted Toadvine, eds. (2003). *Eco-Phenomenology: Back to the Earth Itself.* NY: SUNY Press.

Brown, Jim. (Jan. 11, 2017). "Meryl Streep's speech was patronizing to people with disabilities" for *The 180.* CBC Radio: http://www.cbc.ca/radio/the180/what-not-to-love-about-meryl-streep-s-speech-more-on-ptsd-and-violence-and-reform-politics-not-elections-1.3930068/meryl-streep-s-speech-was-patronizing-to-people-with-disabilities-1.3930082.

Brown, Lydia. (2013). "Compliance is Unreasonable: The Human Rights Implications of Compliance-Based Behavioral Interventions under the Convention Against Torture and the Convention on the Rights of Persons with Disabilities" in *Torture in Healthcare Settings: Reflections on the Special Rapporteur on Torture's 2013 Thematic Report.* Center for Human Rights & Humanitarian Law. Washington D.C.: American University. http://www.wcl.american.edu/humright/center/resources/publications/documents/YESPDF_Torture_in_Healthcare_Publication.pdf.

———. (Feb. 24, 2013). "A Critique of Disability/Impairment Simulations" posted on autistichoya.com. http://autistichoya.files.wordpress.com/2013/02/a-critique-of-disability-impairment-simulations.pdf.

———. (Feb. 11, 2014). "Violence in Language: Circling back to Linguistic Ableism" posted on autistichoya.com. http://www.autistichoya.com/2014/02/violence-linguistic-ableism.html.

_____. (Oct. 20, 2014). "The Crisis of Disability is Violence: Ableism, Torture, and Murder" in *Tikkun*. http://www.tikkun.org/nextgen/the-crisis-of-disability-is-violence.

_____. (2014). "Disability in an Ableist World" in *Criptiques*. Caitlin Wood, ed. Portland, OR: May Day Press. www.criptiques.com.

_____. (Jul. 9, 2015). "The Long Road Ahead for the Autistic Rights Movement" in *The New Idealist*. http://magazine.thenewidealist.com/tag/lydia-brown/.

_____. (Fall/Winter 2016). "Disability and Divergence: Strange Questions Not Asked" in *Asian American Literary Review: Open in Emergency: A Special Issue on Asian American Mental Health*. Mimi Khúc and Lawrence-Minh Bùi Davis, eds. Vol. 7.2. http://aalr.binghamton.edu/special-issue-on-asian-american-mental-health/.

_____. (2016). "'You Don't Feel Like A Freak Anymore': Representing Disability, Madness, and Trauma in Litchfield Penitentiary" in *Feminist Perspectives on Orange Is The New Black: Thirteen Critical Essays*. April Kalogeropoulos Householder and Adrienne Trier-Bieniek, eds., Jefferson, NC: McFarland & Company, Inc., pp. 174–193.

Brown, Charles S. and Ted Toadvine. (2003). *Eco-Phenomenology: Back to the Earth Itself*. Albany, NY: SUNY Press.

Brown, Mike. (Jan. 25, 2017). "Disabled People Are to be 'Warehoused.' We Should be Livid" for *The Guardian*. http://www.theguardian.com/commentisfree/2017/jan/25/disabled-people-disabilities-health-care-homes.

Brubaker, Rogers. (2016). "The Dolezal Affair: Race, Gender, and the Micropolitics of Identity" in *Ethnic and Racial Studies*, Vol. 39, pp. 414–448. Accessed through Taylor & Francis Online: http://dx.doi.org.libezcnr.idm.oclc.org/10.1080/0141987 0.2015.1084430.

Burch, Susan and Ian Sutherland. (Winter 2006). "Who's Not Yet Here? American Disability History" in *Radical History Review*, No. 94, pp. 127–147.

Butler, Judith. (2004). *Precarious Life: The Powers of Mourning and Violence*. NY: Verso Books.

_____. (2010). *Frames of War: When Is Life Grievable?* NY: Verso Books.

Braswell, Harold. (2014). "Family Matters: An Ethnography of Disability and Kinship in US Hospice Care." Unpublished presentation paper for Society for Disability Studies (with permission of author).

_____. (2015). "Euthanasia" in *Keywords in Disability Studies*. R. Adams, B. Reiss, and D. Serlin, eds, NY: NYU Press.

_____. (Winter 2015). "My Two Moms: Disability, Queer Kinship, and the Maternal Subject" in *Hypatia*, Vol. 30, No. 1, pp. 234–250.

Cachia, Amanda. (Dec. 2014). "Disability, Curating, and the Educational Turn: The Contemporary Condition of Access in the Museum" from OnCurating.org, pp. 51–66.

Campbell, Fiona Kumari. (2009). *The Contours of Ableism: The Production of Disability and Ableness*. NY: Palgrave Macmillan.

_____. (2010). "Crippin' the Flâneur: Cosmopolitanism, and Landscapes of Tolerance" in *The Journal of Social Inclusion*, Vol. 1, No. 1, pp. 75–89.

Charlton, James I. (2000). *Nothing About Us Without Us: Disability Oppression and Empowerment*. Oakland, CA: University of California Press.

Cherney, James. (2011). "The Rhetoric of Ableism" in *Disability Studies Quarterly*, Vol. 31, No. 3. http://dsq-sds.org/article/view/1665/1606.

Cogdell, Christina. (2015). "Design" in *Keywords in Disability Studies*. R. Adams, B. Reiss, and D. Serlin, eds, NY: NYU Press.

Cohen, Emily. (2012). "From Phantoms to Prostheses" in *Disability Studies Quarterly*, Vol. 32, No. 3. http://dsq-sds.org/article/view/3269/3103.

Cohen-Rottenberg, Rachel. (2011). "On the Matter of Empathy" on blog: Autism and Empathy: Dispelling Myths and Breaking Stereotypes. http://autismandempathyblog. wordpress.com/on-the-matter-of-empathy/.

_____. (Aug 19, 2013). "The Complexities of Giving: People with Disabilities as Help Objects" posted on Disability.Blog, the official blog of Disability.gov. http://usodep.blogs.govdelivery.com/2013/08/19/the-complexities-of-giving-people-with-disabilities-as-help-objects/.

_____. (Nov. 7, 2014). "10 Questions About Why Ableist Language Matters, Answered" posted on everydayfeminism.com. http://everydayfeminism.com/2014/11/ableist-language-matters/.

Corker, Mairian and Tom Shakespeare, eds. (2002). *Disability/Postmodernity: Embodying Disability Theory*. NY: Bloomsbury Academic.

Crenshaw, Kimberlé. (Jul. 1991). "Mapping the Margins: Intersectionality, Identity Politics, and Violence against Women of Color" in the *Stanford Law Review*, Vol. 43, No. 6, pp. 1241–1299.

Davies, Quentin. (Aug. 9, 2014). "Prisoners of the Apparatus": The Judge Rotenberg Center" posted by The Autistic Self-Advocacy Network [ASAN]. http://autisticadvocacy.org/2014/08/prisoners-of-the-apparatus-the-judge-rotenberg-center/.

Davis, Lennard. (2002). *Bending Over Backwards: Disability, Dismodernism, and other Difficult Positions*. NY: NYU Press.

Derrida, Jacques. (1999). *Adieu to Emmanuel Levinas*. CA: Stanford University Press.

DeShong, Scott. (Jan. 2008). "Ability, Disability, and the Question of Philosophy" in *Essays in Philosophy*. Vol. 9, No. 1, Article 8.

Diamond, Cora. (2008). "The Difficulty of Reality and the Difficulty of Philosophy," reprinted in *Philosophy & Animal Life*, NY: Columbia University Press, pp. 43–89.

Diprose, Rosalyn. (2002). *Corporeal Generosity: On Giving with Nietzsche, Merleau-Ponty, and Levinas*. Albany, NY: SUNY Press.

Dolmage, Jay. (2014). *Disability Rhetoric*. NY: Syracuse University Press.

Dotson, Kristie. (2014). "'Thinking the Familiar with the Interstitial': An Introduction" in *Hypatia* Special Issue: *Interstices: Inheriting Women of Color Feminist Philosophy*, (Winter) Vol. 29, No. 1, pp. 1–17.

Downes, Kathleen. (May 4, 2015). "When the Bus Driver Called Me 'The Wheelchair'" posted by *Estanara Magazine*. http://e-newsletter.pdpi.pk/?p=662.

_____. (Aug. 28, 2015). "Why I long for spontaneity as a Young Person with Cerebral Palsy" originally posted by TheMighty.com [no longer available online].

Ehrenreich, Barbara and Deirdre English. (1973). *Complaints and Disorders: The Sexual Politics of Sickness*. NY: The Feminist Press.

Embree, Lester. (2003). "The Possiblity of a Constitutive Phenomenology of the Environment" in *Eco-Phenomenology: Back to the Earth Itself*. Albany, NY: SUNY Press, pp. 37–50.

Erevelles, Nirmala. (2011). ""The Color of Violence: Reflecting on Gender, Race, and Disability in Wartime" in *Feminist Disability Studies*. Kim Q. Hall, ed. Bloomington, IN: Indiana University Press., pp. 117–135.

Estrich, George (Apr. 2016). "Open Letter to Medical Students." *AMA Journal of Ethics*, Vol. 18, No. 4, pp. 438–441. Available online: http://journalofethics.ama-assn.org/2016/04/mnar1–1604.html.

Faulds, Cas. (Jul. 23, 2015). "Reclaiming the Dignity Lost in a Diagnosis" posted on blogsite, *We Are Like Your Child*. http://wearelikeyourchild.blogspot.com/2015/07/reclaiming-dignity-lost-in-diagnosis.html.

Ferguson, Philip M. and Emily Nusbaum. (2012). "Disability Studies: What Is It and What Difference Does It Make?" in *Research & Practice for Persons with Severe Disabilities*, Vol. 37, No. 2, pp. 70–80. http://www.accessiblefuture.org/wp-content/uploads/sites/2/2013/09/78362125.pdf.

Foster, Sheila and Luke Cole. (2013). "Environmental Racism: Beyond the Distributive Paradigm" in *Reflecting on Nature: Readings in Environmental Ethics and Philosophy*. L. Gruen, et al., eds., NY: Oxford University Press, pp. 122–139.

Foucault, Michel. (1995). *Discipline and Punish: The Birth of the Prison* (Second Edition). NY: Vintage Books.

_____. (1999). *Abnormal: Lectures at the Collège de France 1974–1975*. Graham Burchell, trans. NY: Picador.

_____. (2007). *Security, Territory, Population: Lectures at the Collège de France 1977–1978*. Graham Burchell, trans. NY: Palgrave Macmillan.

Freire, Paulo. (2009). "From *Pedagogy of the Oppressed*" in *The Critical Pedagogy Reader*. A. Darder et al., eds., NY: Routledge, pp. 52–60.

Fuller, Abigail and Sarah Ivy, dirs. (2014). *Do You Dream In Color?* NY: Final Cut Productions, Tenacity Entertainment.

Gaard, Greta. (2014). "Toward New EcoMasculinities, EcoGenders, and EcoSexualities" in *Ecofeminism: Feminist Intersections with Other Animals & the Earth*, Carol Adams and Lori Gruen, eds. NY: Bloomsbury.

Garland-Thomson, Rosemarie. (2005). "Staring at the Other" in *Disability Studies Quarterly*, Vol. 25, No. 4. http://www.dsq-sds.org.libezcnr.idm.oclc.org/article/view/610/787.

_____. (2011). "Integrating Disability, Transforming Feminist Theory" in *Feminist Disability Studies*, Kim Q. Hall, ed. Bloomington, IN: Indiana University Press, pp. 13–47.

_____. (Summer 2011). "Misfits: A Feminist Materialist Disability Concept" in *Hypatia*, Vol. 26, No. 3, pp. 591–609.

_____. (2014). "The Story of My Work: How I Became Disabled" in *Disability Studies Quarterly*, Vol. 34, No. 2. http://dsq-sds.org.libezcnr.idm.oclc.org/article/view/4254/3594.

Gilman-Opalsky, Richard. (2014). *Precarious Communism: Manifest Mutations, Manifesto Detourned*. Brooklyn, NY: Minor Compositions. http://www.minor-compositions.info/?p=601.

Giroux, Henry. (2009). "Critical Theory and Educational Practice," in *The Critical Pedagogy Reader*, A. Darder et al., eds., NY: Routledge, pp. 27–51.

Goodley, Dan and Mark Rapley. (2002). "Changing the Subject: Postmodernity and People with 'Learning Difficulties" in *Postmodernity and Disability*, M. Corker and T. Shakespeare. eds. NY: Bloomsbury Academic.

Greenberg, Julie. (2014). "Beyond Allyship: Multiracial Work to End Racism" for *Tikkun Magazine*, Vol. 29, No. 1, (Winter). http://www.tikkun.org/nextgen/wp-content/uploads/2014/01/Greenberg.pdf.

Grosz, Elizabeth. (1994). *Volatile Bodies: Toward a Corporeal Feminism*. Bloomington, IN: Indiana University Press.

_____. (2005). *Time Travels: Feminism, Nature, Power*. Durham, NC: Duke University Press.

Guenther, Lisa. (Jun. 19, 2013). "Phenomenology as a Practice of Liberation" posted by *New APPS: Art, Politics, Philosophy, Science* blog. http://www.newappsblog.com/2013/06/phenomenology-as-a-practice-of-liberation.html.

Hall, Kim Q. (2011). *Feminist Disability Studies*. Bloomington, IN: Indiana University Press.

Hall, Melinda. (2017). "Response to Commentaries on My Book: *The Bioethics of Enhancement, Transhumanism, Disability and Biopolitics*" posted on the Discrimination and Disadvantage blog (Jun 9). http://philosophycommons.typepad.com/disability_and_disadvanta/2017/06/symposium-on-melinda-halls-the-bioethics-of-enhancement-hall.html.

Hamraie, Aimi. (2012). "Universal Design Research as a New Materialist Practice" in *Disability Studies Quarterly*, Vol. 32, No. 4. http://dsq-sds.org/article/view/3246/3185.

_____. (2013). "Designing Collective Access: A Feminist Disability Theory of Universal Design" in *Disability Studies Quarterly*, Vol. 33, No. 4. http://dsq-sds.org/article/view/3871/3411.

Havis, Devonya. (2014). "'Now, How You Sound': Considering a Different Philosophical Praxis" in *Hypatia* Special Issue: *Interstices: Inheriting Women of Color Feminist Philosophy*, (Winter) Vol. 29, No. 1, pp. 237–252.

Hechler, Andreas. (2017). "Diagnoses That Matter: My Great-Grandmother's Murder as One Deemed 'Unworthy of Living' and Its Impact on Our Family" in *Disability Studies Quarterly*, Vol. 37, No. 2. http://dsq-sds.org/article/view/5573/4651.

Heidegger, Martin. (1962). *Being and Time*. John Macquarrie and Edward Robinson, trans. NY: HarperCollins Publishers.

Heldke, Lisa and Peg O'Connor. (2004). Excerpts from Iris Young's "Five Faces of Oppression" in *Oppression, Privilege, and Resistance*. Boston, MA: McGraw-Hill. http://mrdevin.files.wordpress.com/2009/06/five-faces-of-oppression.pdf.

hooks, bell. (1990). "Homeplace: A Site of Resistance," in *Yearning: Race, Gender and Cultural Politics*. Boston: South End Press: 41–49.

_____. (1994). *Teaching to Transgress: Education as the Practice of Freedom*. New York: Routledge.

Householder, April Kalogeropoulos and Adrienne Trier-Bieniek, eds. (2016). *Feminist Perspectives on Orange Is the New Black: Thirteen Critical Essays*. Jefferson, NC: McFarland & Company, Inc.

Jarman, Michelle, Leila Monaghan, and Alison Quaggin Harkin, eds. (2017). *Barriers and Belonging: Personal Narratives of Disability* (1st Edition). Philadelphia, PA: Temple University Press.

Johnson, Andy J., Ruth J. Nelson, and Emily M. Lund, eds. (2017). *Religion, Disability, and Interpersonal Violence*. Cham, Switzerland: Springer International Publishing.

Johnson, Jenell. (2013). "Negotiating Autism in an Epidemic of Discourse" in *Disability Studies Quarterly*, Vol. 33, No. 2. Available online: http://dsq-sds.org/article/view/3716/3236.

Johnson, Larry. (Jul. 11, 2014). "Treat Emergency, Not Disability" posted by *Express-News*. Available online [accessed 7/15/2014]: http://m.mysanantonio.com/opinion/commentary/article/In-emergency-situations-disabled-people-are-5615774.php.

Jurecic, Ann. (May 2007). "Neurodiversity" in *College English* by the National Council of Teachers of English, Vol. 69, No. 5, pp. 421–442.

Kittay, Eva Feder. (March 2011). "The Ethics of Care, Dependence, and Disability" in *Ratio Juris*, Vol. 24, No. 1, pp. 49–58.

_____. (July 2009). "The Personal Is Philosophical Is Political: A Philosopher and Mother of a Cognitively Disabled Person Sends Notes from the Battlefield" in *Metaphilosophy*, Vol. 40, Nos. 3–4, Malden, MA: Blackwell Publishing Ltd., pp. 607–627.

_____. (Oct. 2005). "At the Margins of Moral Personhood" in *Ethics*, Vol. 116, No. 1, pp. 100–131.

Kozma, Melissa and Jeanine Weekes Schroer. (2014). "Purposeful Nonsense, Intersectionality and the Mission to Save Black Babies" in *Why Race and Gender Still Matter: An Intersectional Approach*. N. Goswami, L. Yount, and M. O'Donovan, eds. VT: Pickering & Chatto, pp. 101–116.

Kristeva, Julia. (1982). *Powers of Horror: An Essay on Abjection*. NY: Columbia University Press.

Ladau, Emily. (Accessed 5/16/2016). "Stuck in the Dirt: Why Advocating for Justice and Access Never Stops." Posted with The Center for Disability Rights. http://cdrnys.org/blog/disability-dialogue/the-disability-dialogue-stuck-in-the-dirt/.

Lalvani, P. and Hale, C. (2015). "Squeaky Wheels, Mothers from Hell and CEOs of the IEP: Parents, Privilege and the 'Fight' for Inclusive Education." *Understanding and Dismantling Privilege*, Vol. 5, No. 2, 21–41.

Lawlor, Leonard and John Nale, eds., (2014). *The Cambridge Foucault Lexicon*. NY: Cambridge University Press.

Leibowitz, Cara. (2014). "Palsy Skinny: A Mixed-Up, Muddled Journey into Size and Disability" in *Criptiques*. Caitlin Wood, ed. Portland, OR: May Day Press, pp. 59–65.

Levi, Primo. (1989). *The Drowned and the Saved*. NY: Vintage Books.

Levinas, Emmanuel. (1998). *Entre Nous: Thinking-of-the-Other*. NY: Continuum.

_____. (1998/1981). *Otherwise Than Being or Beyond Essence*. Pittsburgh, PA: Duquesne University Press.

_____. (GF1998). "Secularization and Hunger" in *Graduate Faculty Philosophy Journal*, Vol. 20, No. 2—Vol. 21, No. 1, pp. 3–12.

_____. (2000). *God, Death, and Time*. Bettina Bergo, trans. Stanford, CA: Stanford University Press.

_____. (2003/1982). *On Escape*. Bettinga Bergo, trans. Stanford, CA: Stanford University Press.

_____. (2003). *Humanism of the Other*. Nidra Poller, trans. Chicago, IL: University of Chicago Press.

Logsdon-Breakstone, Savannah. (Dec. 23, 2015). "Run Down of #Crippingth-eMighty" posted on *Cracked Mirror in Shalott.* http://crackedmirrorinshalott. wordpress.com/2015/12/23/run-down-of-crippingthemighty/.

Lord, Catherine and Rebecca M. Jones. (May 2012). "Re-Thinking the Classification of Autism Spectrum Disorders" in *The Journal of Child Psychology and Psychiatry,* Vol. 53, No. 5, 490–509.

Lorde, Audre. (1984). *Sister Outsider: Essays and Speeches.* Berkeley, CA: Crossing Press.

_____. (1990). Forward to *Wild Women in the Whirlwind: Afra-American Culture and the Contemporary Literary Renaissance,* J.M. Braxton and A.N. McLaughlin, eds., NJ: Rutgers University Press.

_____. (1997). *The Cancer Journals: Special Edition.* San Francisco, CA: Aunt Lute Books.

Lu, Alex. (May 11, 2016). "Deaf People Don't Need New Communication Tools—Everyone Else Does," posted by *The Establishment.* http://www.theestablishment.co/2016/05/11/deaf-people-dont-need-new-communication-tools-everyone-else-does/.

Luczak, Raymond, ed. (2015). *QDA: A Queer Disability Anthology.* Minneapolis, MN: Squares & Rebels.

Mackenzie, Catriona. (2005). "Imagining Oneself Otherwise" reprinted in *Self & Subjectivity,* K. Atkins, ed., Malden, MA: Blackwell Publishing, pp. 284–299.

Marcus, Lilit. (Mar. 28, 2014). "Why You Shouldn't Share Those Emotional 'Deaf Person Hears for the First Time' Videos" posted for *The Wire.* http://www.thewire.com/politics/2014/03/why-you-shouldnt-share-those-emotional-deaf-person-hears-for-the-first-time-videos/359850/.

McIntosh, Peggy. (1989). "White Privilege: Unpacking the Invisible Knapsack" in *Peace and Freedom Magazine,* July/August, 1989, pp. 10–12. Reposted online: http://nationalseedproject.org/white-privilege-unpacking-the-invisible-knapsack.

McKenzie, Mia. (Sep. 30, 2013). "No More 'Allies.'" Posted with Black Girl Dangerous.org. http://www.blackgirldangerous.org/2013/09/no-more-allies/.

Mills, Charles. (2007). "White Ignorance" in *Race and Epistemologies of Ignorance.* Shannon Sullivan and Nancy Tuana, eds. Albany, NY: SUNY Press.

Millsaps, Bridget Butler. (May 22, 2015). "Happy Being Himself, This Little Boy Turns Down a 3D Printed Prosthetic Hand" posted by *3DPrint.com.* http://3dprint.com/66657/boy-happy-without-prosthetic/.

Miserandino, Christine. (2003). "The Spoon Theory" posted on ButYouDontLookSick.com. http://www.butyoudontlooksick.com/articles/written-by-christine/the-spoon-theory/.

Mitchell, David T. (2000). "Narrative Prosthesis and the Materiality of Metaphor" in *Narrative Prosthesis: Disability and the Dependencies of Discourse.* D.T. Mitchell and S.L. Snyder, eds., Ann Arbor: University of Michigan Press.

Mohanty, Chandra Talpade. (2003). *Feminism Without Borders: Decolonizing Theory, Practicing Solidarity.* Durham, NC: Duke University Press.

Moreno, Rosa. (Jun. 11, 2015). "When I Lost My Hands Making Flatscreens I Can't Afford, Nobody Would Help Me" posted for *The Guardian.* http://www.theguardian.com/commentisfree/2015/jun/11/lost-hands-making-flatscreens-no-help.

Nielsen, Kim. (2012). *A Disability History of the United States.* Boston MA: Beacon Press.

Noddings, Nel. (1984). *Caring: A Feminine Approach to Ethics and Moral Education.* Los Angeles: University of California Press.

_____. (2012). Excerpt from *Caring* in *Classic and Contemporary Readings in the Philosophy of Education,* 2nd edition. Steven Cahn, ed., NY: Oxford University Press, pp. 387–391.

Norman, Geoffrey R. (Oct 2000). "The Epistemology of Clinical Reason: Perspectives from Philosophy, Psychology and Neuroscience," in *Academic Medicine,* S127–35.

O'Malley, Kimberly J., Karon, F. Cook, et al. (Oct. 2005). "Measuring Diagnoses: ICD Code Accuracy" in *Health Services Research,* Vol. 40 (5 Pt 2), pp. 1620–1639.

Owen, Randall and Sarah Parker Harris. (2012). "'No Rights without Responsibilities': Disability Rights and Neoliberal Reform under New Labour" in *Disability Studies Quarterly,* Vol. 32, No. 3. http://dsq-sds.org/article/view/3283/3110.

Pfeiffer, David. (2002). "The Philosophical Foundation of Disability Studies" in *Disability Studies Quarterly,* Vol. 22, No. 2, pp. 3–23.

Pieper, Marianne and Jamal Haji Mohammadi. (2014). "Ableism and Racism—Barriers in the Labour Market" for *The Canadian Journal of Disability Studies,* Vol. 3, No. 1. http://cjds.uwaterloo.ca/index.php/cjds/article/view/147/242.

Piepzna-Samarasinha, Leah Lakshmi. (2016). "Making Space Accessible Is An Act of Love for Our Communities." Blogpost on Creating Collective Access (Accessed 5/9/2016). http://creatingcollectiveaccess.wordpress.com/making-space-accessible-is-an-act-of-love-for-our-communities/.

Plato. (1935). *Republic, Books 6–10.* Paul Shorey, trans. Cambridge, MA: Harvard University Press.

_____. (1961). *Plato: The Collected Works.* E. Huntington and H. Cairns, eds. NJ: Princeton University Press.

Plummer, Ken. (2003). "Queers, Bodies and Postmodern Sexualities: A Note on Revisiting the 'Sexual' in Symbolic Interactionism" in *Qualitative Sociology,* Vol. 26, No. 4 (December) pp. 515–30.

Quinones-Fontanez, Lisa. (May 15, 2013). "Five Years after an Autism Diagnosis (Part 1)" reposted for Parents.com. http://www.parents.com/blogs/to-the-max/2013/05/15/autism/five-years-after-an-autism-diagnosis-part-1/.

Reynolds, Joel Michael. (Jul. 7, 2014). "Transability: Or Your Body Is Not What You Think." TEDxEmory talk posted online: http://www.youtube.com/watch?v=nBk8YeJv7Dg.

_____. (Jun. 22, 2016). "Trump's Greatest Insecurity: His Body" posted in *The Huffington Post.* http://www.huffingtonpost.com/entry/trumps-greatest-insecurity-his-body_us_57605683e4b079c7cee63caa.

Robertson, Rachel. "Sharing Stories: Motherhood, Autism, and Culture" in *Disability and Mothering: Liminal Spaces of Embodied Knowledge.* Eds. Cynthia Lewiecki-Wilson and Jen Cellio. Syracuse University Press, 2011.

Rodriguez, Michelle (Oct 2008). "The Challenges of Keeping a World: Hannah Arendt on Administration," in *Polity,* Vol. 40, No. 4, pp. 488–508.

Rothstein, Mark A., Yu Cai, and Gary E. Marchant. (2009). "The Ghost in our Genes: Legal and Ethical Implications of Epigenetics." *Health Matrix,* Cleveland, OH, Winter; 19(1): 1–62.

Ryan, Frances. (Jan. 13, 2015). "We Wouldn't Accept Actors Blacking Up, So Why Applaud 'Cripping Up'?" for *The Guardian* http://www.theguardian. com/commentisfree/2015/jan/13/eddie-redmayne-golden-globe-stephen-hawking-disabled-actors-characters.

Samuels, Ellen. (2011). "Critical Divides: Judith Butler's Body Theory and the Question of Disability" in *Feminist Disability Studies*, Kim Q. Hall, ed., Bloomington, IN: Indiana University Press.

Saul, Jenny. (2013). "Implicit Bias, Stereotype Threat, and Women in Philosophy" in *Women in Philosophy: What Needs to Change?* K. Hutchison and F. Jenkins, eds. NY: Oxford University Press.

Savarese, Ralph. (2010). "Toward a Postcolonial Neurology: Autism, Tito Mukhopadhyay, and a New Geo-Poetics of the Body" in *Journal of Literary & Cultural Disability Studies*, Vol. 4, No. 3, pp. 273–290.

_____. (2013). "From Neurodiversity to Neurocosmopolitanism: Beyond Mere Acceptance and Inclusion" in *Ethics and Neurodiversity*, C.D. Herrera and A. Perry, eds., Cambridge Scholars Press, pp. 191–205.

Schalk, Sami. (Spring 2015). "Transing: Resistance to Eugenic Ideology in Nella Larsen's *Passing*" in *Journal of Modern Literature*, Vol. 38, No. 3, pp. 148–161.

Scuro, Jennifer. (2004). "Illuminating the Ethos of an Artist: Frida Kahlo as a response to Picasso" in *International Studies in Philosophy*, Vol. 36, No. 2, pp. 95–117.

_____. (Spring 2008). "Thinking of Bhopal: Women's Bodies as Waste-Sites" in *International Studies in Philosophy*, Vol. 40, No. 2, pp. 93–105.

_____. (2014). "Theory Can Heal: Constructing an Ethos of Intervention" in *Why Race and Gender Still Matter: An Intersectional Approach*. N. Goswami, L. Yount, and M. O'Donovan, eds. VT: Pickering & Chatto, pp. 179–190.

_____. (2017). *The Pregnancy ≠ Childbearing Project*. London, UK: Rowman & Littlefield International.

Sekou, Osagyefo. (May 19, 2014). "The Master's House Is Burning: Bell Hooks, Cornel West and the Tyranny of Neoliberalism" for Truthout.com. http://www. truth-out.org/opinion/item/23792-the-masters-house-is-burning-bell-hooks-cornel-west-and-the-tyranny-of-neoliberalism.

Sheth, Falguni. (2014). "Interstitiality: Making Space for Migration, Diaspora, and Racial Complexity" in *Hypatia* Special Issue: *Interstices: Inheriting Women of Color Feminist Philosophy*, (Winter) Vol. 29, No. 1, pp. 75–93.

Shildrick, Margrit. (2009). *Dangerous Discourses of Disability, Subjectivity and Sexuality*. NY: Palgrave Macmillan.

Shildrick, Margrit and Janet Price. (1999). "Breaking the Boundaries of the Broken Body" in *Feminist Theory and the Body*. J. Price and M. Shildrick, eds., NY: Routledge, pp. 432–444.

Shiva, Vandana. (Nov. 1, 2013). "How Economic Growth Has Become Anti-Life" for *The Guardian*. http://www.theguardian.com/commentisfree/2013/nov/01/how-economic-growth-has-become-anti-life.

Shlay, Anne B. (March 2006). "Low-income Homeownership: American Dream or Delusion?" *Urban Studies*, Vol. 43, No. 3, 511–531, pp. 511–531.

Siebers, Tobin. (2008). *Disability Theory*. MI: University of Michigan Press.

Silvers, Anita. (1995). "Reconciling Equality to Difference: Caring or Justice for People with Disabilities." *Hypatia*, Vol. 10, No. 1, pp. 30–55.

_____. (Jun/Jul. 2016). "Philosophy & Disability: An Overview" in *Philosophy Now*. http://philosophynow.org/issues/30/Philosophy_and_Disability_an_overview.

_____. (Oct. 2016). "Philosophy and Disability: What Should Philosophy Do?" *Res Philosophica*, Vol. 93, No. 4. pp. 843–863.

Simone, Rudy. (2010). *Aspergirls: Empowering Females with Asperger Syndrome*. Philadelphia, PA: Jessica Kingsley Publishers.

Sinclair, Jim. (1993). "Don't Mourn for Us" in, *Our Voice*, an Autism Network International newsletter, Volume 1, Number 3. Reposted online: http://www.autreat.com/dont_mourn.html.

Smith-Donohoe, Lauryn. (2017). "It's Time to Retire 'Ablebodied.'" Blogpost: Disability Justice. (Feb. 19). http://laurensmithdonohoe.com/2017/02/19/its-time-to-retire-ablebodied/.

Stanescu, James. (Summer 2012). "Species Trouble: Judith Butler, Mourning, and the Precarious Lives of Animals" *Hypatia* Special Issue, *Animal Others*. Lori Gruen and Kari Weil, eds., vol. 27, no. 3.

_____. (Dec. 15, 2013). "Accelerationism, Animal Ethics, and the Factory Farm," for blog, Critical Animal. http://www.criticalanimal.com/2013/12/accelerationism-animal-ethics-and.html.

Stanford Encyclopedia of Philosophy [SEP]. (May 2009). "Feminist Perspectives on Disability." Revised Aug, 2013. http://plato.stanford.edu/entries/feminism-disability/.

Taylor, Ashley. (2012). "Addressing Ableism in Schooling and Society? The Capabilities Approach and Students with Disabilities" in *Philosophy of Education*, Urbana, IL: The Philosophy of Education Society, pp. 113–121.

Taylor, Astra, dir. (2008). Film: *Examined Life*. NY: Zeitgeist Films.

Taylor, Sunaura. (2014). "Interdependent Animals: A Feminist Disability Ethic-of-Care" in *Ecofeminism: Feminist Intersections with Other Animals & the Earth*, Carol Adams and Lori Gruen, eds. NY: Bloomsbury.

Tremain, Shelley. (July 11, 2011). "Ableist Language and Philosophical Associations" posted on *New APPS: Art, Politics, Philosophy, Science* blog http://www.newappsblog.com/2011/07/ableist-language-and-philosophical-associations.html>

_____. (2013). "Introducing Feminist Philosophy of Disability" in *Disability Studies Quarterly*, Vol. 33, No. 4.

_____. (Mar. 23, 2014). "Disabling Philosophy" draft post on *New APPS: Art, Politics, Philosophy, Science* blog. Full version reprinted in *The Philosopher's Magazine* (April 2014). Accessed Aug 2015: http://www.newappsblog.com/2014/03/disabling-philosophy.html.

_____. (Mar. 28, 2017). "Philosophy and the Use of Phineas Gage" posted on Discrimination and Disadvantage blog. http://philosophycommons.typepad.com/disability_and_disadvanta/2017/04/philosophy-and-the-use-of-phineas-gage.html.

Wade, Cheryl Marie. (1994). "It Ain't Exactly Sexy" in *The Ragged Edge*. Barrett Shaw, ed., KY: Advocado Press, pp. 88–90.

Walker, Nick. (Apr. 2, 2014). "April, Autism and Allies" from Blog: *Neurocosmopolitanism: Notes on Neurodiversity, Autism, and Cognitive Liberty*. Available online: neurocosmopolitanism.com.

Ware, Linda. (Mar/Apr 2001). "Writing, Identity, and the Other: Dare We Do Disability Studies?" in the *Journal of Teacher Education*, Vol. 52, No. 2, pp. 107–123.

Warren, Karen. (1990). "The Power and Promise of Ecological Feminism" in *Environmental Ethics*, Vol. 12, No. 2, pp. 125–146.

_____. (2009). "Lead Essay: 2,600 Years of the History of Western Philosophy Without Women." *An Unconventional History of Western Philosophy*. Karen Warren, ed., NY: Rowman & Littlefield.

Wendell, Susan. (1996). *The Rejected Body: Feminist Philosophical Reflections on Disability*. NY: Routledge.

Wiley-Mydske, Lei. (Jul. 19, 2014). Review of the documentary, *Sounding the Alarm: Battling the Autism Epidemic*. Posted on Autism Women's Network blog. http://autismwomensnetwork.org/film-review-of-documentary-sounding-the-alarm-battling-the-autism-epidemic/.

Wood, Caitlin, ed. (2014). *Criptiques*. Portland, OR: May Day Press.

Yancy, George and Janine Jones, eds. (2013). *Pursuing Travon Martin: Historical Contexts and Contemporary Manifestations*. NY: Lexington Books.

Young, Iris Marion. (2005). *On Female Body Experience: "Throwing Like a Girl" and Other Essays*. New York: Oxford University Press.

_____. (reprinted 2014). "Chapter One: Five Faces of Oppression" in *Diversity, Social Justice, and Inclusive Excellence*. Seth Asumah and Mechthild Nagel, eds., Albany, NY: SUNY Press. http://www.sunypress.edu/pdf/62970.pdf.

Young, Stella. (Sep. 2, 2013). "Disability Is No Justification for Murder" posted by *The Drum*. http://www.abc.net.au/news/2013–09–03/young-kyla-puhle-death/4930742.

_____. (Jun. 9, 2014). "I'm Not Your Inspiration, Thank You Very Much." TEDtalk posted online: http://www.youtube.com/watch?v=8K9Gg164Bsw.

Index

About the Authors

Jennifer Scuro has a BFA in painting and sculpture from St. John's University, a MA in philosophy from Boston College and a PhD in philosophy from The New School for Social Research. She is associate professor of philosophy and former chair of the Philosophy & Religious Studies Department at The College of New Rochelle in New York. She continues to work on her art while teaching courses in global and applied ethics, feminist and critical disability theory, and environmental studies. She wrote the final chapter, "Theory Can Heal," for the anthology *Why Race and Gender Still Matter* (Yount et al., 2014) and is author of the graphic novel and philosophical analysis, *The Pregnancy ≠ Childbearing Project: A Phenomenology of Miscarriage* (Rowman & Littlefield International, 2017).

Devonya N. Havis is an associate professor of philosophy at Canisius College in Buffalo, New York. Dr. Havis' publications include "'Now, How You Sound': Considering a Different Philosophical Praxis" in the feminist philosophy journal, *Hypatia*, in its special issue on interstitiality. She also has published "Blackness Beyond Witness" in *Philosophy and Social Criticism*, and "'Seeing Black' through Michel Foucault's Eyes: 'Stand Your Ground' Laws as An Anchorage Point for State-Sponsored Racism," a chapter in the anthology, *Pursuing Trayvon Martin: Historical Contexts and Contemporary Manifestations of Racial Dynamics* (Yancy & Jones, 2013).

Lydia X. Z. Brown is a queer, East Asian, autistic disability justice activist, organizer, and advocate, dedicated to intersectional social justice. Brown authors the blog Autistic Hoya and currently serves as chairperson of the Massachusetts Developmental Disabilities Council. Their publications include the chapter, "'You Don't Feel Like a Freak Anymore': Representing Disability,

Madness, and Trauma in Litchfield Penitentiary," in *Feminist Perspectives on Orange Is the New Black: Thirteen Critical Essays* (Householder & Trier-Bieniek, 2016), and the chapter, "Ableist Shame and Disruptive Bodies: Survivorship at the Intersection of Queer, Trans, and Disabled Existence," in *Religion, Disability, and Interpersonal Violence* (Johnson et al., 2017). They have also published "Autism Isn't Speaking: Autistic Subversion in Media & Public Policy" in the Disability Studies reader *Barriers & Belonging: Personal Narratives of Disability* (Jarman et al., 2017), and "Disability in an Ableist World" for the radical disability anthology *Criptiques* (Wood, 2014).